A GIRL FROM GLASGOW

MORAG'S STORY

A Girl
from Glasgow

Morag's Story

MORAG RIDINGS

The right of Morag Ridings to be identified
as author of this work has been asserted in accordance
with the Copyright, Designs & Patent Act, 1988

ACKNOWLEDGEMENTS

I couldn't have written this book by myself. It's the first and
probably the last book I'll ever write. I had no idea when I started
how incredibly hard and how time-consuming it was going to be.

Without the help and professional skill of my friend Helen Beaton I
couldn't have done it. There would be no book. There are so many
other helpers to thank too:

- My brother Sandy and sister Elizabeth for sharing the Wilson
  family memories
- My lifelong friends Heather, Christine and Angela for allowing
  me to tell their stories
- Jean Miller, my sub-editor, for checking it made sense
- Keith Cuthbert, my son-in-law, for help with the digital images
  and family trees
- My cousin Hamish, my daughter Kirsty, my granddaughter
  Annabel and friends Pat Whitton and Mary Cowan for written
  contributions
- Ian Drever for giving me a book about the Glasgow Academy
- Laura Laing for the author photo on front jacket
- Kinross Golf Club and Kirklands Hotel, Kinross for permission
  to use photos featuring their buildings

First published in 2022 by Stravaigers Press
21 Hatton Green, Glenrothes KY7 4SD
ISBN: 978-1-9164789-1-6

Printed & bound by Imprint Digital, Exeter
https://digital.imprint.co.uk

CONTENTS

For friends and family
who have helped me
over the years

Chapter 1: Introduction

I'm Morag. I'm fourteen years old and it's my first day back at school after the Christmas holidays. I'm standing in the corridor after my teacher, Mrs Lund, told me to get out of her classroom—punished not for *talking* or *misbehaving*, but for—God forbid—the shocking sins of giggling and laughing.

I'm tall for my age, gangly, awkward and flat-chested (like most but not all of the others) with short, wavy, mousy blonde hair and I'm chronically shy.

Only one teacher in the whole school likes me and knows my name. That's the gym teacher, Miss Loudon, who has a soft spot for me, but only because she once knew my aunt, who was an excellent hockey player. But she's a heartless and sadistic bully. One whisper of the words 'Miss Loudon' brings pupils out in icy bumps of fear.

So here I am, standing outside the door in the empty, bleak corridor. I can hear the deafening silence from the adjoining classroom. I don't feel like laughing now.

I balance first on one foot, then the other, hoping no one will come past. I wish I was invisible.

Oh no! In the distance I make out a black-gowned creature emerging from the shadows, her black lacing shoes, *clippety clop, clippety clop,* heading towards me. It's Miss Barker, the Headmistress. Nowhere to hide.

'You, girl—what is your name? You're a disgrace to this fine school! What have you been doing? What would your parents say if they knew you were wasting your time misbehaving, spending your time *outside* the classroom instead of inside?'

I stay silent.

'Answer me girl! What's your name? What would your mother say? Indeed, what would your father say? I'm talking to you, girl! Don't be so insolent—have you lost your tongue?'

I still say nothing.

'Answer me girl—or I really will have to phone home and speak to your mother and your father. Speak girl, NOW!'

I make a huge effort. I mutter, 'You can't ... speak to my father.'

'Don't tell *me*, girl, what I can and can't do. If I want to phone your father, I will. He certainly needs to know what an insolent child you are.'

'You can't phone my father.'

'And why may I not phone your father, you impudent girl?'

In a very tiny voice, I whisper, 'He's dead.'

'Speak up, child. Don't mutter!'

My eyes are filling up. I can barely speak for crying. 'You can't phone him. He's not here. He *died*.'

She finally gets it and ... sends me back to the classroom.

She'll overlook it this time, but I had better behave myself in the future.

Tears streaming down my face, I return to where the other thirty girls and the teacher are engrossed in *A Midsummer Night's Dream*. My friends notice I'm crying but the lesson continues. I make my way to my desk, quietly take out my copy of the play and try to follow what's going on.

⋈

Only one week before this, my father had died in the early hours of New Year's Day. He was in great pain. From my bedroom, I could hear him groaning and my mother talking quietly to him.

Years afterwards, my mother told me the GP had refused to prescribe any more morphine in case he 'became addicted'. (He was dying!) He'd lost his right lung to cancer four years previously. Now his left lung was finished too.

My little sister Elizabeth was eight years old when this happened. It was only recently that she told me about her own classroom experience after he died. In the fifties no-one talked about (or even mentioned) death, in Glasgow anyway. Our mother had notified the school that our father had passed away. Despite this, Elizabeth's teacher still checked the register on the first day of term after the Christmas holidays, asking not only for names but family details as usual. Starting with the 'A's, she slowly worked her way through the register until she came to 'Wilson'.

'Elizabeth Wilson—your father's occupation please, and any change of your home address?' It was a question my little sister never answered. She burst into tears instead. 'Go and sort yourself out, Elizabeth, and come back to the classroom when you've stopped crying. You may take a friend with you.'

Now that we're grown-up, with all of this in the distant past, not one of us can remember ever talking about our fathers' deaths back then. Another school friend, Anne Hamilton, lost *her* father when she was in second year and I can honestly say I knew nothing about it until fifty years later when we were having dinner and a glass or two of wine in a restaurant in Glasgow. What she told me says it all really.

She wasn't permitted to attend the funeral, although she knew he had died. When she came home from school one day, he was simply not there. Frightened of upsetting her mother, she never mentioned it. When his birthday came round, she wrote him a card to say how much she missed him—and buried it at the bottom of their garden. She never told a soul.

It must be almost impossible for a young person today to understand how and why we behaved as we did. When my friends and I meet and talk (and we still do), it's hard for us, too, to fathom why we didn't ask and question and disagree. But the principles of our upbringing were instilled in us from birth. We were to be seen and not heard. We were to do what we were told.

We were Glasgow girls in the fifties in a male-oriented society.

We were expected to *please*.

Chapter 2: My Glasgow Origins

I was brought up in Glasgow in the fifties, and the Glasgow culture of that time is part of my very being, part of who I am. In his book *Made In Scotland*, Billy Connolly, one of my favourite comedians, explains it when he says, 'I didnae come from nothing, I came from something'.

Like Billy Connolly I didn't come from nothing either, I came from *something*. Like Billy Connolly, my 'something', was Glasgow and Scotland.

But there the similarity ends. For a start I was much better looking (as a child) and less hairy (as an adult). But we both came from the north of the Clyde, and in our childhood we lived in tenements. His was in Anderston and mine in Hillhead. He's also two years older than me but I won't mention that. He's famous and funny and I am simply an unknown old lady. But when I read his books, I identify with so many of his experiences: the wonderful freedom of our youth to cycle and explore and camp in the west of Scotland; the joyless, laughterless formal education; the holiday swimming in ice-cold water; the drinking culture all around us; and the unwritten rule that you never talk about yourself or your feelings unless you're blootered, wellied, hammered or stocious.

We learned (unconsciously) how to take the piss out of our friends, to take risks just for a laugh, to make the best of what we had, and to recognise bullshit when we met it. That was our Glasgow inheritance. Glasgow was, and still is, a strange city of contrasts. But first, to understand how I survived my roller-coaster life story, I have to take you back in time to meet my Glaswegian grandparents and my Glaswegian mum and dad.

My granny Wilson (Janet Buchanan Service) was born in 1879 and my grandfather (James Cruikshank Wilson) was born in 1877, his occupation listed before the First World War as a 'Locomotive Works Clerk'. He married my granny in 1908 and apparently never worked after that. They were both clearly affluent, with parents who probably made their money in the industrial powerhouse that was Victorian Glasgow.

If you take a walk today through the city centre, you're reminded at every turn of Glasgow's prosperous past. For example, there's Jamaica Street—named after the island which produced so much rum and sugar for Glasgow merchants. There's the Custom House in Clyde Street, where duties were once charged on imports from the plantations. And, of course, there's the Merchant City, where tobacco lords like John Glassford and Andrew Buchanan used to live and work. Buchanan was my granny's middle name. Is that a clue?

Not long after my grandmother was born in 1879, tram lines were laid along a two-and-a-half mile stretch from St George's Cross to Eglinton Toll (via New City Road, Cambridge Street, Sauchiehall Street, Renfield Street, Jamaica Street and Eglinton Street). I wonder if she was taken as a special treat on one of Glasgow's early horse-drawn trams? How I wish I had asked her these questions when she was still alive! I had plenty of opportunity but—like most young people—I simply wasn't interested.

My Wilson grandparents were married in 1908 and Granny took Ann Jardin, her maid with her. Ann must have lived with them until after World War II. We could never persuade her to call Dad anything but 'Mr Alex' and his sister, my Aunt Betty, was always 'Miss Betty'. Sometime later they moved from 1, Kelvinside Terrace to

6, Colebrooke Terrace in Hillhead near to the Glasgow Academy. My father's home was no tenement flat. It was a Victorian terrace house with five bedrooms, a back parlour, a drawing room, kitchen, pantry, two bathrooms and in the basement, the maid's quarters, a bedroom, a toilet, a coal cellar, and two large sinks for the household laundry.

I loved to listen to Ann Jardin's stories. Here she is, as I remember her talking:

I was so lucky to be with your granny's family, who were real good to me, treated me like a daughter, showed me how to behave and how to speak proper. I was allowed suitors only if Mrs Service approved, but there weren't that many anyway!

She roared and laughed with one of the most infectious laughs I've ever heard.

And I had to be home always by nine and of course it was only on my one day off that I went out at all. I loved being with your granny's family, I felt safe and secure, they were among the best years of my life. And when your granny got married and was allowed to take me with her, I was that pleased for I got to be there for Mr Alex and Miss Betty. I was there helping your granny right through the war and the Depression. It was your granny who found a wee flat just for me and that's where I am now. I never thought I'd have my own place and it's all thanks to your granny.

Ann died in the early sixties, and must have been very young when she first went into service. She clearly accepted social class divisions as simply the way it was. I wonder what she would have thought of Downton Abbey? I remember her as one of the happiest people I have ever met. Is my memory correct? I've no way of knowing but

I can still hear her infectious giggle as she told us tales about our granny. My Granny Wilson was brought up to be 'middle-class', 'a lady', and 'posh'. No 'well brought up' person would ever wear slippers in the house, only in the bedroom. As Ann told us:

A serious problem arose when your granny broke her left toe, Disaster! She couldn't get her foot into her shoe, only her slipper, so what did she do? For three weeks, she walked about the house, right foot in her shoe, left foot in her slipper!

One of Ann's many jobs was to set the table with the family cutlery, definitely no easy task. In the cutlery chest—in the top drawer, steels and dessert knives, meat carvers and game carvers; in the middle drawer, tea spoons, egg spoons, salt spoons, table forks, dessert forks and knife rests; and in the bottom drawer, soup ladles, sauce ladles, sugar spoons, sugar tongs, and table spoons, dessert spoons, gravy spoons, mustard spoons and butter knives, all monogrammed with 'W', as was the custom.

As a child, my grandfather attended the Glasgow Academy, a school that reflected much of Glasgow's West End Protestant history. The school started thanks to two brothers, William and James Campbell, the latter a generous benefactor of the Free Church of Scotland, the Royal Infirmary and the Botanic Gardens.

In 1845, William convened a meeting with Free Church Ministers to discuss the possibility of establishing 'an Academic Institution in the City'. By 1846, a school of forty pupils was envisaged. Some members of the governing committee, including Dr Robert Buchanan (there's that Buchanan name again), were even in favour of 'admitting girls.' The idea was put on the back burner. Almost one hundred and forty-five years later—as late as 1981—girls were finally admitted!

Although my grandparents were clearly privileged, it was in their lifetime that Glasgow grew to become a city of extreme contrasts and strong sectarian attitudes.

Chapter 3: Sectarian Glasgow—A City Of Contrasts

Granny and Grandfather were brought up in a Glasgow where extreme deprivation, exploitation and strong sectarianism attitudes sat side by side with privilege, wealth and numerous benefactors and philanthropists. Glasgow's current prestigious status in architectural terms owes much to the inspiration and funding of the latter group.

In sectarian Glasgow the Orange Walk on July 12th still lives on, celebrating the Protestant victory of King William of Orange over the Catholic Jacobite followers of the exiled King James II at the Battle of the Boyne. Few Glaswegians remember—or even care—that it was in fact a complex struggle for the throne involving the Dutch, the Irish, the French and the English, all disputing the rights of succession. It's only remembered now as a struggle for Catholic or Protestant ascendancy.

The thriving Glasgow of Victorian times offered great opportunities for work, and between 1841 and 1851, the Irish immigrant population in Scotland increased by 90%. Almost 29% of these new arrivals settled in Glasgow. The mainly Catholic Irish were suffering from the aftermath of the potato famine, as well as general unemployment. Many of them ended up in the east end of the city looking for work. At the time, Irish Catholics generally went wherever unskilled labour was needed. The combination of their low status, their willingness to work for less than everybody else, and their Catholicism led to vicious discrimination against them. They were regarded by many as drunken, lazy and uncivilised. 'Typhus' was popularly known as 'Irish fever'. Despite the opposition to them and their poverty, Irish immigrants managed to establish local communities. Within ten years the number of Catholic churches in Glasgow had doubled. Glasgow Celtic Football Club was born out of the poverty of the east of Glasgow, the area that the Irish called 'home' in the 1800s. On May 1888, the first 'Old Firm' match was played between Celtic and Rangers. Celtic won—five goals to two!

To this day when you meet a fellow Glaswegian, one of the first questions you'll be asked is 'What school did you go to?' It's the quickest way to find out whether you're Protestant or Catholic. And now you know that my Glasgow grandparents were Protestant, well off, lived in the west end of Glasgow and went to private schools.

My father was born in 1910, four years before the beginning of the First World War. He grew up in a Glasgow similar to that of his parents, where wealth and poverty, privilege and deprivation were neighbours. Most people lived in tenements and in any tenement building, you would find eight to ten families in apartments off the main stairway. They shared a communal back green and each landing probably had a water closet (the WC or toilet), used by the families on that floor.

The flats were warmed by coal fires and that, plus the constant battle against the mud from outside, meant life for women was a never-ending, continuous and constant battle to keep clean. 'Steamies', or washhouses, were popular and a great place for the women to blether and share their news and worries. Between the tenements on the cobbled streets ran the tramcars. Inside these, women and children generally travelled downstairs, while upstairs sat the men, swathed in tobacco smoke and often coughing productively. In my childhood there was a prominent notice on each tram that read:

SPITTING STRICTLY FORBIDDEN
PENALTY FORTY SHILLINGS

In my dad's time, the trams were electric. Each one had a driver and a fierce and scary 'clippie' (or ticket collector) who took no nonsense from anyone and kept everyone in line. There was no class distinction on a *Glesca* caur (tram)!

When I started looking into my family history, my father appeared at first to have been a very fortunate child—well-off, educated at Kelvinside Academy, and living in Hillhead.

However, I now know better. Alcohol, Glasgow's 'achilles heel', affected the whole household. When my grandfather stopped working, aged only 31, he took to the bottle. Protestant, middle-class alcoholism was like its education—not a happy affair. It was never about singing, dancing, partying, waking the neighbours, and having a good time until the money was gone. It was a miserable family secret to be hidden from the neighbours at all costs (similar at that time to pregnancy out of wedlock). Each day my grandfather, smart, well-dressed, affluent looking, a smile on his face, would go out walking, grasping the ebony handle of his carved walking stick. He would smile and chat to the neighbours who (without exception, I was told) thought he was a charming gentleman.

His wife and children knew better. He was even sent on a trip to America for a 'cure'. It succeeded, allegedly, until just a few days before his ship was due to dock when he clearly needed 'dutch courage'. He had a few wee drams, and a few more, and then a few more. He managed, with difficulty, to walk down the gangway to be greeted by my irate and bitterly disappointed grandmother. When he climbed up the few stairs to the front door, with Granny firmly holding his arm, he staggered only a little.

'Problems with his sea legs after his long trip from America,' explained Granny, smiling at a passing neighbour.

I don't know much about Dad's childhood, but I think perhaps I know what it wasn't. Feelings weren't discussed, or expressed. Laughter and warmth, touching and hugging—these were alien to the Glasgow culture at that time. Middle-class Presbyterianism was cold. It was about duty, about respectability, about What Not to Do. It focussed on appearances and 'what the neighbours would say'.

Meals for my father as a boy were very formal and served in the dark and dismal dining room with its long rectangular brown mahogany table, mahogany sideboard and dining chairs. The walls were papered in textured brown faux-leather paper and complemented by a brown carpet and brown velvet curtains. My grandfather sat at one end of the table, my granny at the other, her back upright and stiff as a ramrod. Even sitting in the parlour in her armchair, she never leaned against the back. 'Ladies don't slump, posture is everything', she would say.

One of Ann Jardin's jobs as family servant was to bring in the meal. Many years later it was still well-nigh impossible to persuade her to sit down and eat with us.

After Auntie Betty was born, Granny decided she didn't want any more children, so having a big house with plenty of room, my grandfather was despatched to his room forever. Perhaps the independence which came from a substantial private income allowed her to make this decision. Was this a result of his alcoholism? Or was it the cause? I'll never know. Since home life wasn't ideal, my dad left his posh school as soon as he was old enough, worked as a mechanic for a while, then joined the Merchant Navy. His father's 'problem' had sorely affected him, and from that time on, he was teetotal, disliking and refusing to drink alcohol in any form. But he made up for it in cigarettes!

Dad used his months and months at sea (an experience not unlike the 2019 corona-virus lockdown but without digital communication) to read widely and also to develop his talent for painting, drawing and model making. I inherited many of his books, which cover a wide range of topics. In his seafaring travels, he must have known people of the Moslem faith and that explains the copy of the Koran brought home in 1931 which, according to my brother Jimmy, he had read from cover to cover.

In the thirties, like most companies, the P&O Shipping Line found itself in the grip of an unprecedented worldwide depression, precipitated by the Wall Street Crash of 1929. By 1932, fifteen million tons of shipping, a fifth of the world's sea-faring capacity lay idle for want of trade. For my father, this seemed an optimum time to leave the seafaring life and find himself a shore job. What to do? Cars were his other great interest.

And so before the war 'Alex Wilson Motor Engineer' was born in Great George Street. The mid-thirties were clearly a good time for my father. He was enjoying himself, free of protocol and rules and happy—well enough off to enjoy an independent life, driving modern cars, sailing, going what we now call 'wild camping' with his friends, and also, hopefully, running his business. To top it all, he met my mother-to-be, Kirsteen Graham. She was fun, carefree, a hairdresser, from the west end of Glasgow and she had also been at a Protestant fee-paying school. No family difficulties there, then? In Glasgow, this was almost as good as an arranged marriage: same class and same religion.

My mother's family was respectable and reasonably well-off, but it was less affluent than my father's. She had a similar west-end Glasgow upbringing, but she was the youngest of five—four girls and one boy, and every one of her siblings has played a big part in my life.

Mum's father was a commercial salesman when he married her mother in 1904 in Cowdenbeath. They were young: he was 25 and she was 22. He worked hard, started his own timber business and was able to provide his children with a good quality of life. According to Mum, he always felt blessed to have married an Edinburgh lady educated at Mary Erskine School. *His* children were going to have a private education like their mother and become ladies.

But it wasn't to be. Aunt Isabel, his first born, went to Glasgow University in 1923, became the Personnel Manager for Ferranti Ltd and lived until she was 89. Her letters written during the Second World War still ring true today: 'Why does the government not do something about childcare? Grannies and neighbours will look after the children during the day but because of lack of childcare, we can't get the women to work in the factory for the back shift and the night shift and we simply must meet our munition production targets'.

Auntie Helen was the 'stay at home' sister, the one who looked after Granny Graham. And then there was Uncle George, the only boy. *He* had his shoes cleaned for him by his sisters. He wasn't expected to do *any* domestic chores.

Auntie Kathleen, the one liked by my school gym teacher (the infamous and heartless Miss Loudon), wanted to be a sports teacher, but her dad insisted she studied domestic science, a good preparation for being a wife. Last but not least was my mother, a happy-go-lucky sociable child, musical—the favourite of them all. It was a cheerful happy household, with evenings spent singing round the piano. Summer holidays were enjoyed in Dollar and Aberdour, playing golf and tennis, picnicking and hill walking.

No wonder my father enjoyed visiting my mother's family. It wasn't long before he and she were engaged, my mother sporting a beautiful ring with three diamonds, and the wedding planned for June 22, 1938.

Chapter 4: The Empire Exhibition, 1938

This was a great year for Mum and Dad. They were both young and in love and they had a day out to remember in May. Not that you would have known it was May. This was Glasgow and it was raining cats and dogs or, as we say in Glasgow, it was pissing down.

Dad borrowed a Morris Cowley Bullnose 4-seater from his garage in Great George St, and drove it to the Exhibition site in Bellahouston Park. Heads turned to look at this tall, good-looking, fair-haired guy in his late twenties as he leapt out of car to open the door for my mum, a young lady in her early twenties, slim and elegant with curly, shiny, chestnut hair. But first he unfurled his huge umbrella to protect her from the rain which was attacking from all sides.

The Exhibition wasn't as busy as it had been two weeks ago on 3rd May when King George VI and Queen Mary arrived for the opening ceremony and 146,000 people came to see them. Glasgow was showcasing Scotland and the Empire, boosting the economy and celebrating trade and developments as the country struggled to free itself from the Great Depression. From May to December, the exhibition attracted nearly thirteen million visitors despite (like everything else at the time) being shut every Sunday, on the Sabbath, the Day of Rest.

When they got out of the car, my parents heard the sound of pipe bands playing in the distance. Looking up was hard while trying to stay dry under the umbrella, but it was definitely worth getting a bit of a wetting. So—what did they see? The first ever skyscraper—the Tait Tower, no fewer than 300 feet (91 metres) high.

The exhibition site stretched for twelve acres and the young couple first opted for a ride on the Mountain Railway in the Amusement Park. Perhaps it wasn't as fast or as scary as the modern Disneyland rides, but the sounds coming from the passengers on this ride, even in the pouring rain, weren't screaming and yelling, but *singing*. It's true!

Now dripping wet, they made for the restaurant where it was dry. As they chatted during their meal, they discussed where to go next. Mum wanted to see the Women's Section in the Palace of Industry, but Dad's interests lay elsewhere—the displays by the army and airforce, the Palace of Engineering and the vintage cars. The only thing they did agree on was that neither wanted to watch the football match. An Empire Exhibition Football Trophy was to be awarded for an international event played throughout the six months of the exhibition (it was finally won by Celtic, the runners up being Everton).

What a brilliant day they had, one Mum never forgot—a day of fun, hope, colour and promise. In only four weeks' time they would be getting married. The date was set: 22 June in Lansdowne Church on Great Western Road.

⚒

Mum's sister (Kathleen) and Dad's sister (Betty) were to be the bridesmaids. They planned to wear hats which were fashionable and elegant. Mum, a trained hairdresser, was the expert on hairstyles. Long hair, unless exquisitely hidden behind curls, was definitely not fashionable in the thirties. Partings were 'in', as were curls. The top of the head was smooth and flat, the sides wavy and the ends curly. Mum herself had wavy, curly hair all her life. When it wasn't curly, we knew she wasn't very well. The best man, George Todd, was also Dad's best friend, and he remained a loyal friend throughout his life. The other groomsman was his cousin Quentin Service.

Grandpa Graham, entirely content with his youngest daughter's choice of husband, was full of pride when he took her down the aisle. Both before and after the marriage, he and my father enjoyed many in-depth 'man to man' conversations about current affairs. But serious chats and weddings don't mix. The guests were there to have a good time—and they did.

Alcoholic drinks were, of course, served at the reception and with the meal. The bride and groom didn't enjoy alcohol at all really but they did take a sherry before dinner, as did Granny Wilson and Granny Graham. Grandpa Wilson was not to be seen anywhere and was probably enjoying a dram (or two, or three, or more) somewhere out of sight of the guests.

The dancing went on until 10.30 but as the next day was Sunday, everything and everybody had to be shut down and cleared away by midnight at the latest.

After their honeymoon (about which I naturally know nothing at all), my parents settled into ordinary married life in a rented flat in Melrose Street in the West End, Mum going to her hairdressing job and Dad to his garage in Great George Street.

But Dad, Grandpa Graham and Uncle George all had grave concerns about events outside Scotland. In February 1938, the German leader, Adolf Hitler, had abolished his country's War Ministry and created the High Command of the armed forces that allowed him direct control of the German military. A few weeks later, the Italian leader, Mussolini, also took control of the Italian army. In March, German troops occupied Austria. (The Julie Andrews film,

The Sound of Music, is set in Salzburg during the occupation of Austria.) In May, Hitler declared his intention of destroying Czechoslovakia by military force.

None of this was good news to discerning readers of the Glasgow *Herald*. My father, Uncle George and Grandpa Graham liked to keep up with the news but their concerns were not generally shared with the womenfolk, although Aunt Isabel—by then aged 33 with a professional career—would have made sure she was included in this chat.

After the Munich Pact of September 1938 when Britain, France and Italy agreed they would not intervene if Hitler were to annexe Sudetenland, the UK Prime Minister Neville Chamberlain returned home triumphantly with the news that war had been averted. His mantra 'Peace in Our Time' was welcomed widely because no one—and I mean no one—wanted another war. Memories of the First World War were still raw for most people. But there were many who, like Winston Churchill, had serious misgivings about the Munich Pact.

One of those doubters was my Grandpa Graham who in his own inimitable style replied to a letter in the *Herald*:

> Sir, —*I confess to a feeling of envy at the complacency of mind that characterises the letter of your correspondent 'P.H.N.' and all of those who may think like him, and who are able to find something new and promising of a more Christian attitude in Mr Chamberlain's efforts at Munich.*
>
> *As I value my skin as much as most folk I feel a certain amount of relief that there is to be no war yet, and I am ready to admit that the Government are in all probability by far and away the best judges of the necessities of the present occasion; but that there is tremendous*

danger ahead and need for unceasing vigilance and effort on our part is only too evident.

Napoleon said God is always on the side of the big battalions, and so it must appear at present. But it would be better perhaps if we keep the name of Christ out of it and sing our 'Te Deums' on a more appropriate occasion; otherwise some of us may be driven to believe that there is a good deal to be said for a German god and his prophet Adolf Hitler.

I am, etc.,

James Graham

After the wedding Dad's garage business—not doing very well anyway—continued to go downhill. He, however, was much more concerned about events playing out in Germany and joined the Glasgow Highlanders, a territorial battalion within the Highland Light Infantry.

Grandpa Graham, also very worried about the possibility of war and what might happen to the Jews, continued to write to the *Herald*:

We have to reckon with a generation of Germans soon to arrive at maturity who have been subjected to authoritarian discipline from infancy, and who have been taught that the all-powerful State is the supreme God, and its leader the tribal god.

Little did he know that between 1941 and 1945 six *million* Jews would be murdered. I'm not sure exactly when in 1938 his letter was written, because the date has been cut off the newspaper cutting. Was it before *Kristallnacht* (the 'Night of Broken Glass')? That terrible event was November 9, 1938, when Nazi-led mobs carried out an assault on the Jewish populations of Germany, Austria and the Sudetenland. They wrecked more than seven thousand Jewish businesses and two hundred and sixty-seven synagogues. Thirty thousand Jewish men were arrested and sent to concentration camps.

While ten thousand mainly Jewish children (from Nazi Germany, Nazi-occupied Austria, Poland Czechoslovakia, and the Free City of Danzig) were leaving their parents forever to come to Britain under the 'Kinder Transport' scheme, my mother was bursting to tell my father her own news.

She waited until after their first Hogmanay party in their very first home together. 'I think I'm going to be having a baby,' she said. 'Probably about July, August. Shall we keep it our secret for a while longer till I'm absolutely sure? Everyone will be over the moon and I'm not ready for all the fuss. So shall we wait until sometime in the new year?'

My dad, absolutely delighted, agreed.

And so ended 1938.

Chapter 5: A Fool's Paradise

Granny and Grampa Graham lived in a house called 'Belhaven' in Church Avenue in Cardross. And Belhaven was where my Mum and Dad (to be) were heading for their Sunday lunch, very excited about finally sharing their secret with the family.

That wasn't the only excitement. Mum's brother George was bringing Elma Borthwick, his tennis and golf partner. The whole family was curious to meet Elma and weren't even sure that he had told her anything at all about them.

Mum's sister Kathleen would be there too; she was teaching Domestic Science, as it was called then, at Hartfield School (later to become Dumbarton Academy) where she'd met the love of her life, a chap from Helensburgh, Gregor Ian Smith.

Kathleen was just bursting to tell Mum about him. 'Kirsteen, Gregor is such an *amazing* chap, a *brilliant* artist and such *great* fun. Mind you I'm not sure Dad approves—he thinks an artist isn't a real job—but Gregor's the one for me, Kirsteen, whatever Dad says.' So Kathleen rattled on and on. 'He's four years older than me and, do you know, he won the Newbury Medal because he was such an outstanding student? I've met his sister Mary and she's the greatest of fun. He really only wants to be a proper artist, he isn't that keen on teaching but we need the money.'

This was all being whispered in the kitchen where the two sisters were supposed to be helping Granny and Helen prepare the dinner. Dad was closeted in the parlour with Grandpa, probably discussing the most recent events in Germany, while Elma and George had still to arrive.

'I hope you girls are helping your mother!' Grandpa's voice could be heard from the parlour, where he and his favourite son-in-law were having a smoke. Helen and Granny Graham were shouldering the brunt of the food preparation. Kathleen and Mum were pretending to be useful while actually whispering and giggling (Kathleen was 25 and Mum 23).

The doorbell rang.

'That must be George,' said Granny Graham, quickly removing her pinny, putting on her welcoming polite face and heading to the door. 'Do come in the pair of you. Your lunch is almost ready.'

Assuring Elma she was delighted to meet her, Granny introduced her to the rest of the family. 'I believe George is going to take you this afternoon to play Cardross Golf Course, and I hear too that you are a very good golfer.'

Granny knew nothing, and cared even less, about golf, but she certainly knew her only and very precious son was a keen and skilled golfer, so she was making an effort. After all, Elma might well become her daughter-in-law.

Mum rang the dinner gong and soon they were all seated round the table, Grampa one end and Granny at the other, with Auntie Helen and Mum fetching, carrying and serving what was to be a splendid Sunday lunch.

First there was Granny's own very special leek and potato soup. Then there was roast beef with all the trimmings, including masses of Yorkshire puddings (Uncle George's favourite).

And to top it all, for dessert it was Queen of Puddings (bread and butter pudding, with jam and meringue topping) with milk poured over it (an old Scottish custom; today we would probably have cream).

The chat flowed back and forwards across the table. Kathleen was unusually quiet, because much of the chat was about golf and she knew she too would have been good at it if she'd had the chance. But she was stuck teaching cooking and housewifery, two of the things she most disliked.

Mum and Dad still hadn't made their announcement, but eventually Granny got round to her youngest. 'What's your news, Alex and Kirsteen? How are you two managing in your flat in Melrose Gardens?'

'We …. ell,' said Mum, and there was an unexpected sudden hush round the table, the whole family sitting up, paying attention. 'We've got exciting news for you,' she said, and blurted it out quickly—almost too quickly—a bit flustered by the attention. 'Keep August free for a christening.'

This was met with delight and pleasure from everyone round the table, especially Granny and Grandpa. Their first grandchild—to be born in only a few months' time!

Elma and George, having given their congratulations, said their goodbyes and headed off to play golf. The moment they were gone, Granny telephoned her absent daughter, Isabel, to tell her about the forthcoming baby: Isabel was away in Manchester working for Ferranti Ltd.

Ferranti's, for any readers who haven't heard of it, was an electrical engineering company, one of the most advanced of its time. Isabel, as Personnel Manager, was in charge of *all* the women in *all* the factories; and by default responsible for any matters that were considered 'female'—health and safety, first aid, welfare, and (in her own words) 'anything else the men considered women's work'. She was delighted to hear she was to be an auntie but, after chatting to her pregnant sister, asked to speak to her father; she wanted to talk about the war news with him and get his views. At this point Mum and Dad decided to head back to Glasgow, calling in on Granny Wilson to share the good news with her.

They got in their car, 'borrowed' from Alex Wilson Motor Engineers, and sped off to 6, Colebrooke Terrace, one in a row of terraced houses, some of which belonged to the Glasgow Academy School. They drove through Dumbarton and before long they were on their way along Great Western Road. Just before they reached the famous Great Western Bridge (a classic of Victorian engineering), they turned into Colebrooke Terrace, passed Colebrooke Place, which led up to Belmont Street—and arrived! There was no problem parking (cars were still rare in 1939).

They bounded up the few steps, Mum noticing the well-polished brass door bell, the letter box and the opaque glass door with its flower vase pattern. The door was opened almost immediately by Ann Jardin who must have been hovering near the window in the dining room while she prepared the afternoon tea.

'Mr Alex *and* Mrs Wilson—what a treat to see you both! Don't you look well? I'll let your parents know you're here, Mr Alex.' She beamed from ear to ear.

'Please call me Kirsteen,' said Mum, but this was not going to happen for a long time. Old habits die hard.

Granny Wilson was absolutely over the moon at their news— *her* first grandchild, too. Nothing was going to be too good for this child.

Mum and Dad stayed for a chat but, having had such a large Sunday lunch (and much to Ann's disappointment), they didn't stay for a meal. Grandfather Wilson brought through a bottle to celebrate the occasion but the young couple preferred their cup of tea. Granny Wilson, a kind and good-natured lady, offered to help them both in whatever way they wanted.

This future child was going to be blessed with a loving and doting family on both sides and wouldn't be short of anything. No wonder Mum was in a great mood when she arrived home that night.

Dad was happy too but he had inner anxieties. He had already joined the Highland Light Infantry Territorials and went regularly to Maryhill Barracks for training. The more time he spent there, the more concerned he was about the future—and he wasn't selling any cars either! He kept all this to himself because that was what expected of him. A man was supposed to protect his wife and shield her from worries.

Mum carried on blissfully unaware. Or perhaps she was aware that he was worrying—who knows?

On August 15th at Park Circus Maternity Home, James Graham Wilson was born. World War II was still an improbable black cloud on the horizon—surely an impossibility so soon after 'the war to end all wars'.

Mum was spoiled rotten by all those around her; there was no lack of luxury or comfort. Nurse de Rochefort, for example, was engaged by Granny Wilson to ensure that she was properly cared for after the birth. Jimmy, the first Wilson grandchild, was wrapped tightly in his two-ply, hand-knitted shawl (of such delicacy it could be pulled through my mother's wedding ring). In fact, he was swathed in a variety of expensive but thoroughly impractical baby clothes as he lay in his black Silver-Cross pram. Surrounded by doting aunties, loving grandparents, and admired by everyone, this irrepressibly curly-haired, blonde, chubby, sweet-faced, strong sturdy boy—with a temper to go with it—was to rule the roost for the next two years in what turned out to be very difficult times.

Very soon after Jimmy was born on August 15, the Soviet Union and Nazi Germany signed a non-aggression pact. This paved the way for Hitler to attack Poland. Despite the fact that Britain and France were quick to pledge their support for Poland, they only succeeded in delaying the German invasion until the beginning of September. War was declared on September 3rd and by the middle of that same month, New Zealand, South Africa, Australia and Canada had joined the fray.

The Second World War had begun, a European war that ended up as a global military combat. It was the deadliest conflict in human history, resulting in over sixty million people being killed. The majority of these were civilians.

Baby Jimmy knew nothing of all this when he was christened on November 19th in Cardross Parish Church by the Reverend McKay. You might have thought that he *did* understand what was going on in the world because—despite everyone's best efforts— he cried before, during, and after the ceremony, without stopping once. Mum was at the end of her tether, having tried everything she knew—burping, cuddling, feeding, walking around with him on her shoulder, patting his back, pushing him in the pram. But there was no way Jimmy would stop howling. Why not give him a dummy, you may ask? Absolutely not! Simply not the thing— whatever would people think?

Events began to move at a fast pace at home. George, realising he would be off to war very soon, proposed to Elma who fortunately accepted. On 15 September they were married, their wedding reception held in the rather splendid new Beresford Hotel in Sauchiehall St, opened in 1938 to accommodate all the visitors attending the Empire Exhibition

Evacuation plans had been prepared before the outbreak of war. Dad had no intention of leaving his defenceless wife alone in a Glasgow flat with a new baby while he went off to fight, so she agreed to go to the Clyde coast—to Granny Graham's house in Cardross. No sooner had she and Jimmy arrived there than they were joined by two little boy evacuees from Clydebank. Mum always remembered how miserably homesick they were. Everything in Cardross was different—the countryside, the food, the people—even the way people spoke. The boys missed their parents dreadfully and Auntie Helen, who loved children to bits, admitted later that despite her best efforts, the young evacuees were inconsolable; she could hardly bear to see them so wretched. When nothing dangerous happened in Glasgow during the first few months of the War, and their parents sent for them, it was a relief to everyone.

The Graham family were thrilled to have baby Jimmy living with them. Granny Wilson, on the other hand, was disappointed that her new wee grandson was no longer ten minutes' walk away. She had so looked forward to pushing his pram—but it was not to be! Before the end of the year, Dad had wound up his business venture, 'Alex Wilson Motor Engineers'. It wasn't making any money and with a war on had no viable future.

Within weeks, the Melrose flat was nothing but a memory. Mum and baby Jimmy settled into their new life in Cardross. Soon Dad had his marching orders—he was off to fight for King and country. But no one knew where he was going. How quickly life had changed!

Chapter 6: The War Is Real

On my window-sill in my little bungalow in Kinross sits a much-prized heirloom—a large cloisonné vase. It came from the 'Big House' (Granny's term) in Cardross. The day it was bought and carefully wrapped and placed in Jimmy's pram turned out to be the beginning of a new lifelong friendship for my mother, Kirsteen.

It was a cold sunny spring morning and the Big House was having a sale in aid of the war effort. Granny Graham very much wanted to go. Mum needed to entertain Jimmy, who was driving her mad, crawling everywhere and roaring when he was put back in his pram, so she agreed to go too (if she kept him busy all morning and stuffed him with food before he left, he'd surely sleep in the pram for a while in the afternoon).

Auntie Helen was meeting a new friend, a widowed gentleman who lived at the end of Church Avenue, and she had absolutely no intention of accompanying them.

My grandmother and my mother Kirsteen, busy pushing Jimmy up the hill in his big black pram, chatted as they went.

'Mum,' said Kirsteen, 'you need to do something about Dad's cough, it's really bad. Can't you persuade him to cut down on his cigarettes, or even smoke a pipe instead?'

'I know, Kirsteen, I've tried—he just won't listen. He's cut down a couple of times. But he thinks it helps him when he's worrying about the War and George and Alex. What you have to remember is that he fought in the War-To-End-All-Wars. I feel so fortunate he was one of the ones who came home at all *and* in one piece. I can't nag him about his smoking. I just can't.'

Jimmy, wrapped in his lovingly hand-knitted hat, muffler and mittens, was still asleep as they pushed up first the steep hill, then the long drive that seemed to go on for ever and ever. Mum parked the pram in a quiet place, and tiptoed quietly away into the big mansion house. The entrance hall was packed with gossiping villagers, scrambling to see what bargains might be displayed on the trestle tables: cups, saucers, plates, vases, linen, pictures, ornaments galore—many of them with a small chip or crack.

In an adjoining room, tables were set out with cups and saucers—but no cakes: war rationing had arrived. Granny sat down to enjoy her cuppa, while Mum popped out to check Jimmy. Alas, he was awake! She could hear him before she saw him. But what most caught her eye was a tall, fair-haired lady shoogling his pram with one hand and rocking her own pram with the other. Mum beamed at her. The woman was talking to Jimmy in what sounded like a foreign language. Could she be Norwegian? Amazingly, she was making Jimmy laugh and smile. What a find! Mum knew she had met a kindred spirit.

The name of the mysterious lady was Flora Thompson. She was from Aberdeen, and while her husband was away in the War, she had taken a job at the Big House. The two first-time mothers talked and talked and talked. Then Mum remembered that she'd abandoned her mother and rushed off to find her, leaving Jimmy with Flora. Jimmy was fascinated by Flora and perfectly happy to be left with her. He hadn't screamed or cried at all. How wonderful!

Just as Mum reached the entrance to the big house, she spotted Granny Graham, carefully carrying a large vase and looking very pleased with herself. The treasure was clearly highly precious so Jimmy was turfed out of the pram and the vase took his place. Flora offered to walk home with them and put Jimmy, who was heavy to carry and preferred crawling to toddling, in the pram with her baby son Gordon. Result! And when they parted, Flora and Mum arranged to meet the next day for a pram outing.

Auntie Helen, clearly in a good mood, was waiting for Granny and Mum when they got back. She'd baked a cake and prepared the High Tea. This was no mean task with rationing as a constraint.

Actually, rationing was political genius. It ensured that everyone, regardless of class and status, had food on a daily basis. The UK government had realised that ships with cargos of imported food would be a prime target for German U-boats, and rationing would reduce the reliance on those imports. There were green ration books for pregnant women, nursing mothers and children under five, to ensure that children got their fair share and were properly fed.

Then there was the 'Dig for Victory' campaign. This encouraged people to home-grow their vegetables, and to keep chicken and rabbits—even pigs—to provide their own meat. It took 50,000 civil servants to police the rationing, and there was undoubtedly some Black Market abuse of the system (by March 1941, 2300 people had been prosecuted). But in general it worked well enough and ensured that the British were fed. Restaurants were set up offering cheap meals to workers and to those whose homes had been bombed.

To return to Auntie Helen's High Tea, this was a meal that everyone in Scotland knew well: a main course of fish and chips (haddock), served with a pot of tea, bread, butter and jam, then possibly scones or pancakes, followed by cake. Butter would be sparse because the allowance was only 2 oz (125 grams) per week. Cakes were also rare, with sugar in short supply. As they sat round the table, Jimmy in his high chair, Auntie Helen recounted the latest family news. Kathleen, now married to Gregor Ian, the love of her life, was hoping to provide Jimmy with a wee cousin, and Aunt Elma was expecting George's child very soon—in June.

Grampa Graham invited them just this once to listen to *his* news. He sorely missed the menfolk (and Aunt Isabel) to talk to. A mild man by nature, he was forced to bang his fist on the table to stop everyone talking about babies. 'Have you any *idea* how serious the war situation is? Will no one take it seriously? Are Churchill and I the only ones? Now that he's Prime Minister perhaps things will happen. I just hope—'

But Jimmy started to try to climb out of his high-chair, and Grampa's war rant was overtaken by family news about people they knew—mother's new friend, Flora Thompson; Helen's new friend, John; and the soon-to-be-born new cousins for Jimmy.

Nevertheless, Grampa Graham's fears were soon proved correct. Throughout the spring and summer of 1940, Hitler became the undisputed master of western Europe. France was defeated, Italy entered the War in June, and between 26th May and 4th June, the British Army—in retreat and surrounded by German forces—was rescued at Dunkirk with the help of a fleet of small boats. Without doubt their escape was a miracle, although certainly not a victory, but it did mean that Britain survived to fight another day.

For Mum and her family, the War was getting closer to home and very real. News of the internment of the Italians had reached Cardross, as had the unthinkable possibility of a German invasion. Uncle George was sent as commanding officer to defend Southend Pier on the Thames Estuary and so wasn't around when Jimmy's cousin Hamish was born in June. My own father had been sent on a mission and wasn't allowed to tell anyone his whereabouts. It was impossible now to pretend the War was someone else's problem.

Cousin Hamish was born on 21st June in Balshagray Hospital. Fortunately Aunt Elma was completely unaware of the air raid alert only four days later when a German bomber was spotted flying over Glasgow. A few weeks after this, isolated bombs were dropped in the city—in Dumbarton Road, Govan and Hillington Estate. Up to this point, no one had been taking the war threat very seriously. The air raid sirens were often ignored, and many shelters were simply not ready.

But in early September, Glasgow endured the first continuous air attack. This finally succeeded in shifting the complacent attitude. Sixteen sailors were killed and twenty-nine injured when the bombers hit HMS Sussex berthed at Yorkhill. An HMS aircraft carrier and its two Clyde-built escorts were sunk in the same month. The War suddenly became personal for every Glasgow man, woman and child—the Germans had bombed their ships. The city finally improved its home defences.

It was clear, after all, that Clydebank would be a target for German bombs: it was central to the war effort in producing not only ships, but also arms and munitions. For example, the Rolls Royce factory at Hillington made Merlin engines, used in the Spitfire aircraft. At the height of the Battle of Britain, over 20,000 people were employed at Hillington, working an 82-hour week, with a half day each Sunday per month, and production frequently interrupted by air raid alerts.

At breakfast each morning, Grampa Graham kept his family up to date with the latest war news—none of it good! Mum had no idea where Dad had been posted; she preferred not to hear all the bad news, and busied herself with Jimmy. She was upset that Dad was missing Jimmy's early years. Had she kept a diary, here's what she might have written:

July 1940

Flora and I took the boys for a walk today. Jimmy can actually walk now, but he's attached to reins, for he just suddenly takes off at great speed in any direction, while Flora's Gordon seems happy to sit in his pram. I think she's an awfully good mum and considering her husband has been declared missing and there's no news at all of him, she's amazing. She speaks very quickly in Doric, although she can speak in English if she has to. I so love listening to her and she does make me laugh, she's just fun to be with. Jimmy must like her too because he's always well behaved when she's around. Flora's husband was an army sergeant when the war broke out, she thinks he must have been in the British Expeditionary Force that went to France. She hasn't had a single letter from him, only the dreaded 'missing in action' telegram. I just can't imagine what that feels like. We hardly ever talk about the War, it doesn't bear thinking about, we just chatter about the boys, the rationing, our school days, our youth and my family (she only has one brother, her parents are dead). We had such a good laugh today remembering the school knickers our mothers knitted for us and how our bottoms had ribbed patterns on them. And how (this really made her laugh) as the youngest of four, I got the 'hand me down' knitted knickers!

Elma came to see us today and we all got a chance to hold Hamish who is a lovely wee baby boy. So thrilled to see George's boy, and didn't want to hand him back to Elma!

August 1940

Kathleen and Gregor Ian came to visit today, Gregor has asthma which prevents him from joining the war effort. Apart from the occasional bout of coughing, Dad was very quiet, saying very little, partly cos he doesn't really know what to talk about. Gregor's talking excitedly about his most recent painting, while Dad clearly thinks he should be worrying about the War and about Kathleen whose baby is due next month.

September 1940

21st—Graham was born today in Rhu, another cousin for Jimmy, Kathleen is fine and Gregor is absolutely delighted.

Great news! A letter arrived this morning from Alex, he's got four weeks leave and will be home sometime in October. Imagine! I am so excited. He'll be able to get to know Jimmy, and simply won't believe how he's grown and that he's walking now. I can't wait!

The Grahams switched on the 'wireless' and listened with horror to the appalling news from London of Hitler's 'Operation Sea Lion' tactics. There were renewed bomb attacks on ships and airfields, not to mention London and Coventry, all to soften up the British before the proposed German invasion. But the invasion never happened. With his famously compelling speeches, Prime Minister Winston Churchill succeeded in firing his country's patriotism. As the great man said, 'Never in the field of human conflict was so much owed by so many to so few.'

The magnificent defence tactics of the stoic, brave, skilled and heroic Battle of Britain pilots, combined with their use of radar (and despite their inferiority in aircraft numbers), saved the nation and inspired national pride throughout the United Kingdom. Dad's visit home was wonderful but it didn't last long.

November 1940

Well Alex is away again and I don't even know where. He wouldn't talk to me about where he was going or what it had been like. I was really upset but he was adamant it would only upset me and I wouldn't want to hear it and said I had enough to worry about just being here and looking after Jimmy and Dad who's really not looking well and has no energy. We did have some great times with Jimmy, he just loved to be carted around high on his Dad's shoulders. But I think he thought Jimmy was spoiled because he does scream when he doesn't get what he wants. 'Too many women running after him,' said Alex. I was really upset for he's just a baby and he's perfect! Alex spent a lot of his time closeted in the parlour with Dad, listening to the radio and discussing the war. It's really becoming very serious. I can't imagine what the Londoners are going through.

Anyway, he has gone and I have to get on with it.

Christmas, not a recognised public holiday in Scotland until 1958, wasn't a big event in Glasgow at the best of times and certainly not in 1940, in the middle of the War. New Year was a public holiday and the Graham family in Cardross carried out the usual traditions. The house was thoroughly cleaned, and the 'First Foot', tall and dark (in fact our ARP warden) arrived just after midnight with his piece of coal and his whisky. In previous years, everyone had sung auld Scots songs round the piano, but nobody felt like it this year and Mum, the piano player, was feeling a bit queasy. She was tired too with running after Jimmy all day. She just wanted to go to bed.

In fact, compared to all previous years, Hogmanay 1940 was a non-event.

Chapter 7: The War Comes To Cardross, 1941

There it was, in small print, in the Notifications on page two of the *Herald*. Grampa Graham simply couldn't believe it.

> *On 17 January, Prime Minister Winston Churchill will be visiting Glasgow, accompanied by Mr Harry Hopkins (President Roosevelt's special envoy to the UK) and Regional Civil Defence Commissioner, Tom Johnston.*

There were no details as to when and where he would arrive, because it was supposed to be top secret. This was fortunate since Granny wouldn't have allowed him to travel anyway—the freezing temperatures and blizzard conditions would have been disastrous for his bronchitis. Apparently Mr Churchill too had a heavy cold and a cough, but he managed to make a rousing speech in which he outlined his determination to wipe out Hitlerism.

At dinner afterwards, Mr Churchill took a liking to Mr Johnston, a Labour MP, a forthright and direct individual, who not so long ago—like many Glaswegians—had been anti-war. Thinking that here was a man who would get things done, Churchill soon promoted him to Secretary of State for Scotland. The Prime Minister was well aware how much Britain needed the help of America to win the war. That was why he was travelling with the American envoy Harry Hopkins, who became one of his greatest fans.

Two days after this political excitement, in the middle of the night Grampa started coughing and coughing, wheezing and gasping, unable to breathe.

Granny phoned for the doctor, who sat with him as his heart petered out. Nothing could be done. Not a thing. In 1941, neither antibiotics nor oxygen were available for acute bronchitis.

It was a very sad household. The love of Granny's life, her rock for thirty-seven years, was gone for good. The only person she wanted near her was her son George. So Helen phoned Elma, who succeeded in contacting him. He was given immediate compassionate leave to come home and bury his father. He arrived the next day, along with Isabel who was unbearably grieved too. She wasn't sure how she was going to cope with the stress and responsibilities of her job without his support. Mum tried to contact Alex, but failed. She thought he might be abroad but how could she know? In his letters, he wasn't allowed to tell her where he was or what he was doing.

Meanwhile there was Grampa's funeral to arrange. Who would be the pall bearers? Granny was adamant it couldn't be strangers. Traditionally it was a male job but the men were all away. Six was the usual number for the task.

However, since caskets were now being made of cardboard and cloth (saving metal and timber for the war effort), they were lighter than normal. Granny finally agreed on four of the family plus Mr Auld, the undertaker. The four were George, Gregor Iain, Isabel, and a reluctant and wretchedly miserable Helen, who had always lived at home and had never known daily life without her father.

Kathleen, Elma and Kirsteen looked after their children and tried to comfort their mum, but without much success. Like Queen Victoria when Albert died, Granny missed him sorely for the rest of her life.

But life went on. Uncle George had to report back, Elma returned to Glasgow. Kathleen and Gregor Iain were off to Helensburgh. Still, before they left, Mum made an announcement—she was expecting again—in June. Granny was pleased. But she'd just lost her husband and this was her fourth grandchild now, so her response wasn't quite as rapturous as the last time.

Shortly after, two letters arrived from my dad, Alex. One was a letter of sympathy to Granny. The other was for Mum. She read it again and again, as she sat at the breakfast table with Helen, Granny and Jimmy. Of course, he didn't even know she was pregnant yet. Some parts of his letter she kept to herself, and others she shared with the family.

'I love to hear all the news,' wrote Alex, 'especially about Jimmy, and I am so sorry I'm not there for you; all our letters are censored but I think I can say that the War is not going well at all, and we need time to build up our strength again, as we are still expecting a German attack. I have been promoted to Acting Captain by the Emergency Commission, as so many men from the regular army have already been killed, are missing in action, or prisoners of war. I'm hoping to get leave some time but I am not in control of my life anymore, so I'll let you know, meanwhile please keep writing to me.'

Mum replied almost immediately with her vital news: he was to be a father again, another baby expected in June. But there was no reply from him for the next two months.

Nevertheless, she and her friend Flora could no longer think of the War as happening somewhere else. In March it arrived on their doorstep. During the nights of 13 and 14 March, Clydebank was bombed extensively, but some of the bombs and incendiaries also landed in Cardross.

It was absolutely terrifying. Granny, Auntie Helen, and Mum— with a wriggling, crying Jimmy wrapped tightly in her arms—hid under the stairs, and waited to die. Mum thought it was the longest and the worst night of her life. Little did she know there was worse to come!

On May 6, at the stroke of midnight, they heard the zooming of planes overhead. Shortly after, a shower of incendiaries fell to the north of Cardross. This was a much bigger attack than the previous one. Bombs were falling everywhere—in the woods, in the fields and all along the shore.

The whole family was better prepared this time—with blankets, toys, food, drinks, a bucket and nappies. They huddled under the stairs, emerging only when the attack stopped. But the very next night the bombing started again, and it seemed like it would never stop. It continued for at least three hours. Then suddenly they heard one enormous crash, incredibly close—an incendiary bomb. They held their breath, waiting for the worst. Nothing. They cooried into each other expectantly, but all they could hear was an eerie silence.

Eventually, Helen bravely decided to venture out of the cupboard. The house seemed ok. The roof was still intact. Her hands shaking, she opened the front door and there—in the field opposite, down by the railway line—was an enormous crater, with shrapnel everywhere. It had somehow missed every house in Church Avenue.

Slowly, people began to come out of their houses and survey the damage. Believe it or not, shaken as they were, they started to clap and cheer. After all, they were still alive!

There and then, Mum decided she wasn't staying in Cardross to have her second baby. A few days later she met up with Flora for a walk with the boys. Surveying the surrounding streets, they were appalled by the damage. So many places were flagged up as officially dangerous that it was difficult to know where to go. They headed towards Cardross Old Parish Church but a bomb had clearly fallen through the roof. Geilston Hall was badly damaged too. Thanks to the rubble and mess everywhere, they couldn't get any further with their buggies. They turned round and headed in the opposite direction towards the railway station, only to find the railway footbridge gone too. Mum was none too nimble on her feet at this stage with her baby almost due.

Still, the boys in the buggies dropped off, and once they were asleep, bi-lingual Flora started talking in her usual, excitable way, at a hundred miles per hour. 'Ah think we hiv tae git oot o here, Kirsteen. Ye'll be haein yer bairn gye seen. Ye cannae bide here, it's jist nae safe. Ah've git an auntie in Moffat wha's husband's jist bin killt in the war. We cuid gang there fer a while—jist till things quiten doon. We cuid tak the loons an ah cuid look after Jimmy while ye heve yer bairn. She wid be gled oav oor clamjamfry an she's a richt guid cook. Her hoos is gey spacious. Ah kid speir her tae borrow bairn stuff fer ye. Fit dae ye think? See if ye kin git haud o Alex, see fit he says. Ah ken he's nae gotten leave fur the drappit—but ye never ken...'

For the first time in weeks, my mother felt excited. When she got home, she told Helen and Granny about Flora's suggestion.

Go and stay with Flora's aunt? *What?* Granny was horrified. She would have phoned Granny Wilson to enlist her help in putting Kirsteen off the idea, but the phone lines were down.

That very same day there was a ring at the door. It was a telegram for Kirsteen.

Everybody knew what a telegram could mean. She froze with terror. She asked Helen to open it for her.

IS EVERYONE OK TWO DAYS WEEKEND
COMPASSIONATE LEAVE GRANTED
ARRIVING FRIDAY ALEX

What a relief! For the next few days, Belhaven was a hive of baking and cooking—they made good use of their ration coupons.

When Dad arrived home, he took charge. He agreed that my very pregnant mum and Jimmy should leave Cardross—the Germans might renew their attacks on Clydebank. All the same, he couldn't understand why Cardross had been bombed at all. It had no airfields, no munition stores, no oil tankers—but the large number of bombs and incendiaries made it unlikely to be a straightforward mistake. Had there been a decoy site somewhere near the Cardross golf course, maybe?

Since Mum couldn't go and stay with Granny Wilson (Glasgow was far too dangerous), she told him about Flora's plan. He agreed it was a great idea and if they could get ready in time, he would accompany them on the train on Monday. He phoned Moffat Cottage Hospital, checked that they would look after his wife and—hey presto! It all happened.

Flora's auntie was very pleased and couldn't do enough for them. Clearly she liked children and she enjoyed having the boys, who loved her and amazingly (mostly) did what they were told.

Baby Sandy was born on 22 June 1941, in Moffat Cottage Hospital. Jimmy wasn't very keen on this new sibling. He took up too much of Mum's attention. So Flora had her hands full looking after the two older children.

Mum's sister Isabel desperately wanted to come and see her new nephew, but the factories were working day and night, and she simply couldn't be spared, the war was at such a critical point.

Then Alex managed a visit. He told Kirsteen he might be posted to Stirling Castle quite soon. It wasn't confirmed and his orders might change, but would she be willing to live in Alloa for a while—then he could see more of his boys? She instantly agreed. But what about Flora, who still had no news of her missing husband?

As often happens in life, especially in war time, events overtook them. Flora got an urgent phone call from her brother. He had been injured while on active service. He was no longer fit for war duty, and was returning to Scotland—planning to rent a cottage on a farm in Aberdeenshire—but he needed help. So Flora went off to Aberdeen to be at his side. Was that the end of the friendship? Definitely not. I remember Flora well.

By June Germany had successfully conquered Yugoslavia and Greece, thus delaying 'Operation Barbarossa' (the code name for the invasion of Russia by Germany and its allies) but by August, Germany was preparing to complete the final offensive on the Eastern Front —the capture of Moscow.

Nonetheless, the tide began to turn against Germany. Hitler's plan to capture Moscow foundered. The harsh winter conditions set in and through November and December, Russia successfully defended Leningrad. Meanwhile, the British captured a piece of equipment which helped them to break the ENIGMA code, the messaging system that had kept enemy communications secure. And on 7 December, the Japanese attacked Pearl Harbour, thus ensuring that the Americans, with all their wealth and military power, joined in the war effort.

Mr Churchill was happy and relieved. There just might be some light at the end of a very long and dark tunnel.

Chapter 8: A Well-Kept Secret: Operation Torch 1942

Now that Flora was up in Aberdeenshire, Mum really missed her. Flora had always lightened the daily grind—she inevitably found the funny side of everything. Mum knew she was fortunate to have so many family around—she had two lovely boys, her two sisters Helen and Kathleen, and her mother—and there were others so much worse off. But she didn't always *feel* lucky.

Helen was working hard every day at Dumbarton Hospital; Kathleen was expecting her second child in June and had a husband at home; and Granny Graham (who throughout her life had had four girls to do her bidding *and* a husband to look after her) certainly wasn't accustomed to boys. This became increasingly obvious, as Jimmy became more mobile and increasingly inquisitive.

Granny was 'not amused' the day she found her favourite mantel clock lying in bits on the floor. Mum had wondered why Jimmy was so quiet but—busy with baby Sandy—had ignored him and enjoyed the moment's peace. Still, she knew she was lucky to have so many other mums with small children living in Church Avenue. Next door was Mrs Carrie with her two boys, Martin and Allan, of similar ages to Sandy and Jimmy, and further along Church Avenue was Mrs Brown, who had a little girl, Gracie. On the other side of the road, next to the field with the bomb crater, were the McBrides, and they had small children too.

Occasionally, Mum took the boys on the train to Glasgow to see their other granny and Ann Jardin. They were received with such delight that it was well worth the effort—although it was not at all relaxing (too many precious and breakable ornaments). Jimmy loved to climb on the chairs *and* tables and—if left unsupervised—

could reach just about anything. Still, Ann Jardin must have saved up all their coupons because she always provided a fantastic spread.

If a letter arrived from Dad, or even a phone call, Mum's day suddenly seemed so much better. She genuinely had no idea where he was, or what he was doing, but she did know he was in the UK, and he kept hinting he might get home.

The news she was hoping for came in July. He was being posted to Stirling and might be there for a few months. Would she be willing to rent a house or possibly stay with her Graham relations in Alloa? The problem was that he had no idea how long he would be there or even why he was being posted to that location. Granny Graham phoned her brother-in-law and he confirmed that he and his wife Grisel would love to have them.

The whole family still missed Grandpa Graham: he had been their source of strength. He would surely have turned in his grave if he had known what the Nazis had agreed at a conference in January—the planned murder of the entire Jewish race!

All the same, I'm not sure he would have enthused about our systematic bombing of Germany's towns and cities, with 600 acres destroyed and countless deaths. Perhaps he might have thought the end justified the means? He would have been pleased that the Japanese expansion in the Pacific had been halted. But he'd have been distraught at the fall of Burma, and worried sick about the fall of Tobruk and what might happen if the allies lost control of the Suez Canal.

What nobody knew at that time was that just before Mum went to Alloa, President Roosevelt and Winston Churchill were busy planning the first combined Anglo-American operation. Churchill was concerned that the territories in North Africa, Morocco,

Algeria and Tunisia, controlled by the French Vichy government, might fall into German hands and prolong the war in North Africa.

So an amphibious operation, on an unparalleled scale, was planned by both countries. General Eisenhower was to take overall command and a three-pronged invasion was masterminded to seize the ports of Oran, Casablanca and Algiers. This operation, code-named 'Operation Torch', was planned for November. It was a very well-kept secret (a bit like the Normandy landings in 1944).

Dad finally got word that he was being posted to Stirling Castle—the home of the Argyll and Sutherland Regiment—in the summer. Mum would move to Alloa, as he'd suggested, as soon as she'd kept her promise to look after little Graham while Kathleen had her second baby. Which turned out to be yet another boy— Charlie—born in June.

After this, Mum and the boys went to stay with Uncle Sandy and his wife Grisel. This was a good time for her and she became friends with Mrs Hammie, a large lady in every way, with a big heart, and a huge infectious laugh, and boys the same age as Jimmy and Sandy. We all remember her well. Dad managed periodic visits home but the training he was going through was intense and arduous, and he still had no idea where he was going, or why. Some of his training involved water, some climbing, some armoured warfare, some endurance—overall an unusually high fitness level.

Just as Mum was getting used to having him around a bit more, and not having to worry about his imminent death, Alex told her he was being posted abroad in November. He didn't know where, or precisely when, or for how long, but he was definitely going somewhere. Mum decided she had probably outstayed her welcome with Uncle Sandy. She would go back to Cardross. But before she left, and before he was posted, they had a day out in Glasgow (always present was the unspoken thought that this might be their last time together). Mrs Hammie and Grisel looked after Jimmy and Sandy.

Mum got dressed up and Dad wore his HLI (Highland Light Infantry) kilt—thus guaranteeing their friendly treatment in the city. First they had a look at the shops but it was war time and rationing so they settled for a good chat and afternoon tea in Cranston's Tea Room in Buchanan Street. Dad wanted to go down by the river (after all he had been in the merchant navy) but there were 'NO ENTRY' notices everywhere. There seemed to be hundreds of people about, and they glimpsed what looked like a cruise ship in the dock, but it was difficult from that distance to see what was going on.

All was revealed when, only two weeks later, Dad—along with seemingly endless columns of men—was marched up the gangplank of the luxury cruise ship MV Strathmore. But the Strathmore was no longer a cruise ship; it had been converted to a troop carrier. All round the coast of Britain and in America, other troop carriers were setting off. No one knew where or why.

We have in our possession Dad's war-time sketches of places in Algeria: Timgad, El Kantara and the Mouth of the Desert. From these, and wider research, it looks likely that he played his part in the Eastern Task Force of Operation Torch, and was one of the 20,000 troops, half American and half British, who left for Algeria in early November, 1942.

Algeria was controlled by the French Vichy government, which was officially under the thumb of the Germans. The British and American forces were hoping that the French forces would see them as liberators, not as invaders. There was a suggestion at one time that the British forces should wear US uniforms: they believed the Americans would be more welcome than the British. In fact, a frontal navy force suffered disaster at Algiers but, despite fierce resistance, the city was soon surrounded and the garrison surrendered on 10th November.

Many lives were saved when the Vichy vice-premier agreed to cooperate with the allied forces and ordered an immediate ceasefire on 11 November and, to the relief of the allies, the French fleet scuttled itself rather than be taken by the Germans.

The battle for North Africa was a long way from being over, but Operation Torch, together with El Alamein, saw the first steps towards ultimate victory in Africa for the allies. This took until May 1943, however, with heavy losses on both sides.

But while Dad was away doing his bit in Algeria, it was an anxious and busy time for my mother. Like so many war wives, she learned to cope on her own, make decisions and take responsibility, a very different person from the trusting, carefree, and fun-loving bride of 1938.

Chapter 9: The Forgotten Army, 1943-1944

W hen Dad returned from Operation Torch, he was war-weary and so was Mum. They decided to spend his leave in Banff near Flora's farm, partly because Mum wanted Dad to meet Flora. They knew this was no more than an interlude, a lull until his next posting. There would be further separation to come before (and if) the War was ever to end.

By the winter of 1943—all too soon—Dad was gone again, this time to Italy. As Mum adapted once more to being a war wife, she discovered she was expecting again, with the baby due in May. Perhaps this time it would be a girl? No one in her family had managed a girl so far.

And where was Dad off to this time? He was sent to join what is often called 'the Forgotten Army'—the soldiers of the Eighth Army, who carried out the advance on the Adriatic side of Italy from September 1943. The fighting there was intense and continuous, from Bari in the south to Milan in the north, but official news of this was thin on the ground. Meanwhile, on the Mediterranean side of Italy, the US Fifth Army was carrying out its well-publicised advance towards Monte Cassino.

By this time Dad had attained the rank of Major. As such, he was responsible for getting soldiers trained—as fast as possible—in totally different fighting skills from those used hitherto. The new terrain was nothing like the huge expanses of desert with which he and his men had become familiar. The Eight Army had instead to confront a succession of fast flowing rivers, with intervening ridges that ran at right angles to the line of advance. So this time, there could be no speedy advance.

Worse still, the geographical features provided ideal defences for the Germans. The cold November weather worked against the allies too.

The advance to the Sangro river at the east end of the famous 'Gustav Line' (a belt of German fortifications) saw them having to cope with icy winds and torrential rain, living in improvised shelters and eating cold rations. Perhaps Dad's experience of wild camping days in the west of Scotland in the thirties proved a positive advantage.

In mid-December, the Eighth Army, delayed by drifting snow, blizzards and zero visibility, finally fought outside Ortona for nine days. Casualties on both sides were heavy but even after this, the Germans still had control of the city itself. The ensuing battle within Ortona, was as brutal as the defence of Stalingrad. It involved similar hand-to-hand fighting, and booby traps. And the end result? Yet another city reduced to chaotic rubble.

All the same, by the end of December Ortona was secured and General Montgomery halted the military advance to conserve resources for the spring campaign. The hiatus over the winter months was hard for the troops. It was increasingly difficult to keep up morale. Meanwhile Montgomery (who was needed in London to prepare for the invasion of France) handed over command of the Eighth to General Leese.

A fierce and much better-known struggle was also happening on the Mediterranean side. The Battle of Monte Cassino resulted in needless loss of life on a scale that beggars belief. The Gustav Line (the line of German defences stretching 100 miles across Italy) was dominated in the west by a Benedictine monastery which overlooked the main route to Rome from the top of a 1700 ft mountain.

Unable to take the monastery, the Allies decided to bomb the town of Cassino. Two hundred and fifty bombers were sent. Within four hours, the town was reduced to rubble. But the bomb craters provided effective hiding places for defending Germans, and the indiscriminate bombing spurred the morale of the German troops, making them more determined than ever. So Allied Command decided to bomb the monastery, in the mistaken belief that the enemy was using it as a fortress.

They were not. It was a Benedictine monastery.

But after the bombing, it *became* a German fortress, strategically dominant in its hilltop position, and the allies needed to take it before they could advance to Rome. The ongoing struggle was fierce and tragic, involving heroic acts on both sides. There was fierce hand-to-hand fighting. Shells and mortar rounds caused a horrifically high number of head, face and eye injuries. The only shelter the allied forces could find was in the natural hillside fissures or by making nests from the rubble. They were unable to bury their dead. Each grim battle was defined by the weather, the terrain and the supply line. Around them stretched a grey, treeless landscape— little vegetation for camouflage and no wood for overhead cover or camp fires to keep them warm.

And so the four battles of Cassino were fought over five months, through winter to the beginning of summer. The warm spring weather brought new problems when the already thirsty troops had to subsist in a parched landscape. However, on May 14 (four days after I was born in Glasgow) the Polish troops finally took the battered monastery at the summit. By the 23rd of that same month, the First Canadian Corps had advanced on the Hitler Line, and secured the bridgehead at the Melfa River.

Finally, the allies were able to advance to Rome. But at a cost. The capture of Monte Cassino had resulted in 55,000 allied casualties. The German losses were far fewer (estimated at around 22,000 killed and wounded).

So far as Dad was concerned, his active service continued on the east side of Italy into the following year. But as Mum discovered when he eventually arrived home, he was a deeply damaged and troubled man. The futility and brutality of his war-time experiences affected him deeply.

Mum may never have fully realised how traumatic it had been, and she didn't seem all that interested. She had her own responsibilities—two boisterous boys and another child on the way. Besides she had her own challenges. She wasn't feeling too well during this third pregnancy. She had recurring kidney pains in her back and was advised to rest. The grannies took charge. This time, Kirsteen was not to disappear to Moffat to have her baby. They had other plans.

Towards the end of April, she was persuaded to leave the boys in Cardross, and go to Granny Wilson's. A bed was made ready for her in the drawing room and Nurse de Rochefort was engaged to help before and after the birth. Needless to say, Ann Jardin was over the moon. 'I can't believe Mr Alex's bairn is going to be born here at 6 Colebrooke Terrace!' she said.

Dr McCutcheon, the GP, who lived in Whittingham Drive visited to check up on Mum. How was she?

She was fed up—frankly bored to tears. Also she had too much time on her hands, time to be worried sick about Dad. She'd thought she would enjoy some peace and quiet without the boys but in fact she missed them both dreadfully. She did enjoy a blether with Ann—but Ann was always busy, while Granny Wilson was killing her with kindness. The best (and only?) good thing about being there was the piano. Mum couldn't read music but she loved to play her favourite tunes by ear. 'Wouldn't it be wonderful if I could go to a musical?' she said to her GP. 'I won't get much chance after the baby is born.'

'Leave it with me,' said Dr McCutcheon. And that's how, three days later, my mother was taken to the cinema by her doctor.

The very next time she saw him was somewhat different. She was in labour and it was the middle of the night and a beautiful and perfect baby was delivered in the drawing room of 6 Colebrooke Terrace, and this time it was a girl—*me*! My official name was to be Kirsteen Morag Wilson but they would call me Morag (so as not to be confused with Mum).

Allegedly, I was 'no bother' compared to the boys, but it's possible that Mum by this time was simply more experienced. Before long, I obligingly did what all new parents need and long for: I slept right through the night.

As she had done for my two brothers, Granny Wilson opened a National Savings Account and deposited in it the huge sum of £100. The accounts she opened were to prove a godsend for each of us in the years to come.

Mum decided at this point to move back to Glasgow permanently and have some independence. Four years of living with her mother in Cardross was not what she'd expected or planned when she got married in 1938. So we settled into a new home at 25, Kelvinside Terrace. It was a rented three-bedroomed flat in a four-storey tenement with a communal back green and we stayed there for the next twelve years. We kids liked our flat. It was second from the top, and there were children to play with, particularly the Campbells, a large family who lived in the basement. One up from us, at the top of the building, were Mrs Clark and her daughter Helen.

But Dad was still in Italy. His war hadn't finished yet and he still hadn't seen his beautiful daughter (me). Did he even know I existed? I'm not sure. For him, some of the toughest fighting had yet to come. Over the summer months, the Eighth army advanced first to the Trasimene Line, winning a battle at Arezzo, then—when the bulk of the army was switched to the Adriatic sector—they occupied the south of Florence,

On August 25, 1944, they attacked the Gothic Line, which they breached west of Pescaro. In September, they sustained heavy casualties at the Gemmano Ridge. Finally, on 21st September, the allies captured Rimini. Through the months of November and December, they took Cesena, Ravenna and Fraenza.

The Eighth Army line now ran from Monte Grande along the Senio river to the Adriatic coast. At this point, some of the divisions were withdrawn and sent to the Western Front, but others stayed. Dad was among the remainers. Dog-tired and war weary, they spent the cold winter months in Italy, preparing for what they hoped would be their last battle.

But first they had to celebrate Hogmanay. And so, as 1944 came to an end, my now not-so-teetotal Dad was celebrating with a dram or two in Italy, while Mum—finally settled in her first real home— invited in the neighbours, the first of whom arrived with the traditional bottle of whisky, black bun and lump of coal.

Chapter 10: The War Ends

Mum, who was very much aware of the huge contribution Glasgow had made to the war effort, could see the weariness in the people all around her. It wasn't surprising they were tired. Throughout the war, the Clyde shipyards (along with those on the Tyne) had produced 994 naval ships and 503 merchant vessels, not to mention rockets, bomb cases, gallon drop tanks, and transporters, as well as 600,000 pairs of boots, 1,100,000 tins of powdered milk, and endless packets of cigarettes.

There had been a few industrial demarcation disputes on the way, not to mention the ongoing perpetual struggle for a decent living wage. At times union leadership had struggled with the influential, but often unpopular, communist influence. After four years of long working hours, rationing, shortages and loss of loved ones, constant anxiety was taking its toll on all of Glasgow's people—including my mother who had heard nothing from Dad, not even a letter. Did he know that he had a daughter? Was he even alive?

These troubling thoughts might have kept her awake but she was so tired by bedtime she literally dropped off the moment her head hit the pillow.

So where was he?

With the benefit of hindsight, we now know that he must have been with the Eighth Army somewhere on the fringe of the Lombardy plains. The contingent was smaller than before, some divisions having been withdrawn to the Western Front.

Was he part of the offensive which began in April 1945 when the Eighth successfully crossed the Senio, Santerno and Sillaro rivers and by 19th April, had routed the enemy from the Argenta Gap?

The evidence suggests that he was. Once the River Po was within range of their guns, it was full speed ahead. The Polish troops entered Bologna on the 21st, and by 29 April, the Eighth Army had entered Venice.

A few days later, on May 2nd, the German Commander in Chief surrendered. That was my father's last battle and officially 'victory in Europe' had arrived. Dad's war service in Italy was over. Theoretically, he could go home—though it wasn't quite that simple.

By the time he was demobbed (officially released from service) and returned to his family in Glasgow, it was the end of 1945. His external battles were over, though the internal conflict had barely begun. But at least he was alive!

Uncle George, Mum's only brother, was stationed in Lucknow, in India, and he didn't get home until the following year. My cousin Hamish, six years old at the time, remembers how scared he felt—and yet wildly excited too—as on October 4 he waited to meet his father off the train at Queen Street Station. He clung to his mum with one hand, the other tightly gripping his prize possession, the precious war-time letters from his Dad.

For some, the War didn't finally end until the atomic bombs that were dropped on Hiroshima and Nagasaki in August 1945 forced the Japanese to surrender. World War II had left Europe in ruins, with millions of its inhabitants dead. Perhaps one of the most tragic outcomes was that Poland, the country the UK had gone to war to defend, was abandoned to Stalin's soviet-controlled eastern Europe. It wasn't what Churchill wanted but at the Yalta Conference, his wishes were overruled by his allies, Roosevelt and Stalin.

For most people in the UK, the War officially ended in May, and VE (Victory in Europe) Day was a momentous occasion. After nearly six years of hostilities, it was time for a national party, and there were celebrations all over the country.

Glasgow was no exception. Along the length of the Clyde, ships used their sirens to sound out the morse code for V for Victory. In George Square, lit by floodlights, there was a display of rockets and squibs, and on Hope Street a hundred thousand people danced to the music blaring from loudspeakers. There they were, dancing reels, dancing for the joy of it, forming human chains, jumping on and off the buses and trams, linking arms and whistling and singing. All you could see was a mass of red, white and blue everywhere, girls with their coloured berets, bunting draped on the shop fronts, the vendors doing a wonderful trade in Union Jacks, and here and there, bonfires burning effigies of Hitler. (The day after the party, three tons of empty bottles were collected in George Square.)

My Aunt Helen was in the city centre, celebrating in person with her new friend John, the widower. And even though she was still desperately worried about her brother George, she never regretted going along. It was, she said, 'a once-in-a life-time experience that I'll never forget, so much unrestrained joy and abandon, after such misery. Even the policemen joined in. It was just so good to laugh and dance again, just to be carefree.' She recalled soldiers climbing on statues and either wrapping bunting on them, or sticking a Union Jack wherever they could. Thinking now of the Donald Dewar statue in Buchanan Street, almost always topped with a traffic cone, perhaps it was the start of a Glasgow custom?

Was my mother there? Unhappily no. She had three children to look after. Still, everyone in the tenement hung out their bunting and their flags, and shared a wee dram (apart from Mum who didn't drink at all). Our upstairs neighbours, Mrs Clark, and her daughter

Helen walked down to the floodlit university to see it mirrored in the river Kelvin, where thousands had gathered to see the lights after years of blackout.

Mum knew by this time that Dad was alive and that he was coming home as soon as he could—to meet his new daughter for the first time ever, and of course to see his two growing boys.

But one of the first jobs facing her was to enrol Jimmy for school. Which school should she choose? The Glasgow Academy School (boys only, of course) was only ten minutes' walk away. It was highly regarded, and given that his grandfather was a Glasgow Academical, it was really a no-brainer, especially when Granny Wilson offered to pay the fees.

That same Granny duly took Jimmy off to Copelands in Sauchiehall Street to kit him out with his school uniform. She continued to do this for all of us (always one at a time) throughout our school days. And school shoes? Twice a year we were taken to a shop called Vernon's in Great Western Road.

At the beginning of term, Mum dutifully delivered Jimmy to the school. He was curious and wanted to find out what this thing called 'school' was like, so he went in eagerly. Once he'd changed his shoes (and he *could* tie his laces), his teacher stood all the little boys in a line and marched them into the classroom. Jimmy liked marching so that bit was good, but next he had to sit down and stay sitting at a wee desk (and he was a big boy) and not allowed to speak unless he put up his hand.

This was not so good and soon he was very bored. When Mum picked him up after what seemed to him like a very long day, he informed her he had no intention of going back THERE. He had been accustomed to roaming free in the Cardross garden, exploring, touching, running, climbing and playing with Martin, the boy next door. Years later, he likened school to being put in a strait jacket. As in the army, discipline, obedience, conformity were the cornerstones of the school system, and there were dire consequences for those who rebelled. ('Consequences' is a modern word: it was called 'discipline' and 'punishment' in the forties, fifties and sixties.)

When Dad eventually arrived back at the end of the year, Jimmy was a miserable school boy, Sandy was a contented toddler, and then there was me—a docile, smiley little soul of eight months. The boys weren't used to having a man around telling them what to do, so they didn't take kindly to having him in their house *and* in their mum's bed.

For his part, our Dad, who for two years had lived for this moment of coming home, found it almost impossible to feel he belonged. He had been in another world, witnessing the unspeakable horrors of war. He had endured extreme physical deprivation, too. But he had been supported by the comradeship of his fellow soldiers, the mutual trust, the feeling of unity and family.

When he was away, he'd dreamed of getting home. Now he was home, he was withdrawn, unable to talk to anyone. For him, it was like being on another planet, like watching a movie about other people in a distant place. He could hardly sleep. He didn't consider talking about his difficulties to anyone, particularly not to Mum— his job was to protect her. What was he to do for the rest of his life? He was only 36.

He found that keeping his hip flask filled and taking a wee dram to cheer himself up was something that helped. It made him relax enough to communicate, to get through each day, and it numbed the turbulent emotions that bubbled below the surface. (The term post-traumatic stress disorder—PTSD—was mentioned first in 1980, in a medical textbook on mental disorders. In 1945, it didn't have a name, which meant officially it didn't exist.)

Unsurprisingly, Kirsteen and Alex, my mother and father, were not the same people they had been before the War. They wanted to be—and they tried to be—but their different war experiences and lack of communication had created an ocean of ignorance and misunderstanding between them.

And now there was a third person in the marriage—alcohol!

My Grandfather Wilson was awarded this book as a prize by the Glasgow Academy in 1887.

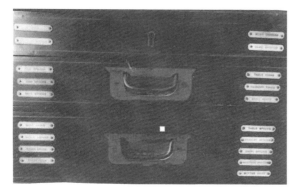

← 1908 A cutlery chest—a wedding present for my Wilson grandparents. Granny Wilson was also allowed to take her maid Ann Jardin with her & one of her first tasks was to learn how to set the table correctly using the cutlery from this chest.

→
This photo of my father Alex, his sister Betty & their mum (my Granny Wilson) was taken at the end of World War I, 1918.

← In the 1930's, Dad left the Navy, trained as a mechanic & started up his own business: 'Alex Wilson Motor Engineer'.

→ On June 22, 1938, Mum & Dad were married in Landsdowne Memorial Church in Great Western Road

← My brother Jimmy, born in 1939, the first Wilson grandchild, here attended by his mum & both doting grannies.

← It's 1939. Is Grampa Graham worrying what the future will hold for wee Jimmy, his first grandson?

→ A letter from Grampa Graham in 1939 to the Glasgow *Herald:* shows he had reservations about Neville Chamberlain's Munich Agreement

Dangers Ahead

Belhaven, Cardross.

Sir.—I confess to a feeling of envy at the complacency of mind that characterises the letter of your correspondent 'P. H. N." and of all those who may think like him, and who are able to find something new and promising of a more Christian attitude in Mr Chamberlain's efforts at Munich.

As I value my skin as much as most folk I feel a certain amount of relief that there is to be no war yet, and I am ready to admit that the Government are in all probability by far and away the best judges of the necessities of the present occasion; but that there is tremendous danger ahead and need for unceasing vigilance and effort on our part is only too evident.

Napoleon said that God is always on the side of the big battalions, and so it must appear at present. But it would be better perhaps if we keep the name of Christ out of it and sing our "Te Deums" on a more appropriate occasion: otherwise some of us may be driven to believe that there is a good deal to be said for a German god and his prophet Adolf Hitler.—I am, etc.,

JAMES GRAHAM.

1940: the war is not going well

Ardenbank
Ashley Road.
Altrincham.
Cheshire.
15 . 8 . 40.

Miss I. G. GRAHAM,
Personnel Manager.
(Women)

Dear Bride.

It was nice to get your letter out of the blue and hear what has been happening to you all these years.

Aunt Isabel (above), Personnel Manager in the Ferranti Moston factory, writes:

Here in Munitions we have 5000 women and girls working 6 days of eleven and a half hour shifts day and night. Long hours and night shifts are particularly hard when women have homes and children to look after. My suggestion of a government organised Child Minder scheme was dismissed after a Ministry of Health report stated that 'minders' for the most part were unsuitable people to care for children.

← Dad gets leave to see his second son Sandy born on 22 June 1941 in Moffat Cottage Hospital.

A family photo before Dad goes back to war. →

← Dad in Algeria in 1942.

Operation Torch November 1942

↑
Dad's paintings of North of Batna & the Mouth of the Desert
suggest he was in Algeria.

The Forgotten Army, 1943-1945

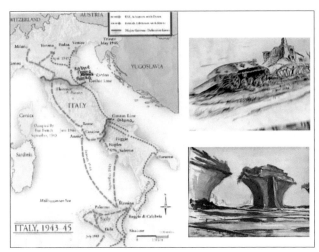

ITALY, 1943-45

Italy is finally defeated & Dad comes home

Dad's painting of a bombed bridge in Cattolica (near Rimini) is dated 1944; on the back, in his hand-writing, *11 Mobile Section 8th Army*
←

← Left to right: Sandy, me, Jimmy. I arrive May 14, 1944 when Dad is fighting in Italy, four days before Monte Cassino is taken

After the War

←
1949 Mum, Sandy, me & Jimmy holidaying in beautiful Portincaple on the shores of Loch Long

← Left to right: Sandy, Jimmy holding baby Elizabeth (born July 14, 1950) & myself.

Sandy and I in Kelvinside Terrace in our school uniforms. At this time boys and girls were educated separately. The girls' school was in Garnethill St, the boys' in Elmbank St →

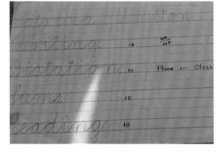

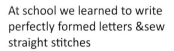

At school we learned to write perfectly formed letters &sew straight stitches

1954: a Jubilee Celebration of the Glasgow High School for Girls
Back Row: left to right (ringed): Jean Lindsay, Diane Muir, Elizabeth
Dalziel and Sheila McVey *Middle Row*: left to right (ringed):
Elizabeth Dickie, Pat Whitton, me &Heather Craig

We have no
income & a rent
to pay so Dad
returns to work
in the Merchant
Navy on the
MV Hannington
Court, launched
in 1954. This is a
painting he did of
the ship.

Chapter 11: A Tenement Flat in Hillhead

I don't recall much about my pre-school years in Kelvinside Terrace. Dad was there but I barely remember him: he was a remote distant figure who appeared at meal times, then vanished. Jimmy had started school in 1944, the year I was born. Sandy went to the Glasgow High School for Boys two years later in 1946.

Soon I had to start my education too, and in August 1949, I was sent to Park School, an independent girls' school, the same one Aunt Isabel and Aunt Helen had attended. And I really liked it. My teacher, Miss Robertson, was kind, and since I had two older brothers, I wasn't accustomed to kindness, or attention, or praise. I was, however, accustomed to being teased or ignored. I have vivid memories of having my pigtails (plaits) tied to the bedpost while I slept—not to mention the time I was lifted up on top of the wardrobe. My screams soon brought Mum to sort the boys out. So next time they placed, not me, but my much loved and cherished doll up there, well out of my reach.

My new school was girls only—and girls liked to play with dolls, not bows and arrows, guns and toy soldiers. An enjoyable new experience for me!

For the first term I came home at lunch time and Grandfather Wilson was waiting at the school door for me every day as per instructions. I felt quite proud of him, so well dressed and sporting his ebony handled cane. I had trouble keeping up with him as we walked from the school in Lynedoch Street to the foot of Belmont Street.

Before long, I was expected to find my own way home, using the tram or caur. I got the hang of it fairly quickly but there's one tram trip I remember well. 'Fares pal-leeze!' called the well uphol-stered 'clippie' in her serge-green corporation uniform, a scary creature for sure. It was lunch time, the caur wasn't busy and the clippie waited patiently as I looked under my blazer for my school purse which should have been attached by a cord round my neck and— horror of horrors—it wasn't there! I must have left it in the gym changing room.

So without my purse, I didn't have my halfpenny fare. And what did I do? Burst into tears, of course. A kind lady intervened and paid the fare for me. I never forgot my purse again. Nor have I forgotten the kindness of an unknown Glasgow lady.

Following the war and long afterwards, Glasgow was a grimy and smoky place, everything blackened by decades of coal fires in factories and houses. People smoked cigarettes inside and out, and lung diseases like TB were widespread. It was certainly not a healthy place to live and in the summer of 1949 we were fortunate to escape for a while.

When I was five, after my first year at school, we holidayed in the most beautiful place ever—a place called Portincaple, a hamlet on the shores of Loch Long in Argyll and Bute. To get there, we took a tram to Anniesland, a train to Helensburgh, then to Gare-lochhead, and from there we boarded the single-track West High-land line to Whistlefield. Our home for the holiday was a tiny But 'n Ben right on the shore. The lady who owned it lived beside us in an even tinier caravan. We were able to use her rowing boat to fish, and the water was teeming with mackerel (at one time Portincaple had been a fishing village).

Our cousins, the Smiths, who lived in Helensburgh, sometimes joined us: boys and more boys. Was I fed up with them? Yes! Jimmy, Graham, Charlie, Campbell and Sandy all had a great time, jumping in and out of the boat, fighting army battles, playing cowboys and indians, shooting at each other and leaping out from behind the trees, yelling and waving sticks and guns—it was never-ending. In genuine child's play—not the kind devised and controlled by adults—there's a natural pecking order learned and accepted by all children. I was a girl and the smallest. That says it all.

One lovely memory was when Granny Wilson and her sister, Auntie Teenie, came to visit us. They came in a car as far as the Green Kettle at the top of the hill in Whistlefield, driven by Granny's nephew Hamish Service, a minister in Kilmarnock. We all had to wear our best clothes. My hair was specially dressed with ribbons and I got to wear my party dress. The boys were not so happy!

Dad visited us too for a couple of days and that was really exciting because we went out fishing. The boys had to row the boat, but I was allowed to hold the thick string fishing-line that we pulled along behind us. There were fluttery things attached to it. Were they feathers, I wonder? Whatever they were, they attracted the fish and every night for tea we had mackerel, dropped alive into a pan of boiling water, then served on a plate and accompanied by tatties. We ate the lot. We were hungry.

The other highlight of Dad's visit was the model boat he brought with him, a replica of the famous Cutty Sark. He had made it himself (the original was a clipper-ship built on the river Leven in Dumbarton in 1869). The story of the Cutty Sark would fill a book all by itself, so I'll just say its history is fascinating. The boys spent hours and hours playing with the small boat in the water. Whenever the wind or the tide swept it out to sea, Sandy or Jimmy would row out and bring it back. Throughout their lives they loved sailing. Their understanding of the effect of wind on sails and their respect for the strength of the tide were probably learnt on the shores of Loch Long in Portincaple. Like so much important knowledge we acquire in our lives, it wasn't taught; it was unconsciously learned.

Back in Glasgow, Dad had started up a shop in 200, Great Western Road, selling domestic appliances—mainly fridges and washing machines. Undoubtedly a clever and inventive man, he had even built a washing machine. He never patented this (one hand-built washing machine was never going to be a money maker). He was absolutely right, though, that domestic appliances were the future and after the War the demand for them was high.

Initially his shop was profitable but this didn't last long. Soon Dad met a chap called Jimmy Scott and they decided to go into business together, selling second-hand cars and making side-cars for motor bikes. And so 'Scott and Wilson' was born, with its premises in Grovepark Street in Maryhill. This venture was never to make much money—for a number of reasons: a slow turnover, cash flow problems, wealthy customers who didn't pay their bills, and profits disappearing as Dad kept filling his hip flask with usquebaugh. Like so many Scots, he loved the poems of Rabbie Burns, especially 'Tam O' Shanter' which he often recited by heart at Burns suppers. He understood all too well the magical powers of a wee dram:

> *Inspiring bold John Barleycorn*
> *What dangers thou canst make us scorn!*
> *Wi tippeny, we fear nae evil*
> *Wi usquebae we'll face the devil!*

In the summer of 1950, Jimmy, Sandy and I were sent to Cardross to Auntie Helen and Granny Graham. We were accustomed to Cardross and I don't think it occurred to any of us to ask why we were there. I was six years old by this time, so as soon as we arrived I went along Church Avenue to see if any of the Brown Family (Gracie, Isabel and Sheena) wanted to come out to play, while the boys played next door with Martin Allan and John Carrie.

Apart from the bomb crater in the field in front of the railway line, it was a safe place for kids and we were allowed to roam freely, so long as we showed up promptly for dinner (at noon) and high tea (late afternoon).

One day, as we were getting stuck into our bacon and eggs for tea, we heard the wheels of a car crunching on the drive. We didn't have a car and we didn't know anyone who did, so we all rushed to the door—and there were Mum and Dad! We were pleased to see them, of course, but our feelings were mixed. Would we have to go home to the city?

Suddenly we were distracted by a squeaky, crying noise coming from a white bundle in Mum's arms. The 'bundle' was our new little sister, to be called Elizabeth Helen. What we didn't know was that Mum had been seriously ill with kidney complications in a nursing home in Clairmont Terrace. This time Dad had been on hand for the birth—though not actually in the room. Men at a birthing? Not in 1950, and for many years after, they were kept well out of the picture. After all—so the thinking of the time went—what could men do except get in the way?

For me and Sandy (I'm not sure about Jimmy) childbirth was definitely the best-kept secret ever. Maternity clothes were designed to cover the bump, and how babies came into this world was a complete mystery—one that didn't even interest us. Women were always having babies. So what? It was a topic never really mentioned or discussed. A bit like the rain or the sun, it was just something that happened.

Mum was now responsible for the finances, and with three children, a new baby, and a husband spending too much money on drink, she was finding it harder to pay the bills. To save money, in August 1951 I was transferred to the Glasgow High School for Girls (a Glasgow Corporation School with minimal fees but entry dependent on an entrance exam). It was the same school Mum and her sister Kathleen had attended.

Each morning on his way to work, Mum's brother, Uncle George first dropped his son Hamish off at the Glasgow Academy, then Sandy and me at the Beresford Hotel.

Sandy trotted off down Elmbank Street, while I climbed up Garnethill Street to the bleak, dark building that was to be the hub of my life for the next eleven years.

Chapter 12: The Glasgow High School For Girls

At first I was very happy at my new school. My primary three teacher, Miss Bissett, was kind and gentle and I wasn't scared of her. I had to sit at a little desk with a hinged lid and an ink pot, and use a pen with a nib. Painstakingly, slowly and with much blotting paper and ink-covered fingers, I learned to write beautiful script—no mean achievement.

My jotters had two dark, parallel lines, with fainter lines below and above. Any letter with a top or a tail had to just touch exactly the line above or below. I spent a long time learning to put tails on letters so that my writing was 'joined up'.

But I have a sadder tale to tell about my handwriting. Last year I decided—for fun—to write the address for my friend Angela's Christmas card in my best school-learned, joined-up handwriting instead of my usual printed label. I took the envelope to the Post Office, handed it to the young girl and asked if she would find the post code for me.

She looked at it, screwed up her face and returned it to me. 'I'm so sorry. I can't read your handwriting at all.' I didn't think she would appreciate me telling her it had taken a year out of my life—not to mention untold pain and practice—to learn to write like that. As we oldies often do, I just zipped the lip and printed it out in caps.

From primary one onwards, we learnt to count, spell, write, and read. And for that I am extremely grateful. These skills are undoubtedly essential tools for survival, and for continued learning. I am not convinced, however, that it had to be such a joyless painful experience. Our primary four teacher, Miss Wood, was not as kind as Miss Bisset; in fact she wasn't kind at all, and most of us endured the school day in a constant state of anxiety and fear.

Her main teaching method was firing questions at the class. If you didn't know the answer, and so didn't put up your hand, then you were a sitting duck. Naturally you would be picked on to provide the answer you clearly didn't know, and then criticised because of your ignorance, while the rest of the class (relieved that they *hadn't* been picked) were encouraged to laugh.

It was Catch 22. If you raised your hand *as if* you knew the answer, and then got chosen, and looked blank, then you were 'telling lies'—which was a heinous offence. Most of us remember with horror the fate of one girl who fell into this trap. She was ordered to stay outside the classroom on her own for two whole days, and the rest of us were told not to speak to her even at break times. I'd like to think we disobeyed the instruction but somehow I think we were too scared.

Did our parents know any of this? I doubt it. The general parental view prevalent in the fifties (and in the sixties) was that if you were in trouble, then you must have deserved it.

Playtime, lunchtime and after school were when we had fun and made friends. In my year, five of us had an amazing and very exclusive club. Unsurprisingly and with a complete lack of originality, it was called 'The Secret Five'.

Heather was Captain, because her dad, as a journalist, had the badges made and engraved at his work. Naturally, she had 'Captain' and 'Number 1' on her badge.

The official purpose of our club was to save up with a particular treat in mind. Once a month after school we aimed to have 'afternoon tea' (a cup of tea, and a cake too if we could afford it) at the

City Bakeries above the furniture shop in Charing Cross. I suppose we were copying our mums.

Every month we turned up at the tearoom after school, wearing school hats and blazers. What we talked about none of us can remember, but it was a very exclusive club (or at least we thought so). We even used to leave a tip for the waitress under the saucer like our mums did. As we were all just eight or nine years old at the time, it was a big deal for us, and it was fun. We were well-mannered but very shy, and neither the waitresses nor other customers could persuade us into a conversation of any kind. We knew most adults were best avoided because they asked boring, unanswerable questions like, 'How do you like school?'

Heather's dad was often at home when we got back from school and sometimes obligingly helped us with our homework. I adored going round to Heather's because her mum always made a cup of tea just for us, with a plate of bought cakes on the table (my mum never *bought* cakes) and they had television too. I had to reluctantly rush off home in time for my tea at six. It was a twenty-minute walk from Barrington Drive, off Woodlands Road, to Kelvinside Terrace, but I always made it on time.

In our house, there were six of us and we were supposed to eat whatever was on the plate. Food generally was something you ate when it was put in front of you (it was never considered interesting enough to talk about). I drew the line at tripe, though, and to this day I can't stomach its taste, smell, colour or texture. Mostly we dutifully ate what we were given because we were hungry, except occasionally when Jimmy, who disliked sloppy mixed-up food, refused to eat mince and tatties. If he was *forced* to eat it (and he was a very stubborn boy), he used to rush to the bathroom immediately afterwards and vomit it up. The retching noises made us gag as we sat at the table, our appetites defeated, but still dutifully pushing the food round the plate. Jimmy always triumphed in the end, and would be given something different to eat. If I stayed for tea at Heather's, her mum used to ask us what we would *like* to eat. No wonder I loved going there.

Weekends for me were good times. Simply not having to go to scary school was a treat in itself. Heather would cycle round from Barrington Drive on her brother's bike. I had Sandy's old blue bike and we spent hours spinning up and down Kelvinside Terrace and Doune Quadrant, showing the young Campbells from the basement how to balance and stay on the bike. A favourite pastime was speeding up and down with a small passenger balanced on the handlebars. For sure there were a few grazed knees, and occasional tears.

The back greens, the tenement closes, the wash houses, the streets and the 'Pleasures' were the playgrounds for us children. Children in the fifties were never entertained as such; they were simply sent out 'to play'. The Pleasures were our name for the sloping ground leading down to the dirty, deep and rat-infested River Kelvin directly opposite our tenement block. The river was dangerous and absolutely forbidden, which as we got older, made it even more appealing.

Interesting characters who wandered in the Pleasures down by the river, but more often in our street, included Prince Monolulu, the only black person we ever saw (he was a peripatetic bookkeeper who collected bets) and Hairy Mary (every district had one), an alcoholic lady who walked about carrying a clinking shopping bag, muttering and talking to herself.

Other regular visitors were the gas lamp lighters, the rag and bone men, the coal men with their carts and horses, and the milkman with his cart. Jimmy delivered milk before he went to school to earn some money. He had started to smoke like Dad and somehow the £100 deposited in his savings account by Granny Wilson at his christening was disappearing fast.

Chapter 13: The Arlington Baths & The Coronation

If we weren't playing in the streets, we were fortunate enough (thanks to Granny Wilson's money in the bank) to be able to go to the swimming baths. In Glasgow's west end there were two private swimming clubs—the Arlington (which I went to) and the Western.

Sandy and Jimmy belonged to the Western, which had set days for boys, and different ones for girls. Along the length of the pool there were ropes, with rings at the end hanging from the rafters. At the deep end there was a trapeze, and a high diving board. A supervisor/lifesaver (Mr Jamieson) did exist, but he was rarely to be seen and spent most of his time hiding in his wee smoke-filled office at the side of the pool.

Once we could swim we spent hours just playing in the baths and I think this is possibly where I learnt to love the water. It was never about competition, or racing, or personal bests, or keeping fit, although I do vaguely remember an annual swimming gala. Our Arlington bathing costumes were bright red, practical and functional with a large 'A' emblazoned on our flat chests. Definitely not sexy.

When it was too wet to play outside, I escaped to another world by reading a book. I was fortunate to have Helen Clark in the flat above—she ran a lending library just for me. As soon as I finished one story, I was upstairs asking for the next and she had a vast library of girls' books.

In our own house we had all the Arthur Ransome volumes because Jimmy too loved to read. (Sandy preferred to play with his collection of lead soldiers.) Dad had lots of books of his own but I was too young yet to enjoy any of them. Every week he would buy the boys a copy of the *Eagle,* the comic they loved, and as soon as I was eight, I was allowed *Girl,* which I devoured eagerly.

On Sunday afternoons, there was a different kind of school in Stevenson Memorial Church—Sunday School. Heather and I wouldn't—and didn't ever—speak one word to our teacher Miss Rolland, although she was a lovely young girl. When asked a question, we would look at the floor, blush, wriggle and refused to open our mouths. In the end she gave up trying and left us alone. As a result my biblical knowledge is flimsy. All I remember is us giggling a lot, and shuffling our bottoms along the bench so the end person fell off onto the floor.

Sandy and Jimmy's religious education didn't fare much better. They were sent to Crusaders, at a Byres Road Church opposite the Botanic Gardens, until one Sunday Sandy was spotted skiving and playing in the Botanics instead. When this was reported to his mother, that was the end of Crusaders. However, they somehow still managed to attend the Crusader Camps, and possibly picked up some religious education there.

Occasionally on a Sunday we visited Dad's Aunt Teenie and his sister, my Auntie Betty. This was special and we wore 'our Sunday best'. Scrubbing up and catching the train to Ayr on time was a challenge for us all. Auntie Teenie lived most of the year in Ayr in Arnsheen Hotel on Racecourse Road, and spent the summer in the Kyles of Bute Hydro in Rothesay—but more about that later.

Elizabeth and I always enjoyed our days out in Ayr. First we had lunch in Teenie's hotel, where we were all admired and fussed over and we girls were treated like celebrities. Then we were taken to a dress shop to choose a dress and a coat and a hat for Sundays. The boys were measured for kilt outfits, though this wasn't something they relished. After our shopping, we would visit Auntie Betty, Uncle Willie and their yappy Corgis.

Another enjoyable visit was to a relation we always called 'Cousin Dorothy'—a wealthy Buchanan relation. Her house, Torwood Cottage in Rhu, the gardens and her dog Nigel were the main attractions, although we undoubtedly liked Dorothy too. Born in Partick in 1901, she was the only daughter of a coal merchant who—thanks to his profitable business—had the foresight to buy a couple of pubs in Glasgow's east end. As a result, his only daughter was what you might call 'comfortably off'. She was a single lady and provided my first introduction to the sort of person who lives for their dog and treats it just like a child. Although this was long before 'poo bags' were in use, I do remember being amazed and disgusted that although she didn't pick up the poo, she would wipe the dog's bum personally. I don't think there ever was such a spoiled (or 'loved' if you prefer that description) dog as Nigel.

Towards the end of the school term in June 1953, the Queen's Coronation took place, an historic occasion celebrated nationwide and, for the first time ever, televised. Those of us who didn't possess a TV managed to watch the grainy black-and-white moving pictures of the occasion somewhere—somehow—on a 12-inch screen. And it seemed like a miracle to have the young Queen and Westminster Abbey in your front room.

My friend Elizabeth Dickie remembers going with another pal (Hope Gregory) to Liz Dalziel's house around that time. The three of them ran about the garden with homemade crowns and dressed up in red crepe-paper cloaks. They took turns 'crowning' each other. Picnics, parades, concerts, bonfires and street parties took place all over Glasgow, and there were trestle tables laden with cakes and sweets at the street party in Simpson Street behind Maryhill Road. Perhaps the best treat for most of us were the green tins filled with toffees and given to every child in Glasgow. On the lid was a picture of the Queen and the Duke of Edinburgh.

Glasgow loves a party and the night before the Coronation there was a party in George Square to rival Hogmanay. The Lord Provost even toured the city to thank everyone for their magnificent red, white and blue decorations. But not all was perfect. Some Elizabeth II coronation mugs were deliberately smashed in the street. Why? A political point was being made. If you were Scottish, the Queen was the *first* Queen Elizabeth, not the second. Elizabeth I, the Tudor Queen, was Queen of England, not Scotland. It wasn't until 1603 that the two crowns (and countries) were united under the Stuart King James VI of Scotland (James I of England)

A crowd of 60,000 people, dressed in their Sunday best, gathered on the terracing at Hampden Park. There were performances of dancing and gymnastics, and lots of choirs singing. To top it all, there was an inspection of the guard of honour of the Glasgow Highlanders, Dad's old regiment. It was a really sunny July day and many people fainted with the heat. This unaccustomed sunshine had undoubtedly helped to create a holiday atmosphere, with children running around the grass in their swimming costumes.

A one-off football tournament was also organised to celebrate the occasion, bringing together the four best English and the four best Scottish football clubs at that time. There was no European football in those days, so this was a great chance for the clubs to measure themselves against another country. Perhaps you could guess which teams were selected as the four best? From Scotland, it was Hibs, Aberdeen, Rangers and Celtic. The English teams were Arsenal, Manchester United, Newcastle United and Tottenham Hotspur. And the result? In the semi-final, Celtic beat Man U, 2-1, and Hibs beat Newcastle United 4-1. In the final, Celtic beat Hibernian by two goals.

There was yet another excuse for Glasgow to party when the young Queen and her husband toured Scotland a few weeks after she had been crowned. One of my schoolfriends, Pat, remembers the excruciating disappointment of their visit. She waited an interminably long time—hours and hours—and when she finally caught a glimpse of our new Queen, she wasn't even wearing a crown or a gown—just a blue outfit and a hat!

The summer holidays were spent partly in Glasgow, partly in Cardross. Kelvingrove Park boasted municipal tennis courts: for sixpence, you could hire racquets and balls. There was a roller-skating rink, too, where you could hire rollers, strap them onto your sandals and skate around for an hour. Highland Fling classes were also available (sixpence a lesson). You turned up at the hall, paid your money, stood in a line and copied the teacher. Which I did. To this day, I can remember the first three moves.

At the end of the summer break, it was hard to return to the routine and discipline of school. We now had to get there by tram because Uncle George, who had given us a lift, was seriously unwell. In October Mum visited him for the last time. Terminally ill from lung cancer, he died on October 8, 1953 at the age of 44. Little Hamish had known his dad for such a short time, Aunt Elma was a young widow, Granny Graham had lost her only son, and my mother sorely missed her brother, the person who had been such a support to her in the difficult post-war years.

CHAPTER 14: A Boat Launch & Some Guisers

The fourteenth of May, 1954 was my tenth birthday and it was a school day. I'm sure there would have been a birthday present and possibly a home-baked cake for tea—but for other reasons, this was a very important date in the school calendar. Why?

Because the Glasgow High School for Girls was going to celebrate its Diamond Jubilee Year in Glasgow Cathedral. Believe it or not, the original school was founded in around 1124 as the Choir School of Glasgow Cathedral, and later became known as Glasgow Grammar School. The name was changed again in 1834 to the High School of Glasgow, and in 1872 it was transferred to the management of the Glasgow School Board. From these early beginnings, The Glasgow High School for Girls was founded in 1894.

Sixty years on, there we were, singing our little hearts out in Glasgow Cathedral. Having practised all year, we knew every hymn by heart, particularly 'Praise, my soul, the King of heaven.' It was a favourite hymn of the late Queen and was even played at her wedding in 1947. We had to sing 'Praise Him!' no fewer than four times, and each time round it had to be sung louder, so by the fourth time we were really belting it out. The ceremony finished with the singing of the national anthem, 'God Save the Queen'.

The service of thanksgiving didn't do the school much good in the long run. Twenty-four years later it was reorganised on comprehensive lines and the Glasgow High School for Girls became Cleveden Secondary, a mixed comprehensive. When it came to the closure of the Glasgow High School for Boys, this was met with anger from former pupils. But the day after the closure, a new and independent co-educational high school came into being, following a merger involving the former pupils' association and Drewsteignton School in Bearsden. They have been asking me for money (unsuccessfully) ever since.

But to go back to our Diamond Jubilee in May 1954, a class photograph was taken to commemorate the occasion. Naturally, I have a copy, and could probably name even now every child in that class. Many of them are friends to this day.

Although this school occasion was quite a big deal, a much greater highlight of my year was 'The Launch of the Morag'. The late Queen Elizabeth and I had certain things in common. She was somewhat richer (and older) than me, but we were both grannies and both had boats named after us— although you would probably call hers a ship.

In the spring of 1954, Dad was spending most of his time at Grovepark Street in Maryhill. He wasn't feeding the cart horses stabled opposite his premises. Nor was he making money. So what was he doing? Believe it or not, he was making a sailing dinghy. The first my mother knew of it was when she returned home from a visit to her friend Vera Greig's.

The TV programme *Watch with Mother* was popular in the fifties and the Greigs had a TV. So it was a great treat for my four-year-old little sister to watch Andy Pandy, Teddy and Looby Loo (or was it Bill and Ben and the Flowerpot Men?) while Mum had a good long natter with Vera. I won't make too much of the fact that when the programme was finished Elizabeth cried all the way home. Poor wee girl! I do understand that feeling of flatness and disappointment when an totally absorbing film or book has come to an end.

As Mum entered our home, there was nothing untoward until she reached her kitchen, but then—oh dear—what met her eye?

An ocean of wet washing draped over the kitchen chairs! Where was the clothes pulley, over which the wet clothes should have been hanging up near the ceiling? Not a sign of the pulley—not even the ropes, and the thick, wooden clothes pole had vanished too. Where on earth had they gone?

I'm not sure if Dad would have survived as long as he did if he'd been there at that moment. To anyone who knows sailing dinghies, the solution to the disappearances was simple. Dad's boat, 'The Morag', needed a mast and a boom and, for that matter, sails too.

Dad later hijacked Granny Graham's old Singer sewing machine and he and Jimmy spent hours using every old sheet they could get hold of, and bound the pieces together to make a strong mainsail and jib. Towards the end, they got help from Hamish, who attached the cleats and the bolts onto the deck.

Burns is for me, as for my father before me, my favourite poet (and possibly the *only* poet I know much about). So here are some words from the bard to sum up the occasion, a day when not everything went entirely to plan:

> 'The best laid schemes o' mice an' men gang aft agley'
> (To a Mouse)

> 'Nae man can tether time or tide'
> (Tam 'o Shanter)

The detail of the story belongs to someone who was actually there on the day, namely Hamish Graham, my cousin. What follows on the next page is his account of the launching of 'The Morag'.

Hamish's memory of the launch:

It was June 1954 when daylight stretched long into the evening. I don't know how the boat was brought to Belhaven but we were up very early to catch the ebb tide down to Ardmore Point. Sadly Alex had got mixed up in the summer tide timing so when we arrived at the shore, there was a vast expanse of muddy sand stretching for about 300 yards to the water in the old channel. By the time we got the boat in the water and floating and ready to sail, we were nearly at Ardmore Point.

By this time the tide had started to flood up the Clyde, which was against where we wanted to go. With no wind, we had to paddle across to Roseneath, mostly against the tide, which then turned at about 17.00 hours, and once we had got level with Rhu Pier, it was ebbing out of the Gairloch. We had to paddle all the way to the Rhu narrows with no windhead, and managed to get a back eddy into the Gareloch near Silvers boatyard, and headed for Clynder as planned. We arrived on the beach opposite the Clynder Hotel about 23.00 hours, pulled it up, turned it over and got the mainsail set as a cover for Alex to sleep under. Jimmy and I then managed to get to Garelochhead and back to Cardross after midnight

I can add some background to Hamish's account. Mum was worried sick when there was still no news from the boat launchers by teatime. After all, they had left early—at 5.00 am—to catch the tide. I don't think it ever occurred to anyone at that time that life jackets would have been a useful sailing aid. No one wore them, or even thought about wearing them.

Mum knew nothing at all about winds or tides, but she did know they should have arrived by 5.00 p.m. According to Dad, they were never in any danger and were always going to get to a safe shore, but against the tide it was going to be a long haul.

Worrying and panicking, Mum finally decided to phone the coastguard. She was assured that The Morag and its crew were safe but would be very late. That night she waited and waited in Cardross for the phone call. It eventually came about midnight.

Jimmy and Hamish had hitchhiked to Garelochhead, where they found a phone box and straightaway called Belhaven. Granny, Aunt Helen and Mum must have been standing next to the telephone because they picked up on first ring. All Jimmy and Hamish had to do now was wait for the car to take them safely home to Cardross. What a relief! Did Aunt Elma know any of this, I wonder?

The next day Dad sailed The Morag across to Gullybridge, Rhu, and pulled her up onto the shore. Very soon, he was surrounded by three old sea-dogs, fags in their mouths, all busy discussing what to do with the vessel. Everybody knows that boat owners and dinghy sailors love to exchange stories about their seafaring exploits, about the winds, the tides, the weather, boat bits—and that's just for starters. Much later, after some cheery and convivial chat, one of them offered some space in his garden. With Dad carrying the weight at the stern, one at the bow and one on each side, they managed to move The Morag into the garden, turned her upside down and left her there. Prompted by Mum, Dad's friend Noel Greig arrived in his car and drove him home

That summer, Dad *did* sail The Morag with Jimmy and Noel Greig, but there were more pressing and urgent problems. The failing Grovepark Street business (not to mention the cost of constantly refilling his hip flask) was a constant drain on the shrinking family finances, and had to be sorted straight away. Jimmy's pre-school milk round didn't quite pay enough to feed us all. Dad's solution was to return to his pre-war occupation. He applied for a job in the Merchant Navy. He had watched with interest the progress of one particular ship (the Hannington Court, built in Sunderland and launched in July 1954), and he applied for a job as second mate. By Hallowe'en he was back at sea.

⬚

What I liked best about Hallowe'en was 'guising'. Heather and I used to dress up as char ladies (cleaners), with aprons wrapped and pinned around us, and scarves on our heads tied with a knot at the front and curlers showing. For the loot we hoped to collect, we carried a galvanised metal bucket—which was quite heavy, as I remember. We'd first call on most of the folk in the close, then head out to the streets.

A new girl had joined our class that year: Carole Ann Newby. She was English and most of us had never met anyone English before. Probably all we knew about England was that the Queen lived there, in Buckingham Palace. Heather and I—in our blissful ignorance—decided to go to Carole Anne's house and invite her out guising with us.

The night was drawing in, and our new schoolmate's father answered his doorbell to find two miniature char ladies standing at the door. One of them piped up, 'Would Carole Anne like to come out guising?'

'I'm afraid she's in her bed. It's a school day tomorrow.'

Heather and I were not socially competent. We had no idea what to say and just stood there looking glaikit. Fortunately, Mr Newby took pity on us.

'Would you like to come in and explain to us about guising? I'll call Carole Anne. I'm sure she'd love to talk to you; just give her a minute.'

Mrs Newby made us welcome with biscuits and a drink, so we began to feel less tongue-tied as our school-friend appeared in her dressing gown. We weren't quite sure how to explain the guising procedure though—i.e. that the guisers were now supposed to do a party turn, and then get a reward.

But kindly Mr Newby, by his gentle questioning, eventually got the hang of it, and asked if we would like to say a poem or something. He probably also noticed that there were oranges and monkey nuts in the bucket already. We had prepared our 'turn', of course, but he may not have been over-impressed by our poetry, which went as follows:

> *I'll tell you a story of Jack and Nory*
> *And now my story's begun*
> *I'll tell you a story of Jack and my brother*
> *And now my story's done.*

Just to make her feel part of it, Carole Anne came up with a poem too, a slight improvement on ours, but not all that impressive as I remember. And then off we went to the next set of victims.

One of our classmates, Pat, remembers in her street there was a childless (she thinks) couple, Mr and Mrs Cullen. They warmly welcomed guisers and gave each of them two shillings—a *huge* amount for us back then. As she pointed out, nobody ever missed going to the Cullens. So much for Hallowe'en and guising.

Soon it was back to school routine, and we were saddened to learn that Auntie Helen and Granny had decided to sell Belhaven.

By the spring of 1955, they had moved into Whitegates, a bungalow with fewer bedrooms. It was more practical and easier to look after. That same year, the last visible reminder of the terror of war was removed.

The bomb crater was finally filled in.

Chapter 15: Billy Graham Comes To Glasgow

In Primary Six and Seven, our teacher was Miss Young. I wasn't traumatised by her this time. I was simply scared. In fact, most of the time it was fine, although we'd already become a class of obedient, frightened and gutless little girls.

Miss Young used to go to the staffroom for a fag and, on her way out, would instruct one girl to stand at the blackboard and write down the name of anyone who talked. This way there was no noise, and the headmistress (Miss Barker) wouldn't know she was skiving. Can you believe we sat like little lambs, not saying a word until she returned?

Even at this early level we had exams that assessed all subjects taught, including art and music. What a nightmare for the unartistic, tone-deaf and unmusical among us, namely me. To add to my miseries, the whole class was ordered to audition for the choir. This involved the horrific experience of having to sing for the sarcastic Miss McAdam with her piano. She would strike certain notes, which we had to replicate—loud enough for the whole class to hear. Then she would deliver her unflattering opinion of the singer's musical talent, or lack of it. Easy for some, I'm sure, but certainly not for Jean, Heather and me.

At home, Sandy, Elizabeth and Mum could all play tunes on the piano by ear. But not all of us took to music so easily. Jimmy and I, from a very young age, were painfully aware of our musical inadequacies. Needless to say, at school Heather, Jean and I were not offered a place in the choir and it took me many years to have the confidence to sing. That same sarcastic music teacher was, much later in her life, referred to a physiotherapist who (by sheer chance) happened to be her former pupil Heather. *Yesss!* Medical ethics prevent me from telling the rest of the tale, but I can say with authority and pleasure that there's a natural justice in this world.

Once a year, our exam results were totalled up. We were given class placings according to achievement, and that was how our seating was arranged until the next time. Top of the class sat at the back, bottom at the front beside the teacher. Most of the time I remember being comfortably in the middle. Perhaps a good life lesson was learned there because I certainly never wanted to be top. Nor did I want to be bottom.

Miss Young told us we had to attend Scripture Union at lunchtime and so we did, once a week, for years and years. Religion seemed to play a large part in life in the mid-fifties. When the world-famous American evangelist Billy Graham came by train to Glasgow in March 1955, he was met on the platform by a large crowd singing the twenty-third psalm 'The Lord is my Shepherd'. His Good Friday rally was broadcast live from Kelvin Hall, attracting an audience second only to that of the Queen's coronation.

The Billy Graham visit was supported by the Presbyterian Church of Scotland, and so there was an army of stewards, counsellors and choristers to support him, not to mention his own team of followers. Heather went to the rally with her Dad, who was covering the event for his newspaper. She watched Graham preach from his flower-decked platform to an audience of fifteen thousand. She remembers it as a unique, one-off experience by a mesmerising, charismatic speaker, the atmosphere reaching her very core. The session built to an emotional climax as Graham invited members of the audience to step forward and declare their faith. Heather perfectly understood why folk were moved to do just that.

In fact, Mum was there too and later she confessed to rising from her seat and starting to move along the aisle towards the front. Then something changed her mind, she didn't know what, and she turned back. Heather's abiding memory (she was only twelve at the time) was of being emotionally overwhelmed by the singing of the choir. And this was Glasgow in the fifties, where—with the exception of roaring football crowds—any display of feeling (a 'Glasgow kiss' is anything but friendly) roused instant suspicions of affectation and insincerity.

Indeed, Glasgow was Scotland's biggest city and also, according to the press, 'the most sinful place in Britain'. Did Billy Graham's visit change anything? Well—presbyterian church attendance five years later was still 50% higher than it had been in 1954. Anecdotally, there are numerous stories of how 'Billy Graham' had undoubtedly changed some lives for the better. However, on balance, the 'mass hysteria' methodology of the Billy Graham movement has become discredited over time.

Religious practices of one kind or another, however, affected all our lives as children. It would be nice to think that we gained some spiritual enlightenment from our primary school Scripture Union meetings, but I can't recall a single thing. There was an enticing 'carrot' for those who attended regularly, though—the Scripture Union Camps. They were cheap too, and to fund the trips, I could dip into the Granny Wilson savings account. Heather, Doris, Diane and I were to enjoy quite a few Scripture Union excursions in the years to come. To all the good people who organised these camps, I confess with regret that Christian education was not what motivated us. What we wanted was freedom, and a holiday on our own without family and parents.

So if we weren't learning religion, what *did* we learn in the later years of primary school? Well, by the time we reached secondary, we could all spell reasonably well. We knew our parts of speech (nouns, pronouns, verbs) and had a reasonable vocabulary. We knew the difference between a phrase and a sentence, could construct a correct grammatical paragraph and could punctuate—more or less. We knew our times tables, and we could count and we could knit and sew. But about life—we knew nothing.

Our sewing lessons were neither creative nor fun. They were practical, designed to teach us the basic sewing stitches. The ultimate aim of our needlework was to create large, unusable and extremely ugly cotton knickers and lap bags. But first we had to learn the stitches. Each child was asked to sew six small, straight tacking stitches, then show them to the teacher. Not straight enough? Unpick them and do them again.

Nature Study wasn't too great. A book with colour illustrations was provided by the BBC to accompany a radio programme about birds, plants and animals. Being townies, we never actually saw any real birds or animals, apart from dogs and cats, starlings, and the occasional mouse.

My primary schooling did, nevertheless, give me the tools to learn more. That, on reflection, was a good thing. As a granny myself, I have had the good fortune to watch the education of seven grandchildren, all in state schools (some in England, others in Scotland) and I have the greatest admiration for their teachers who, without exception, made their experience for the most part not only educative but also enjoyable.

How very different was my brother Jimmy's experience in the fifties! Perhaps some of his disenchantment with education was connected with the school discipline policy. In his penultimate year Mum had already put in a written complaint to the Headmaster, an extraordinary occurrence in our family, and against the norms of the time. The reason?

Jimmy had come home from school once too often with bruised and broken skin on his wrist from being repeatedly 'belted'. Mum had had enough. Punishment by the tawse (a leather strap) was at that time an acceptable and legal part of discipline, but brutality was quite another matter, and there were many examples of it in the fifties, including (perhaps even particularly) in boarding and private schools.

I'm not sure what Dad, a gentle man by nature, but toughened by the bloodshed and carnage of his harsh war experiences, would have had to say about it. But he was away at sea, so yet again Mum had to make her own decisions, and that formal complaint was one of them.

Jimmy had always hated school, and he left as soon as he was 15. At the age of 16, he joined the Merchant Navy like his father before him and soon became a cadet on the SS Prome.

Meantime Dad had been at sea too—on the MV Hannington Court, which was expected to dock in Liverpool soon. Unsure of the exact date, Mum was surprised when the phone rang and it was him. He could barely breathe or speak, had severe chest pain and was too weak to walk. Would she come down to the docks immediately and help him home?

Yes, she would—and did—a taxi to Central Station, a train to Liverpool and another taxi which took her straight to the docks.

The driver assisted him into the taxi and a kindly stranger helped her support him to the train, where he slept intermittently.

When they finally arrived back in Glasgow, Mum told the taxi to go straight to the Western Infirmary where Dad was admitted as an emergency case. He was diagnosed with lung cancer. There was no time to waste and within a very short time they removed his right lung.

After six months he was on his feet, and back at sea. This time (still fragile after his operation but medically 'fit for work') he signed on with the Burns and Laird Line which did shorter and more local ferrying trips. He was home more often but for shorter spells. Incredible as it seems, his cancer had cured him of his dependence on a 'wee dram' to get him through his day.

Although she was heartbroken to see him suffering, Mum found the love of her life returned to her: the artistic, gentle, well-read, sensitive and funny man she had married—but now he was frail, and tormented by his inability to support his family.

That same year, I was old enough to join the Girl Guides. Was it because of the unhappy events going on at home that I embraced everything on offer at Stevenson Memorial Church? I don't know the answer to that.

The 128th Glasgow Girl Guide Company was well run by a lady we all called 'Doc'. Once I passed my 'promise' and learned the guide laws, you just couldn't stop me. I made more friends, revelled in all that was on offer—the games, the maze marching, and the camping.

I learned a huge amount and worked to achieve every accolade I possibly could, including my Needlewoman's Badge. For this I had to sew a blouse, with inset sleeves, a collar and button holes. Mum didn't sew, so once again Helen Clark, our upstairs neighbour, came to the rescue and taught me all I needed to know.

Eventually I ended up as a Queen's Guide, no less. I even liked *singing* at the camp fires and joined in enthusiastically. For me, camping was simply brilliant fun. Not all would agree with that, I know, but I have loved it ever since that time. Only in the last ten years have I reluctantly come to the conclusion that it's a pleasure for which at last I am too old.

Chapter 16: The Glasgow TB Problem In The Fifties

Moving on to secondary education wasn't as big a deal for me as it is for pupils today. We didn't have to change schools; we just moved to a different building. One or two new pupils joined us and the classes we ended up in were determined by the results of 'The Qually' (similar to the English Eleven-plus). Miss Young advised us all to take French and Latin, and naturally most of us did as we were told. So 95% of Primary Seven joined the first-year class group called 1 Classical, and the 5% who chose German as their second language ended up in 1 Modern. For the first time, we had a timetable, and the day was divided into different subjects all taught in the same classroom, except those subjects requiring specialist facilities—for example, science, music, art and PE.

Like all schools, our teachers varied dramatically, some being very strict. Our gym teacher, Miss Loudon* (the only one that liked me), was one of the latter. Not all our teachers were bullies. Most were chronically boring. A few were fun. The occasional one couldn't keep control at all—a wonderful experience for such a previously strictly disciplined class! We didn't really see teachers as human beings and, I'm ashamed to say, we took full advantage of a raw, quiet-voiced Geography teacher, who made the dreadful mistake of knocking on the door and asking if she could come in.

Like a lamb to the slaughter, that young woman experienced a miserable existence in our hands. How quickly our new-found power taught us evil tricks to play, which—sad to say—we enjoyed enormously. But to this day, my geographical knowledge is sparse: in writing this book, I needed a world map on my study wall to understand the territories of the World War II campaigns.

The secondary-school day was marginally more interesting than primary because it was more varied. Any distractions or deviations from the norm were welcome, with one well remembered exception. This was the day of the Heaf Gun Test, when a spring-loaded instrument with six needles arranged in a circular formation was inserted into our wrists to check for tuberculosis (I'd forgotten to get my permission form signed and was delighted to escape this procedure)—and nobody checked!

Glasgow in the fifties—unlike England—still had a major TB problem (the incidence had actually increased since the end of the War). For every 100,000 people, 139 to 200 contracted the disease. Like Covid 19, it was spread by droplets in the air and was more common where there was overcrowding, malnourishment and poor health care. In Glasgow, 41% of the population lived in crowded one or two-bedroomed tenement flats, while the packed pubs helped spread the infection. In 1957—as well as the Heaf Gun test for 13- to 14-year-olds—there was a massive chest x-ray campaign with 37 mobile radiology vans converging on the city from all over the country.

I found out something about TB treatment from my friend Angela. We'd chatted about it one day on the tram to school after I had admired her leather satchel. Not long after her father had died of a heart attack on the golf course, she showed her mum a wee lump on her collar bone. She was whisked off to the GP, there was nasal aspiration and TB gland tests and—before she knew it—she was in the TB sanatorium ward in Killearn Hospital. I think she must have been one of the last to endure the 'sanitorium treatment'.

Angela's treatment cured her for sure but it beggars belief just the same. It involved a rigorous regime of fresh air and rest. For three whole months, she was confined to bed (bed-baths and bed-pans were the norm). She confessed to me that one morning when she was alone, she swung her legs off the bed and on to the ground just to see if they still worked (they did).

During the day, and also *at night,* her bed was outside. Dressed in flannel pyjamas and covered in layers of woollen blankets, she was protected from the worst of the weather by screens. Interestingly, she doesn't remember feeling cold. After lunch, there was rest time when she wasn't even allowed to read. Her widowed mum was working full-time as a comptometer operator, so she only had visitors at the weekend—the visitors always had to sit outside.

Part of Angela's treatment was occupational therapy and one of the therapists had helped her make a beautiful leather satchel, the very satchel I later admired. The holes were punched for her by the occupational therapist but she sewed every stitch herself. As she completed her task, she saw each stitch as one step nearer home. And after three whole months, they did let her out. This was Glasgow in the late fifties, and that was Angela's story. Two of my other friends, Heather and Pat Morton tested positive but this was a year later and they simply had to attend a centre where they were successfully treated with drugs—the 'triple therapy'.

My personal acquaintance with TB is a story for later, but at this time I was healthy and fit (I hadn't started smoking yet). One evening at the beginning of term, I returned from Guides to find a brand-new bike sitting in the hall, a Raleigh. Wow! Dad's Auntie Teenie was the donor. It wasn't Christmas and it wasn't my birthday but there it was—and what a brilliant surprise! As soon as my friend Heather had a bike too (courtesy of her Uncle Sandy) there was no holding us back.

Our first adventure was to cycle to Cardross to visit Auntie Helen. One Saturday, we set off, our panniers stuffed with the basics for an overnight stay, and a few sandwiches and an apple. I had been lots of times to Cardross, but mainly by train (and occasionally on a lorry borrowed by Dad from his garage). I knew roughly how the journey worked. Anniesland Cross, the switchback, Dumbarton, then Cardross. Easy!

As everyone knows, and we had still to learn, distance measured in time feels very different depending on the form of transport. The journey on our bikes (about fifteen miles) took a lot longer than we expected, but we made it, and it was a first. It was scary—possibly even dangerous—but tremendously exciting. It left us with that 'feel good factor' which accompanies a new achievement. Looking back on the experience, it's more than likely that Helen was frantic with worry, but since mobile phones hadn't been invented, there wasn't much she could do.

And when we arrived, what a wonderful welcome we got! She was the best kind of auntie. For a start, she listened to us. Then she was always ready with her 'Lucky Bags', packed with forbidden bad things: rude tricks, favourite sweets, comics, and sticky chocolate cakes. She was the aunt who—when we were younger—took us to Dumbarton Fair, and what child doesn't enjoy a fair? Best of all, when you visited Auntie Helen, she admired everything about you. What a tonic for us when our school system functioned mainly on competition, criticism and disapproval. Her Christmas presents were the toys that we longed for, while Aunt Isabel's gifts were more serious, more worthy, more educational—and often more expensive too, I suspect. Aren't kids ungrateful wretches? Heather and I were starving after our long bicycle ride. We sat down to a table laden with home bakes, chatting happily to Granny and, of course, Helen—who couldn't wait to show us our quarters. We were to sleep in the attic. Helen knew what would appeal to us: she had made up camp beds with war-time sleeping bags. We had our very own towels, and there was even a plate of biscuits and a drink of juice by the beds. We simply weren't used to such attention and revelled in it—an unforgettable experience.

Christmas this year was different, and not in a good way. For the first time ever my big brother Jimmy wasn't there. He was at sea on the SS Prome, heading towards Aden, then Port Sudan, where he would endure 80 degrees in the shade. In his December letter, he said 'it doesn't feel at all Christmassy'. I wasn't in the least surprised. Apart from the heat and the food (mainly curry and no ice cream), one of the crew had mental health problems (not Jimmy's words) which meant he had to be watched day and night. This chap thought everybody was stealing his wife, and at night he was obliged to beat her up (or anyone else he could find) for running away from him. For months, the whole crew had had to work alternating four-hour shifts to ensure his (and everyone else's) safety. They simply couldn't wait to reach Port Aden, where he would be taken off, and the crew could return to alternating shifts of eight hours. They were all absolutely exhausted.

When Dad was home on leave, it was obvious that he was getting progressively weaker. He and Mum decided the best way forward was to return to his childhood home at 6, Colebrooke Terrace and move in with Granny and Grandfather Wilson, who agreed unconditionally to the arrangement. There would be enough room for all of us, there would be no rent to pay and Dad wouldn't have to climb the stairs in the close. There wasn't really any other option.

Not much had changed in the Wilson house since before the war—although Ann Jardin was gone. It is true that electricity had finally been installed. But—to the end of their days—my grandparents said they switched on the 'gas' when they meant the lights. There was a phone, but it was a two-piece, hand-held device located on the table in the back parlour where the Wilsons sat. No one dared phone—or answer the phone—when Granny and Grandfather were listening to *The Archers* on the radio every evening after high tea at a quarter to seven.

The large, formal dining room with its brown carpet, brown curtains, textured brown wallpaper and beautiful, mahogany sideboard was the same as ever. The drawing room, parlour and dining room still had coal fires, as did the double bedroom on the top floor. There was no fridge, but there was a pantry for keeping food cool. Above the pantry door, there was a mahogany-cased servants' bell indicator (disconnected now, but in its heyday it would have shown the workers which room to scurry to). The kitchen had a Belfast sink, an old kitchen range very soon replaced with a gas cooker, and for the wet washing, a huge pulley hanging from the ceiling. In the basement next to the boys' bedroom was the coal cellar store room, its main area reserved for the washing, two large sinks and a manual clothes wringer. Next to the sinks was a small flushing toilet.

Ann Jardin's basement bedroom was to be for the boys, while Elizabeth and I each had our own bedroom on the top floor. The best double bedroom was reserved for Mum and Dad. On the middle floor were two bedrooms, one for Granny and one for Grandpa, and—next to the bathroom—was the drawing room where I was born. The piano was still there, too, waiting for Mum to play it.

Chapter 17: Carry On Camping

When we moved to Colebrooke Terrace, it was Mum's life that changed the most. As far as I was concerned, my friends stayed the same, my school stayed the same, and I was still very much part of the life of the Church and, particularly, the guides.

The house itself was large and spacious but really it belonged to a different age. 'Not fit for purpose' would be the modern verdict. So *much* needed to be washed so often. Net curtains on the windows were grimy and grey from the smog outside, and from the coal dust inside. Anything white needed frequent and vigorous washing (a 'petticoat' hanging below your skirt revealed a dirty black rim at the end of the day).

The brass doorstep, letter box and doorbell were polished every day (mainly to impress the neighbours). The brass stairway rods, the cutlery and the silverware were polished regularly, while the coal had to be hauled up the stairs from the basement coal cellar to fireplaces in the drawing room, the parlour and the dining room. Someone had to do the cooking, washing, shopping and ironing—not to mention the daily dusting.

I now had a bedroom to myself and in it there was a two-pin socket. This was a big deal, as not every bedroom had one, and from somewhere I'd acquired a one-bar electric fire which I used very occasionally when I was numb with cold. The process of putting on the fire terrified me. When I put the plug in the socket, it would spark and sizzle before the red bar heated up. To this day, I'm frightened of electricity—but back then it was a case of 'needs must' and 'ignorance is bliss'.

Dad was still managing his short trips to various ports in Scotland with the Burns and Laird Line, but each time he came home, he was weaker and frailer. It was a relief to him that we were all safely housed at Colebrooke. Grandfather was by now an old man, almost 80, who spent most of his time in the parlour, drinking sherry, reading the paper and listening to the wireless. Despite the family stories about his love of alcohol, I never ever saw him drunk. And he did have one very important job—winding up the grandfather clock. His other favoured pastime didn't win him any popularity prizes. We would be sitting comfortably in a room when the lights would suddenly go out. Occasionally it really was a power cut, but mostly it was Grandfather following us round, turning off *his* electric lights. This could be awkward if you had friends round, but after he left the room, we simply turned them on again. In his favour, he saved silver sixpences all year round and—come Christmas time— each one of us was presented with a brown envelope filled with a pound's worth of silver sixpenny coins, every one of which we usually spent on New Year's day at Kelvin Hall Fairground.

Granny Wilson was 77 when we moved in and she decided that although the days of maids were long since gone, and there was no spare room anyway, she would engage a cleaner six mornings a week to help my mother. This is how and why Mrs Kirk arrived and became a valued member of our family.

But she had difficulties of her own. Her husband had been a Japanese prisoner of war, and occasionally when something triggered his horrific memories, he would go to the pub and drink excessively to help him forget. He would then stagger home, smashing everything and anything in his way, until he finally collapsed unconscious on the floor. At these times, Mrs Kirk would salvage whatever she could, and escape to our house until it was all over. In the interests of damage limitation and recovery, she always kept her savings in our kitchen drawer, away from Mr Kirk's clutches.

From Mrs Kirk we learned about a way of life completely new to us. She told us about her friend Jeanie in the flat above who increased her meagre income by 'having gentlemen visitors' (only later did I understand what was meant by 'gentlemen visitors'). Her kids were happy; they were given money for a treat, for chips or sweets (or both on a good day), and told to play in the street until their mum opened the window and called them home.

Home was where you slept, ate your meals, were looked after and felt safe. But real life (or so I thought) was about exciting adventures outside the home and away from the family. Scripture Union camp was such an adventure, and on the first day of the Easter holidays, Heather, Doris, Diane and I set off for Dunbar. I have only two clear memories of our trip. The first is of buying condensed milk and eating it at midnight feasts. The second is of trying (and failing) not to giggle during the two-minute silence when we were supposed to be saying private prayers. So much for organised religion. I hope (and pray?) that we were the exception.

An abiding memory for all of us marks the end of that trip, the moment we got off the train and walked through the barrier at Central Station to find our mothers standing in a huddle, waiting for us. As we got nearer, I heard Heather beside me make a kind of gasping noise as she clocked what her mum was wearing: a black suit with short jacket, straight skirt and a black hat. All our mothers—including Heather's—stopped talking as we approached, turned their attention to us and asked us about our holiday.

As soon as I was home, Mum explained matter-of-factly, and without emotion, that Heather's father had died and his funeral had taken place while we were in Dunbar. I was upset—but she told me firmly that the loss was Heather's, not mine. My job was simply to be there for her. That was me told. It was Friday, it was Guide Night, and Heather's mum believed it was important for her to carry on as normal. Before Heather turned up at the door (at 7.15, as usual) to go to Guides, I had been warned not to mention her father in case I upset her. Believe it or not, we never talked about his death until recently. Her mum—who was a wonderful mother and devoted to her children—simply wanted to protect Heather from pain and sorrow. How different things are today!

I was not the only one who had to move house. Heather, too, had to adjust to a major life-style change. Shortly after she'd lost her father in April 1957, her widowed granny died, leaving two grown-up sons (Sandy and Jimmy, the same names as my own brothers) with no woman to cook for them. They'd always been looked after by their late mother, and her role was soon filled by their sister, Heather's mum, who had only a small widow's pension, a rent to pay and two children to support. So she moved in with her brothers, taking Eric and Heather with her. They never liked their new house nearly as much as their former family home.

Heather's Uncle Sandy was a large, jovial guy with a big personality and, like many Glaswegians, he enjoyed a drink or two, or more. He owned a pet shop in Eglinton Street, kept greyhounds and, to me, seemed very well off. 'Uncle' Sandy would put his hand in his seemingly bottomless pockets, pull out a wad of notes or loose change, then give each of us a half crown—or occasionally a ten-bob note. This was a shock to the system and a new way of doing things but it was very welcome, and we put it to good use, like buying knickerbocker glories.

That first summer after Heather's dad died, I had a holiday in Dunbar again. This time it was with Heather, her mum, her brother Eric and her new family, Uncle Sandy and Uncle Jimmy. We swam most days in the outdoor swimming pool. I was skinny, with no fat to act as blubber, and so goose bumps (followed by 'chittery bites') were normal and expected. No one ever hung about after swimming. Clothes on straight away was the name of the game. The only way to get into the water was to take a run and jump and—splash!—you were in. Or, if you were very brave, you could slide down the chute. At first, your whole body felt numb and you thought you were about to die. But after a while—as long as you kept moving and stayed under the water—your body adapted to the freezing (and I mean *freezing*) temperature.

Once in, we used to swim out to the long greasy pole in the middle of the pool and try to see who could walk along it the farthest without falling off. Pushing and shoving was fair play, so no one lasted long on the pole, some slithering, others dramatically plunging back into the ice-cold, unheated pool. Sometimes small tins of fruit were thrown into the water, and if you swam quickly enough, you might get one. As I remember, Heather's brother Eric (he was bigger, stronger and more confident) was most likely to be successful.

It occurs to me now that Heather's mum must have been really sad the whole time we were away. After all, first her husband and then her mother had just died. The 'cure' for grief and loss in the fifties, however, was not to talk about, or dwell on, your misery, but to 'keep busy' and 'pretend' all was well. We were certainly kept busy. From that time on, Heather came more often to my house for tea. It wasn't always an enjoyable experience for her, however, and there was a good reason for this.

On one occasion when she had stayed to tea and was sitting at our big, long dining table, I kept wondering why she kept wriggling and her face was quite red. Only afterwards did she show me the water dripping down her legs.

Don't get me wrong. She *hadn't* wet her pants. Throughout the meal, my brother Sandy had been busy with his water pistol, firing continuously, relentlessly and accurately at her legs under the tablecloth. But we all understood that you didn't tell tales, you just suffered in silence.

On another occasion when we got off the tram on our way home to Colebrooke Terrace for our tea, there was a wee bauchle of a man standing in the doorway of Hubbard's the Baker's. We both clocked a wee, red, rumply thing sticking out of the fly of his trousers.

Not a word was said until we got round the corner into Belmont Street. Then what did we do? We had a fit of the giggles—almost uncontrollable by the time we rang my door bell.

Mum wanted to know the cause of our hilarity, of course. When we told her, she insisted that after tea Sandy must walk Heather to the tram stop.

It's difficult to know who was more embarrassed—Sandy or Heather. He *did* walk behind her and make sure she was safely on the tram—but chat? I don't think so.

At that stage of our lives, being walked to the bus by a boy was infinitely more traumatic than seeing a drunk's funny wee red thing sticking out of his trousers.

Chapter 18: Colebrooke Terrace Is Modernised

School was different this year. Now that we were in fourth year, we'd all chosen different subjects and were in different classes. I had rejected all the sciences and opted for languages, taking up a new subject, Greek—for two reasons. First, I liked the idea of using an alphabet no-one else understood. Second, I fancied the minister's son, Johnston McKay, and he was studying Greek at the Boys High.

As my poor teacher soon discovered, I wasn't really interested in Homer's *Odyssey*, or Aristotle, or even the female poet, Sappho. If I'd been told Sappho was born on the island of Lesbos and was most famous for her love poems for women, might I have been more interested? The answer has to be 'no'. I wouldn't have understood one word of it, having had no education about topics like sex and gender. Until 1981, homosexuality was illegal in Scotland, and as far as many people were concerned, it didn't exist. (The possibility of sex between women had never occurred to me.)

There were only four of us in our Greek class. I didn't like the sarcastic teacher and never volunteered a single remark all year. With the benefit of hindsight, she probably didn't enjoy trying to teach me either. However, I did somehow win the Beginners' Greek Prize, for which I was awarded the *Oxford Companion to Classical Literature*. This has turned out to be one of my most useful books through the years.

I now think that history is fascinating and wish I knew more but, oh, I remember it as so boring at school. Our uninspiring (and fundamentally lazy) History teacher read the text book and told us which important paragraphs to underline—and that was it. I can remember her showing animation once and once only—in 1961 when President Charles de Gaulle vetoed the UK's application to join the EEC (the European Economic Community). Miss Barlow was not a Francophile—that I do remember.

We had two years to prepare for our final school exams in fifth and sixth year. In most subjects we had a marked exercise each week as practice, and so we were well prepared. After all, we'd been taking internal tests since we were eight years old, so another one was not such a big deal—although we were left in no doubt that it was important. Neither of my parents had ever had much interest (or success) in academic achievement, and as a result Mum was mainly surprised—but also delighted—when any of us did well. Having said that, we were definitely encouraged to get qualifications in *some*thing, so that we could earn our own living.

Mum herself was by this time what we call 'a working mother' but this made no difference at all to my life. My breakfast was cooked for me, my tea was on the table at six in the evening, and my clothes were washed and ironed. I do believe we had to put away our own clothes, and we did help clear up after the evening meal. As dishwashers hadn't been invented then, we had a sink with hot, soapy water for washing dishes, and tea towels to dry them with. Granny and Elizabeth would carry the dishes from the dining room to the kitchen. Then Mum washed; I dried. What did Sandy do? He sat on the kitchen unit and played his guitar, Lonnie Donegan's 'Putting on the Style' being one of our favourites.

I wasn't a 'latch-key kid' (the name for children who went home to empty houses). Mum chose a job—like so many women then and now—that fitted around school hours. Besides, Granny was there all the time too, although I can't remember her actually doing anything—not even making a cup of tea. I never went straight home from school anyway.

That was because Heather, Doris, Diane and I had discovered Fusco's café on Cambridge Street, which had a tiny little table upstairs where no one could see us. Most weekdays we went there, drank Coca Cola, smoked cigarettes and talked—mainly about school and boys, although we did know a little about each other's families.

Another after-school pastime was standing at the corner of Colebrooke Place and Belmont Street with Angela 'putting on the style', in the hope that we'd be noticed by the Glasgow Academy Boarding School boys who lived in Belmont Crescent. There weren't many of them and they were mainly older boys whose parents were abroad. I'm sure sex education wasn't on their syllabus either and, since they attended a boys-only school, they *were* certainly interested.

We'd meet up in Kelvinbridge Café in Great Western Road and if we agreed to go for a walk with a pair of them, the rest of the boys would follow about ten yards behind. We thought this was a great laugh and a fun way to spend an evening. I had another motive for standing at this corner—I still fancied Johnston McKay, the minister's son. He, too, lived in Belmont Crescent.

Changes were taking place at home too. Grandfather, by now 82, died of a heart attack during the Easter holidays and it was soon after this that we acquired Bonzo, a cocker spaniel. He was supposed to be a guard dog, but in fact became the devoted follower and champion of my now not-so-little sister Elizabeth.

Bonzo got no awards for bravery. When the door-bell buzzed, he would race upstairs and cower under the bed. But he was a past master at stealing food, with a particular penchant for tissues in waste-paper bins.

When Jimmy came home on leave, he moved into Grandfather's old bedroom and Sandy was delighted not to have to share any longer.

Slowly the house was modernised. Gas fires were installed, the parlour was converted into a dining room, and the dining room (redecorated with a nondescript green and beige wallpaper) became a comfortable downstairs sitting-room with a three-piece suite.

The upstairs drawing room was transformed by a deep red carpet, and some of the bedrooms were freshly painted (but unfortunately still not heated).

The two-piece, candlestick dial-phone was replaced with a modern, black, rotary affair.

Finally 6, Colebrooke Terrace was no longer Victorian. Bonzo adored stretching out in front of the gas fire beside Granny Wilson (not quite so upright now), who was often to be found there in her armchair having forty winks.

Chapter 19: Good Times Followed By Bad

Both Heather and I were kept busy in the holidays and when we returned from Dunbar we were off to our first Girl Guide camp in Portavadie, a beautiful spot on the shores of Loch Fyne, a few miles from Tighnabruaich. One evening, with the sky a blanket of stars, we set off from base camp, with sleeping bags and rucksacks, to experience sleeping outside. For a group of girls brought up in the Glasgow smog, it was an occasion to be remembered for the rest of our lives. But waking up in the morning surrounded by cows *did* scare the life out of us. The truth is we were more accustomed to coping with drunks on a tram, than cows in a field.

The difference between camping and a weekend adventure that summer was huge. Cousin Dorothy Buchanan and her dog Nigel met Heather and me in her car at Helensburgh train station. But her 'baby' was Nigel, a much petted and spoiled dog and as he needed his walk before we were whisked off to Torwood Cottage in Rhu, we had to stop and walk him on Helensburgh Prom. Back in the car, with Nigel in pride of place in the front seat, we drove up a narrow track, through a gate and along the drive to Torwood Cottage, Dorothy's house.

We were accustomed to rows of joined up terraced houses and tenement flats with back greens. So what was this building? A palace? A mansion? Well no—just a very large house sitting in acres of grounds, which were of even more interest to us than the house itself. Stretched behind the house were vegetable patches, an orchard, and endless rows of ripe strawberries and raspberries waiting to be picked and eaten. Then there was a tennis court at the side of the house inviting us to play and, at the front, a croquet lawn.

After dinner, we made for the games room, full of Dorothy's presents from her doting parents: elegantly crafted sets of chess and draughts, then board games (Monopoly and Scrabble) and the most exquisitely dressed china dolls. We chose cards and, with Nigel nestling on Dorothy's knee, settled down to an evening of Canasta.

This was not my only experience of the high life that summer. The trip to visit my Aunt Teenie in the Kyles of Bute Hydro, in Port Bannatyne, was unforgettable. Arriving alone off the steamer at Rothesay, I was met by the wee bus that ferried guests back and forward from the hotel, which in its heyday, would have offered hydropathic therapy to the wealthy. It still boasted a magnificent suite of salt and fresh-water baths, with ladies and gents carefully segregated (this was 1958). A cluster of staff was in attendance, filling your bath with various lotions and bath salts and providing soft white towelling robes, slippers and towels.

To start with, I was a bit wary of all this—I was used to looking after myself. But I soon discovered that being pampered was a luxury—to be enjoyed rather than endured. Auntie Teenie was an old lady by this time, not able to entertain me as such, and I was adopted by a family with one lonely child. Wherever they went, I went, but I ate my meals and chatted to Teenie at meal times. To be more accurate, I suspect *she* chatted to me and I listened.

The only painful memory I have is how I felt about having to tip everybody when I was leaving. Uncomfortable doesn't describe it. The table waitress, the housekeeper, the hydro attendants, the kitchen staff and the porters—they all had to be tipped. I was given clearly labelled envelopes which I had to hand to each named individual, and make sure that I thanked each one for a lovely holiday. Even now I shudder at the excruciating embarrassment.

It occurs to me now that Dad's single unmarried relations, Cousin Dorothy and Auntie Teenie, were each in their own way trying to help our family through difficult times. When I arrived home from the Kyles Hydro, Dad was noticeably weaker. The cancer was slowly destroying his other lung. It was a slow, painful, miserable, downhill journey, only eased by Mum, who was there for him day and night. In the beginning he managed a couple of meals in the dining room with the rest of us, but two flights of stairs soon became an impossible hurdle, although (with help) he did join us occasionally in the drawing room.

In the end, even the top flight of stairs was too much and he was confined to the bedroom. Terminal cancer treatment in those days was pretty basic. You were offered minimal pain relief, and that was it. Doctors feared patient addiction to morphine, and that meant the limited dosage they prescribed didn't even provide adequate analgesia. No one ever wants cancer—not then and not now—but at least today we have palliative care, one part of which is effective pain management.

In my sitting room today, on top of the corner cabinet, sits a model galleon. The sailing ship was made by Dad from old bits of canvas, paper, string, various bits of wood—even buttons—and anything else he could find (remember this was the same man who borrowed a clothes pulley as a mast for his home-made sailing dinghy, the Morag). We never thought much about his hobby. He had always made amazing model boats. It was just what he did, and painting too.

My brother Sandy got a shock one day on his way home from school. He was wandering aimlessly, schoolbag on his back, socks wrinkled round his ankles, dragging his trench coat along the ground and gazing in every shop window, when suddenly his eyes nearly popped out of his head. There—for sale and placed right in the middle of Lyons shop window—at the corner of Elmbank Street and Sauchiehall Street was one of Dad's model galleons. We had absolutely no idea that even on his death bed he was supplementing our income in this way.

That year there were no Hogmanay celebrations at 6, Colebrooke Terrace. By midnight, Dad was unconscious most of the time, occasionally opening his eyes for a second, then slipping back into oblivion.

On January 1st 1959, at 3.30 am, he finally passed away.

☒

I wasn't expected to go to Dad's funeral but I was given a choice of alternatives. Cardross with Elizabeth—or the crematorium with my brothers, Jimmy and Sandy. For me, there was no hesitation. Cardross was my instant choice.

How different it was for my friend Angela, whose dad had a graveyard burial. Women didn't go to the graveyard in those days, only men. On the day of his funeral, undertakers collected Angela's dad's coffin and carried it down three flights of stairs while the women stayed in the flat. Angela—looking on—was traumatised by watching her father carried off on his final journey without his 'girls'.

'I'm going with him!' she announced, throwing on her navy-blue school hat and coat, and heading down the steep close stairs. The church minister, the Rev Johnston McKay*, sitting in the car behind the hearse, simply opened his door and let her in. She remembers very little after that, but at least she was there.

Mum now had an income—a widow's pension and family allowance—but she definitely felt she needed to work. A job that suited her came up right across the road in the dining hall of the Glasgow Academy school. Our neighbour Donnie Macrae was the school janitor. He told her there was a vacancy for an assistant school dinner cook and introduced her to the Chief Cook, Mrs O'Hara, who was to become her new boss.

A plan was agreed that would work for all concerned. Mum—living so near—would cross to the Academy at a very early hour, turn on all the ovens, then nip home, make our breakfast and return later. That way Mrs O'Hara could arrive a bit later and feed her own children first before they went to school. Going to school without a mum-cooked breakfast was unheard of in our house. Even when Elizabeth was over twenty and at college, she wasn't allowed to leave the house without a 'proper breakfast'.

Later when Mum helped at Glasgow Academy functions in the evening, she recognised parents she'd known when Jimmy was there. Some of them totally blanked her when she was wearing overalls and serving the food. Meeting them in the street or elsewhere, these same folk would be friendly and stop to chat.

During such conversations, Mum would take a wicked delight in talking about her new job. Not long after this, she decided to 'upskill' and attended evening classes at Glasgow 'Dough' (Domestic Science) School, where she learned that she knew absolutely nothing about cooking. According to Miss Rimmer, every single thing she'd done in the kitchen since she was married was wrong. She only lasted one term.

Despite her failure in the evening classes (or perhaps because of it) she applied at the end of the school year for the job of School

Meals Supervisor at Kelvinside Academy—and got it. Her whole summer was spent worrying—and learning new skills: ordering, financial records, and book keeping.

Chapter 20: Learning Some Useful Life Skills

It wasn't difficult going back to school after Dad died because nobody knew anything about it. So I wasn't treated any differently—until the fateful day of being threatened with the phone call home to my father (see chapter 1).

What *was* tough and painful was my journey to school. No, I wasn't being bullied. The source of my anguish was Granny Graham. Aged 77, she was in the Royal Beatson Cancer Memorial Hospital, terminally ill from cancer of the tongue, and she would be propped up by the nurses and sitting at the window every single morning—waiting to wave to me as I walked to school up Hill Street.

At weekends we visited her in a family group. I don't remember this as anything but miserable. The hour seemed interminable, with Mum and Aunt Helen and whoever else was there, strenuously cheerful. Long silences, interspersed with sudden bursts of news, covered up their sadness. Granny—now a yellowish colour—was desperate to speak but her words were incomprehensible. She died at Easter, three months after Dad. I was heartily relieved I didn't have to do any more hospital visits.

I much preferred to spend my time swooning over Pat Boone, Lonnie Donegan and Tommy Steele. Some of us belonged to the Pat Boone Fan Club and we flaunted much prized badges. We were older now and cringed with embarrassment at the thought of our previous badges (as members of the Afternoon Tea Club).

Jimmy (now the man of the house) brought presents when he came home on leave—wrist watches for each of us, a transistor radio for Elizabeth and our very first family record player. The most frequently played record, after Lonnie Donegan, was probably Fats Domino's 'Blueberry Hill' which (along with 'Westering Home') became a signature tune for Mum on the piano.

At school in third year, my friends and I weren't the swinging, boy-mad type—the ones my daughter would later call the 'tits oot' brigade. 'Late developers' and 'blue stockings' might have been a better description for most (but not all) of our class. Heather, Angela and I played hockey on a Saturday morning, while the better-off 'trendy' girls went to meet boys at the mixed ice-skating at Crossmyloof in the south side of Glasgow. We had no skates and couldn't afford it anyway.

I thought I enjoyed hockey but now I'm not sure why. I well remember the process of trailing across the city at some ungodly early hour by subway or tram, arriving finally at a bleak, unheated sports hut, donning a skimpy gym tunic and special hockey socks—not the most enjoyable way to spend a cold, wet Saturday morning. But it was worth it if we won (which happened only rarely).

Our hockey mornings inspired camaraderie, mutual consolation on losing and often much hilarity. At best they were a bonding experience. At worst, they were a recipe for pneumonia. After the game, we had to sit and talk to the opposing team, who were expected to provide a drink and sandwiches. If—for any reason—we failed to show, we'd have to reckon with the fearsome Miss Loudon on Monday morning. So although we couldn't play very well, and mostly lost the games, we always all turned up—whatever the weather. On reflection, this was probably a crucial life lesson.

I was keen to earn money and Aunt Isabel found me a job in Ferranti's. During the Easter holidays, at the age of fifteen, I swanned off on the train to Manchester to work in the catering section, where the company lunchtime eating arrangements were hierarchical. I started working in the elite Directors' Dining Room. It took me no time at all to realise what a food numpty I was. My non-existent culinary knowledge was immediately obvious. I don't know what they were expecting but they were in for a big disappointment. (It was perhaps fortunate my aunt was the boss.)

They tried to break me in with easy tasks. For example, would I like to make some tartare sauce to go with the fish?

This was my first job. I was keen to be as helpful as possible. However, I thought fried fish was always accompanied by tomato ketchup. I had to confess I'd never heard of 'tartare sauce'.

In that case, they would be happy to show me, but first would I fetch some gherkins?

Gherkins? Never heard of them.

And some capers, too, while I was there.

Capers?

And some shallots.

How was *I* supposed to know 'shallots' were onions?

My next challenge was the Middle Management Dining Room. The crockery and cutlery were not quite so classy as the Directors', but far superior to the Staff Canteen. Perhaps the Management Dining Room staff had been warned about my culinary skills? My main job there was to set and clear the tables and Granny Wilson had seen to it that I could at least do that.

My final job was to manage the Brock Trolley in the huge Staff Canteen. This trolley was used for stacking dirty plates and scraping left-over food into a 'brock bin' ready for a pig farm. I enjoyed this because most of the staff were full of banter, ever ready to joke and tease. But the best part of the whole experience was the small, brown, sealed envelope full of my very first earned money. Nevertheless, I had no desire to work again for another three years.

I did learn another new skill (but not perhaps a life skill) that year when we went to Guide Camp on the now disused airfield at Turnberry Hotel. Our friend Christine (definitely not a camping enthusiast) came to visit us on Visitors' Day, armed with a rucksack full of goodies. As soon as we could, we set off towards Turnberry Lighthouse, which is near the golf course and the prestigious Hotel, but I'm not sure we even noticed either of these as we headed for a quiet spot.

We had cokes, sandwiches, and home-made cakes—thanks to Christine. A feast and a treat for hungry campers. After that, there was the final exciting challenge. Lighting the cigarettes in the wind was tricky but since practice makes perfect, we had them glowing in no time at all. As soon as we'd smoked the first non-tipped Olympic almost (but not quite) down to the end, Christine told us to unpin our well-polished, gleaming, trefoil tenderfoot badges from our Guide ties. So we did—but why?

She had a new skill in mind. We had to push the badge pin into the end of the cigarette so that we could smoke it right to the end, without it getting soggy and bits of nicotine ending up on our tongues. Effortlessly, we managed this. Another useful life (or death?) skill achieved. But our time was running out as we sat there, at peace with the world in our Guide uniforms decorated with numerous Guide badges. Before we knew it, Heather and I had to return to camp, while Christine had a bus to catch back to Glasgow. What a pity no badges were awarded for smoking!

While smoking our cigarettes, we plotted our next adventure— youth hostelling. One week later, Heather and I were sitting on the bus on our way to Balloch (sensible Christine had opted out). It was a fair walk from there to Rowardennan Youth Hostel. When we arrived, our feet red and sore with blisters, we had to wait our turn to cook our bacon and eggs on the gas stove, be allocated a bunk to sleep on, and be given a chore for the morning. On the plus side, it was inexpensive and clean, with a warden who made sure everybody did what they were told.

The next morning we set off across the shoulder of Loch Lomond to Loch Ard Youth Hostel. We walked uphill for a very long time and after each hill there was another one, and then another. We were only supposed to be going over the shoulder of Ben Lomond. We expected to go downhill at some point. But it didn't happen, we just kept going up.

Yes, we were lost. Did we have a map? No, it never occurred to us. After all, I knew semaphore, and I could read the compass direction from the stars. But this wasn't of much use in the day time with no one around for miles.

All we could see in front of us were endless hills and we'd no idea how far we'd come. What we hadn't realised was that hill walking is very different from walking along a road or a path. It was summer and so the nights were long and light, but we were beginning to think a long, cold, hungry night outdoors was a possibility. It was Heather who spotted a stream in the distance and although we didn't know much, we *did* know that water doesn't flow uphill.

Having run out of other ideas, we followed the stream for what felt like for ever, searching for some sign of people. Eventually, like a mirage in a desert, a group of buildings took shape. As we got nearer, one of the shapes turned out to be a wee shop.

Positively ecstatic with joy and relief, we dumped our rucksacks, and tentatively pushed open the door. Bedraggled, weary, and damp from intermittent drizzle, we must have looked a sorry sight. The shop lady was kindness itself, telling us the quickest way to the hostel, and offering to phone up and make sure they kept us a bed.

We looked round for something to buy for our evening meal. What had she got in the shop freezer? Our eyes popped out of our heads when we spotted a ready-cooked, frozen, roast chicken meal with all the trimmings. In 1959, such a thing was only served as a special treat.

An hour or so later, settled in at the hostel, now warm and dry and glowing with our achievement, we feasted like kings on our roast chicken, much to the envy of every other hosteller. That was to be the first of many youth-hostelling holidays.

That same summer after Dad died, Mum, Elizabeth and I joined our Smith cousins on a holiday in a croft which was so far north and so isolated that it was unreachable without a car. Aunt Isabel drove us there but—oh!—the journey seemed interminable. Barren landscape as far as the eye could see, with not a tree in sight, not a bird, nor a single living creature. For city dwellers even as long ago as 1959, this lifestyle belonged to a bygone age. Our warm unpasteurised milk arrived in a jug mid-afternoon because we had to wait till the cows came home to be milked.

Our croft in Sheigra was at the end of the road so when the butcher finally arrived, in his van, having enjoyed a sociable 'wee dram' at most houses on the way, he would fall asleep among the dead carcases until he sobered up.

The rain, too, was a problem. How were we to dry the clothes and heat the croft? No trees meant no wood. Crofters didn't buy coal, they burned peat. Uncle Ian used to simply appear, his arms laden with cut peats. Where did he get them? We never knew and we never asked. Part of a crofter's tenancy was access to a peat bank, and each croft had a peat stack which they themselves had harvested, cut and stacked—an extremely hard, tough and dirty job.

Mum and Auntie Kathleen spent most of their holiday feeding all the hungry mouths, because there were an awful lot of us. We had porridge and eggs for breakfast, then two or three loaves of jam sandwiches for the picnic, and enormous pots of soup in the evening, and stews if the butcher had been in his van.

Every day—no matter what the weather, and each carrying our own food—we set off for Sandwood Bay, one of the most beautiful beaches in the whole world, its golden sands stretching as far as the eye could see. The water was cold, but we mostly swam anyway. Then we tucked into our soggy, wet, gritty, sandy jam pieces (sandwiches), a peculiar (but not unpleasant) phenomenon unique to Scottish picnickers in the fifties and sixties.

On the journey home to Glasgow, Mum was unwell and Aunt Isabel decided we couldn't carry on. We were only a few miles from Grantown-on-Spey, so she booked us into the Grant Arms Hotel. Talk about going up in life: from a croft to a hotel!

While Mum suffered in her room, attended by Aunt Isabel, Elizabeth and I were left to roam the establishment. The lift was a novelty. We went up and down (up one, down two; down two, up one), dodging the other guests whenever we could, until eventually we got bored.

Then we were allowed to go and choose what we liked to eat. After nearly two weeks of porridge, bacon rolls, and soggy jam sandwiches, having a choice was exciting. The bedroom, too, was spacious and grand. Sadly, it was a one-night stand only. Next day Mum felt well enough to travel and we had to leave hotel life and return to 6, Colebrooke Terrace—and school.

The holidays were over.

Summer 1955: we holiday in Clynder
& sail in the 'The Morag', built by
Dad & Jimmy. Sitting in the boat
above, Heather & Elizabeth.

↑A letter from Jimmy to Aunt
Isabel written Xmas 1956 (he
was a cadet on the SS Prome
on his way to Aden)

↑1955: Jimmy leaves school &
joins the Merchant Navy

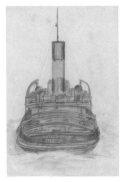 

Dad, recovering from lung cancer, joins the Burns & Laird Line so he can be home more often: these are two of his drawings of Burns & Laird ships; Dad sailed on the Campaigner
←

The last model Dad made before he died ↓

←
Elizabeth & Dad when we move to 6, Colebrooke Terrace, where I was born in 1944

1958: I am sent for a holiday with Aunt Teenie in the Kyles of Bute Hydro in Port Bannatyne, by Rothesay ↓

1961: sixth
year at
Glasgow
High
→

Jimmy home on leave
with wads of spare
cash buys his first car: a
Singer Tourer, 1960
←

At sea, Jimmy makes
detailed model replicas
of the ships he sails in:
this is the MV Arisaig
[see note page 426]
→

- 151 -

At Tighnabruaich in 1961: Elizabeth & I
meet the talent in Susie's cafe →

Elizabeth & Bonzo enjoy the view of
the Kyles of Bute, from holiday house
'Fairy Bank'
↓

I work at Turnberry Hotel
before I go to uni
→

1962-1965
I am a student
at St Andrews
University

St. Salvator's Ball

← Kate Kennedy procession in St Andrews, 1962. Left to right: me, Wendy Johnson, Marlene & Bev &, on top of the cabin, Janette Kerr (who reappears in chapter 48)

1966: David & I are now engaged & he visits me in Colebrooke Terrace →

1965, Heather, Christine & I enjoy our last singles holiday in Newquay before we get married ←

1968: David & I get married and so do all our friends: it would have been unthinkable in the sixties for couples to live together *without* a wedding first!

↑Left to right: Elizabeth, David, me, John Hunter (David's great friend) & Heather.

Jimmy giving me away ↓

Heather & Stewart ↑

↓ Sandy & Sheila

Christine & John ↑

Kirsty, the first Dalrymple grandchild, born in February 1970 is admired by both widowed grannies (Granny Wilson right, Granny Dalrymple above)

←
Fiona is born in Glasgow in November 1971

Kirsty loves having a real dolly, her little sister Fiona, to push in her buggy →

Left to right: Karen (Heather's child), Fiona & Kirsty playing in the garden ↓

My sister Elizabeth marries
Craig Campbell in the
Grosvenor Hotel, 1973

David & I pop
down from a
holiday in Dornoch
for Elizabeth's
wedding, leaving
Stewart & Heather
to look after Kirsty
& Fiona
→

Holidaying in
Wormit: left to
right: Kirsty, Anne,
Fiona, Catriona
(born July 1974) &
Karen
(Anne & Karen
are Heather &
Stewart's children)
←

1975: Stewart
& David doing
what men do
best
→

←
Kirsty & Fiona show
their little sister
Catriona how to
skip.

Chapter 21: Dirty Dismal Glasgow vs. Denmark & St Andrews

At the end of June 1960, I set off on my very first trip abroad, funded by Glasgow Corporation and the Girl Guide Movement. I had never been out of Scotland, apart from my wee job in Ferranti's in Manchester when I was 15, and for that I didn't need a passport. But the two-week International Guide Camp in Denmark was for me a real foreign expedition.

The Guide Captain, 'Doc', drove me to the station. Heather and quite a few others came to wave me off. Apart from unprecedentedly rough waters across the North Sea from Newcastle to Esbjerg (not something I would ever want to suffer again), the fortnight was packed with new sights, sounds, people and the most unforgettable experiences. I couldn't believe how clean and bright and airy Denmark seemed compared to Glasgow, so much more colourful—as if all my life so far I had been looking through dirty lenses.

I was linked up with a young Danish Guide—Alice Jacobsen. When I arrived at Alice's house, there was a feast awaiting me. Never in my whole life had I seen such a huge bowl of strawberries (strawberries were seasonal and counted out at home) and we could eat just as many as we wanted! The table was laden with smørrebrød (open sandwiches), topped with various meats, cheese and garnishes, as well as cakes and more cakes, and everything decorated with tiny Danish and Union Jack flags.

Starving and by now recovered from my journey, I devoured the unfamiliar foods in front of me. Meanwhile everyone was talking at the same time, trying to say things to me with their hands and their faces and their limited English vocabulary.

Alice's three little siblings—Alan, Ann and Axel—were by far the best at communicating. With their antics, acrobatics and funny faces, they made everyone laugh, which made them try even harder. The wee one, Alan, soon became my shadow and interpreter.

When we arrived at the camp after a two-mile march from the train with all our kit, the huge field was teeming with guides and more guides, and strange unfamiliar languages all around us. French was the only one I recognised. Each country was allocated a space and a tent. The rest was up to us. In no time at all, since we were well practised in the art of camping, the 'Scotland' site was ready to be inspected.

During our time in Denmark, we were visited by various VIPs. Lady Baden-Powell flew in by helicopter and the Danish Queen Ingrid arrived for a formal inspection and to watch our display of international dancing and songs.

The young and pretty Danish Princess Margrethe also arrived unexpectedly for an informal visit. We liked her. She wasn't like royalty as we knew it. She was informal and friendly, chatting to us about tartans and kilts.

Each country celebrated its own culture and we Scots entertained the others with Scottish country dancing.

By the end of the holiday, hundreds of mostly Danish guides were attempting the Gay Gordons with little skill but lots of energy, noise and laughter.

⊠

Although I was sorry to leave my new friends and travel home, I was thrilled to be picked up at the station by Jimmy in his very first car. After years of lugging cases on and off the tram or the train, it felt amazing to speed along Great Western Road in an open topped Singer Tourer. I felt like royalty and longed for someone to recognize me. What a poser!

When we arrived back at the house, Aunt Isabel was there and she had an exciting plan. She wanted to visit her newly born nephew, Duncan*, first, she said—but after that, what about a girls-only holiday?

Soon after that, Mum, Elizabeth, Aunt Isabel and me were off to St Andrews, staying in a hotel for the whole time (a first). Jimmy was due back at sea and Sandy had his own plans to earn money in the summer holidays.

In fact, while we were in St Andrews, Sandy was working for the Tay Fishing Company in Newburgh. By 1960, salmon stocks were beginning to dwindle in the River Tay, but it was still a major industry. The work was hard, and dependent on the tide and the high water. A gaffer and a crew of four worked the river with one rowing boat. One person, the 'towman', held one end of the net on the shore, while the others rowed the boat in a loop. The net was then pulled in at both ends to catch surprisingly large salmon.

Sandy was one of such a team, along with his friend David Cuthbert. There should have been three pals working together, but they had been driven to Newburgh by the third lad's mum who—when she saw inside their living quarters, a bothy—forbade her son to take part and whisked him off home. (Bothies are basic shelters usually left unlocked and free for anyone to use. The reason for this is simple: there's nothing in them except bunks and a stove to cook your food.)

Since St Andrews wasn't far from Newburgh, Aunt Isabel brought Sandy to our hotel for a meal, some fresh clothes and a wash. Elizabeth remembers him wolfing down a two-course dinner and Mum asking him if he would like another. The answer was, 'Yes please.' He then effortlessly—and with gusto—scoffed his second meal.

We were impressed. This was probably his only decent food for the duration of his salmon-fishing venture—he was never allowed time off again.

I thought he was paid well, all the same—he got a weekly wage of ten bob (ten shillings), 50p in modern money. But what could he buy with that in 1960? It's hard to be accurate, but even taking the inflation of the decades into account, it wasn't really a generous pay. A loaf of bread cost about one shilling, and Sandy and David were expected to feed themselves out of their wages. No wonder he enjoyed his meal at the Royal Hotel in St Andrews!

St Andrews, like Dunbar, had an open-air swimming pool, called the Step Rock Pool (you can still see it, but now it's part of the Aquarium and you can't swim in it). It was icy cold but we swam there because that's what you did on holiday.

I took a great liking to the town. It seemed so fresh and clean and sunny, compared to damp, dreich, dirty Glasgow. And the idea of living by the sea, while still having shops and cafes, was the best of both worlds as far as I was concerned.

In fact, those two weeks in St Andrews were to affect the rest of my life. When I came to contemplate going to a university, it was the first place I thought of. Lack of money wouldn't be a barrier. These were the sixties, the time of social mobility, of student grants, when parents were means-tested. I knew Mum's income was low enough for me to be eligible for a full grant from Glasgow Corporation.

Only a small percentage of young people went to university anyway because of all the other options. There were the competing temptations of paid employment and plenty of it, all sorts of apprenticeships, and other vocational training such as radiography, domestic science, physiotherapy, primary school teaching and more.

How lucky we all were!

Chapter 22: Tighnabruaich & Turnberry Hotel

In the final years of high school, we were expected to take some responsibility. There were all sorts of official appointments with important titles: House Captains and Vice House Captains, School Captains and Vice School Captains, Prefects, Hockey Captain, Librarians—and others I can't even remember now. I was given the honour of captaining a not very successful hockey team. There were special privileges in the final year, too, one of them being access to a space called 'The Tower' at the top of the school, where we could make coffee and talk. That was all there was to it—but we certainly felt a bit special.

My social life at home was much the same, except I had exchanged the Guides for the Young People's Society (our fancy name for a youth club) organised by the previously mentioned minister's son, Johnston McKay. Since Johnston was running it, I was an enthusiastic member, and soon we were officially going out together. He was everything my brothers were not—academic, a classicist, a church goer, and definitely not sporty—and so I never had any inclination to invite him home. We spent much of our time walking in the Botanic Gardens, and sitting in cafés. In the winter months, it was baltic.

It was baltic too on Hogmanay that year but we didn't notice the weather. Despite sad memories for me, the 1961 celebrations were fun. Christine's family had moved up in the world from her flat in Melrose Street to a semi in Kelvindale. On Hogmanay she bussed it back to Belmont Street to meet us all at the Café de La Paix and invite us to her new house. On our way there, we linked arms and stretched in a line across the car-free road, bellowing any song we could think of loudly and unmelodiously. We were all Lonnie Donegan fans so it was mainly 'Putting on the Style' and 'My Old Man's a Dustman', with 'I belong to Glasgow' thrown in now and then for good measure.

On our way, we passed 'first footers' of all shapes and sizes: old codgers clutching their bottle and hanging on to their missus; mums and dads with their prams and weans heading to their pals or their granny's house; West End ladies dressed in their Sunday best (hats and costumes/suits), their bottle tucked discreetly in their bags. A unique atmosphere of goodwill, banter and humour pervaded the streets as we all shouted *Happy New Year* to each other, sometimes even crossing the road to shake hands. The traditional Scottish reticence and inhibitions seemed to disappear, some of it undoubtedly thanks to the booze, but not all—and certainly not in our case because cafés didn't sell alcohol.

In fact, we were all sober, including our first foot. I can't now remember his name but I do remember he was tall, dark and handsome (or at least Christine thought so). As our merry band of sober revellers walked up the path, Christine's dad was waiting at the door for his piece of coal, and her mum had a splendid spread awaiting us, with a wee glass of Babycham for the girls, and a can of Tennents for the boys. We brought in the bells there and you could have heard our untuneful rendering of *Auld Lang Syne* for miles.

We sang and walked and talked all the way home. A night to remember.

The next two terms at school were mainly exams but most of us managed to pass enough to go where we wanted next: Heather to study physiotherapy in the Glasgow Royal Infirmary, me to the University of St Andrews, Doris to Glasgow University, and Diane to the 'Dough School' in Glasgow. I had no idea what I wanted to study or what I wanted to do for a living. I knew even less about university life and what might be expected from me.

Only one schoolmate, Mary Burton, was also destined for St Andrews. She had been the Dux (top academic achiever) of our school but I didn't know her well because she lived on the other side of town. Interestingly when she answered the phone from home about hockey on a Saturday morning, she spoke with an English accent. At school she sounded just like the rest of us.

By this time, Mum had enough money to go on a holiday of *her* choice. She was no longer her big sister's charity case. Mum, like me, had gone to the Girls' High School, and although she left at the age of fifteen to become a hairdresser, she'd stayed in close contact with her friend Landa, an only child, whose parents had serious aspirations for her. Landa fulfilled their expectations by completing a degree at Glasgow University and marrying well ('well' in those days meant a husband with money, position and status). She may have married for love too—that I don't know.

Landa's life with her husband in the Foreign Office took her all over the world, and her husband felt their three boys would only get a good education if they were sent to boarding school. His choice was Gordonstoun (that same school so loved by the late Prince Philip as a child, and so hated by his son Charles).

Landa was heartbroken by the decision to send her boys away. She had always hoped to be a 'hands-on' mum and missed them dreadfully. So she persuaded her husband to buy a house in Tighna-bruaich, in the hope of providing both roots and some sort of holi-day home. Fitting into local village life is a difficult challenge for outsiders and she was over the moon when her old school friend

(Mum) decided to rent a holiday house called Fairy Bank for a month in July.

None of us knew how good that month was going to be. To get there, you either drove or sailed 'doon the watter'. Mum had neither car nor driving licence as yet, so it was the paddle steamer for us, by which I mean Mum, Heather, Elizabeth and me. (Jimmy was away at sea and Sandy was working elsewhere).

Sailing on the paddle steamer (the Waverley) in those days could be an amazing and unforgettable experience. I recall being on deck listening to their band playing such favourites as 'Song of the Clyde' and 'I belong to Glasgow' (I don't remember anyone ever singing along to the music but perhaps our sailing time was too early and everyone was relatively sober).

The River Clyde has some of the most stunning views in the world, although I would be lying if I said I noticed the scenery at the time.

On the other hand, the steamer experience *could* also—quite often—be wet, cold, dreich and miserable, with the passengers packed tightly inside a smoke-filled lounge.

When our steamer docked at the pier, I don't know who was more excited—the locals waiting to see the talent and greet their relations, or the visitors arriving to find a curious, welcoming reception committee. Heather and I couldn't believe our eyes. There was a gaggle of good-looking local boys standing on the pier, eyeing up the new arrivals, and we seemed to be the only teenage girls coming off the boat.

We liked our rented holiday house, which was near to Landa's. From the time we arrived, our holiday went from good to better and simply never stopped improving. On the first morning we went straight out to explore and we discovered Susy's tea room, Lena's magnificent ice-cream and then—a notice on the police station:

POLICE ON HOLIDAY, APPLY ROTHESAY

Police on *holiday*? What a wonderful opportunity for the two local young men who possessed cars (there were no traffic lights and no pedestrian crossings and very few pedestrians). As it began to get dark, young drivers would appear from nowhere, scrubbed up in their best gear, ready to race along the main street, and sometimes as far as Caladh.

It has to be said that boys with cars came first in our popularity stakes. These same cars ferried the favoured to various ceilidhs in Kames, Millhouse and Tighnabruaich itself. This was the main source of entertainment—and when we got there, the ceilidhs were wild. Heather and I knew our highland dances (courtesy of scary Miss Loudon) but we'd never known them like this—rough and crazy, joyous and uninhibited, catapulted from partner to partner while trying not to bump into the occasional toddler strapped into a buggy. Now *that's* what I call Scottish country dancing—not for the faint-hearted!

After we got home from the ceilidh, nursing our bruised arms, we would play Ricky Nelson's 'There will never be anyone else but you' over and over again, or Buddy Holly's 'It doesn't matter anymore', or even Tommy Steele's 'Singing the Blues'—depending on how the evening had gone. This would continue until, from her bedroom directly above, Mum would knock on the floor with a broom handle. Her message was clear: time for bed.

At some point during the holiday, Jimmy arrived unexpectedly in his own motor. I was seventeen, I was old enough. Here was a chance for me to learn to drive. At first, Jimmy was enthusiastic about the idea. He took me to the old airfield and cranked up the engine.

I stalled it.

He cranked it up again.

I stalled it.

And so on, until he simply waited for me to get the engine to cough into life and then jumped in—though not without choice expletives.

To change gear, I had to learn how to double-declutch. This meant more stalling, and more swearing from Jimmy about the state of his clutch. It was, after all, his hard-earned and very precious new motor.

Several years, and four driving tests later, I finally got my driving licence. By this time, I had bought my own second-hand car.

During our second summer in Tighnabruaich something else improved our holiday even more. The First Boys Brigade lads from our very own home church, Stevenson Memorial, were camping in their hut in Portavadie. Neither they nor the local boys had ever seen anything quite like my Danish pen-pal, who was visiting from Esbjerg.

Her Guide uniform now a thing of the past, Alice had transformed herself into a striking young beauty, dressed in fresh, light-coloured garments, auburn hair twisted on top of her head, with curly locks escaping to frame her face.

She had a hesitant and gentle voice and—thanks to her Danish intonation—she raised her voice ever so slightly at the end of each sentence, as if she was asking a question. She could have had the pick of any one of the local lads. They were all spellbound.

We were no competition for Alice, but fortunately she fancied someone neither of us even liked much.

This summer was different from most. It was longer for a start, because I didn't start university until the autumn. Angela's radiography course didn't begin until October either, so we decided to apply for a job at Turnberry Hotel (we had both admired its grandness when we holidayed in Mary's caravan in the nearby village of Maidens).

And so August found us struggling off the bus with our suitcases and lugging them up the very long drive to the hotel, with absolutely no idea what to expect. 'Staff induction' hadn't been invented back then; we were expected to start the next day.

Angela was on room service, including breakfasts. I was to serve afternoon teas and table drinks in the lounge in the evening. This proved easy because I was allocated the four tables beside the revolving entrance door. Every time someone came in, there was a cold draught, and so hardly anyone ever sat there, with the exception of Mum and Elizabeth, who came to visit me occasionally.

It was more than your life was worth to go near tables allocated to other waiting staff. They belonged (along with the cash tips) to the permanent waitresses. 'Their' guests would call out *Miss! Miss!* as you stood idly by. The first and most important lesson was to pretend they were invisible, and appear to be busy.

When I served drinks in the evening, it was a free-for-all, but I had a lot to learn there too. I conscientiously wrote down the customer orders, then took the slip to the bar.

The barman gave it a cursory glance. 'We don't do *eggs*,' he said.
'But the customer *asked* for an egg.'
'Well go and tell him it's a bar, he can't have it,' was the reply.

'Of course you serve an *aig*. It's a bar, isn't it?' said the hotel guest to me in his (to me) strange accent.

At this point one of the permanent and more experienced waitresses drew me aside, a broad grin on her face. 'The man's a Cockney. He means a Haig. A Haig *whisky*'.

Ouch! But I soon learned the names of the different drinks, and to understand different accents too. In the sixties we didn't even hear a range of voices on television: all the presenters were required to speak in the approved 'RP' (Received Pronunciation) way.

Our pay at the Turnberry Hotel was quite good. We survived the experience and learned a lot. Ever since that time I've had every sympathy with waiters and waitresses. Poor service is rarely their fault but—being on the front line—they usually have to endure the hassle from customers.

Chapter 23: Strange Traditions In St Andrews

After I returned from working in Turnberry Hotel, it wasn't long until I was off to the next stage of my life—St Andrews, this time as a student. I had absolutely no idea what it would involve but was fair chuffed with myself and I cringe now to think how I flaunted my university scarf wherever I went. There was a snag, however—I needed a red undergraduate gown, and they were expensive.

This problem was solved by Mum, who used to chat in the street to a chap called Gordon Carruthers (known as Jock), a bachelor teacher at the Glasgow Academy. In fact, Jock was not simply a teacher; he was more of an institution. A leading light in the CCF (Combined Cadet Force) Christmas Entertainment, he famously played the Dame in the annual pantomime. When they met, Mum used to ask Jock about the boarding school boys (since she knew Angela and I had been chatting to them) and would enjoy telling him how Sandy was off to Aberdeen University to study Forestry, while I was bound for St Andrews. It was never a short—or one-sided—conversation because Jock was always ready to off-load some of his own concerns.

But it was through Jock that I acquired my mandatory undergraduate red gown. A St Andrews alumnus himself, he was both delighted and determined to lend me his, and lend it he did. So armed with all the right gear, I set off to St Andrews by rail (in those days the train line ran right into the heart of the town).

Mum saw me off at Central Station, giving me a packet of fags, a packed lunch and a *Woman's Own* to read on the train. My trunk had been sent ahead to my student residence, and she had arranged for a tall, third-year, rugby-playing friend of my brother Sandy to meet me. Which he did.

And that was how I turned up at my new home, Wardlaw Wing, with Hugh Begg carrying my suitcase. When I rang the bell at the main door, I was greeted by Janette, my future room-mate. She had been watching all the new arrivals with interest and was suitably impressed that I 'already knew a male student'.

As she and I compared notes over the first of many coffees, we discovered that both our mums were widows, and we'd attended similar schools—so perhaps some thought *had* gone into the room pairings. Janette was most interested in finding out how I had already acquired a male escort and I explained the connection with Sandy. But Hugh had asked to be my 'senior man', I told her—what did that mean? Janette, well informed about St Andrews traditions, enlightened me. He would be a kind of mentor and all new students had one. From that time on, Janette and I were pals—a friendship which has lasted to this day.

Wardlaw Wing, named after the University's founder and first Chancellor, Bishop Henry Wardlaw, was to be my home for the year. It was small, no more than twenty girls, all in shared rooms and all—apart from us—from south of the border. In no time I'd learned about R.P., Nouveau Riche, Grammar Schools and Boarding Schools, and about Sally, Alex and Wendy from Roedean, Benenden and St Swithins, who for the first time in their lives— like the rest of us—were hearing a wide range of accents. My Turnberry Hotel experience had taught me that people from different parts of the country spoke differently, but some of the other students had never been out of their home area and were suspicious of strange ways of speaking.

Janette and I found all this fascinating. Our Scottish accents exempted us from any assumptions about social status because none of the other students had ever known a Scottish person before. Throughout the year, as we all lived together and got to know each another, we ceased to notice our differences. Really, we were all the same, looking out for a man and trying to pass our exams.

Living in a university residence at that time was like staying in a hotel. A full, cooked, buffet breakfast was available every morning. Then there was lunch at midday, and in the evening, dinner with table service, when the wearing of your red gown was obligatory. Every so often we had to sit at the High Table with the Warden and other staff. This was very formal, intended to ensure our social skills at dining were up to scratch. I didn't mind the formality involved with using the correct cutlery for the correct courses, but I did find the conversation a strain, as well as tedious, superficial and boring.

Academically, I was ill-prepared for university life. My school qualifications were Highers, but most of the other students had A levels which meant they'd had an additional year's study. For Higher English I had studied Shakespeare's Hamlet and Burns's 'Tam o Shanter', Dad's favourite. I was now presented with Chaucer and Milton, and Shakespeare's *Love's Labour's Lost*. I had no idea how to do anything other than read them and pick out the odd simile or metaphor. Wendy, who was to get a First in English (and married a boy from Madras College, a marriage of brains and looks, not money or class), showed me how to analyse text and do a detailed study. What a shock!

In Greek, I fared worse. I found myself in a class of twenty-six English boys and one other Scottish girl who had been at school in St Andrews. To me they all came across as swotty Greek-loving geeks. You may remember I chose Greek because I liked the idea of knowing Greek letters? Well, that came back to haunt me.

On the first morning we filtered in, and sat round a long desk waiting for the eminent Greek scholar, Professor Dover, to arrive. He welcomed us warmly and I immediately took to him (he had an amiable face and a twinkle). But then he handed each of us a piece of Greek script, and invited us to read it out. My eyes nearly popped out of my head. I didn't recognise a single word. It was written in upper-case Greek letters (caps) and I'd only learned lower case. Some of the characters looked similar—but not enough to make any sense. The Professor, a kind man, must have noticed my reaction because he simply asked for volunteers to read and translate. I was able to sit, eyes down and say nothing.

The hour was interminable but finally it came to an end. I didn't consult anyone about this fairly major difficulty. Who were you supposed to speak to anyway? No one in my family had ever been to university except my Aunt Isabel. Being accustomed to solving my own problems, I came up with a simple solution—I would give up Greek. After at least five minutes' thought, I decided to study Latin instead. A wise decision.

History was my other subject. The first essay I handed in for assessment received a Gamma Delta. Pretentious academia didn't use simple numbers or letters to tell you how you had done. Well, yes, they did—*Greek* letters. I knew enough Greek to know that Gamma Delta was the lowest mark possible.

Fate and good luck saved me. Who should I meet at the Saturday night hop (dance) but a fourth-year Honours History student. On the way home he probably didn't *want* to talk about history essays but for me this was a case of needs must. He agreed to show me his recent work (awarded a top Alpha Beta). He gave me a formula for essay writing. You had to consider all the evidence on both sides of the argument, he explained—in the context of the norms and values of the time—then come to an indeterminate conclusion at the end. For example: 'On the one hand Alfred was Great, but on the other he wasn't so great.' That was the essence of it. The lesson worked, and I never looked back.

Having sorted out the Greek problem, learned how to survive and having zero intention of continuing to Honours (an ordinary degree would suit me fine), I was able to join in first-year university life with gusto. At the friendly police station, Janette and I acquired bikes already painted and numbered. All we had to do was pay out a couple of pounds from our grant and register them in our names.

We swanned and strutted about St Andrews in our red gowns, on the look-out for good-looking male students. Tradition demanded that the undergrads from each year should wear their gown in a particular style. Elitist final-year students had theirs draped from both elbows and trailing along the ground. Third-years wore the gowns draped over one elbow only. Second-years wore the garment higher up, hanging off both shoulders, while bejants and bejantines (first-years) wore it firmly over both shoulders.

Bicycles and gowns didn't mix well—frequently the fold of material got caught in the spokes. I worried that I would tear Jock Carruther's borrowed garment. However, it survived the three years. In fact, we wore our gowns most of the time, partly because we were show-offs but also because they kept us warm.

I had by now acquired an 'academic family'—a senior man, a senior woman and an academic brother and sister. Our 'parents' were expected to act as mentors, our siblings as friends. Luckily, I liked my academic brother, while Hugh Begg, my academic father (AKA senior man) was very willing to show me the ropes.

There were many strange traditions for new students to learn. For example, on 'Raisin Monday', the bejants were required to give their parents a gift of raisins. In return, they received a receipt written in Latin on a strange object. Mine was written inside a child's potty. If stopped in the street on that particular Monday, first-year students had to sing the graduation song 'Gaudeamus Igitur'. Many years later, I enjoyed showing off at the graduations of two of my daughters at Glasgow University when I carolled it lustily (and probably out of tune), as one of the few parents who knew the words by heart.

One weekend I took Carol Williams, a fellow student from Leatherhead in Surrey, to visit my Glasgow home. Being a polite girl, she kept her views to herself, but later she told me how horrified she'd been by the dirt and the dreariness of my home city. Still, she ended up as a GP in Dundee, so it can't have been that bad.

To study medicine in 1962, Carole had to pass O Level Latin. With little or no understanding of Latin, but desperate to be a doctor, she'd learned her prescribed text off by heart. She was the only person I have ever known who—after a drink or two and a bit of encouragement—could recite long passages from Julius Caesar's *Gallic Wars*, a riveting story (not) of his military campaigns.

Chapter 24: St Andrews Uni—A Marriage Bureau?

B y the second year in St Andrews, I was much more confident. I'd settled happily into university life, sharing a room in the Old Wing of University Hall with Beryl from Durham.

Each day maids brought two buckets of coals to our room for the open fires that were the only source of heat. Rules were strict in female residences and men were allowed in only at certain times. At 10 p.m. you would hear the ultimatum: *Time gentlemen, please!* Any females loitering outside had to dash in before the building was locked for the night, and dishevelled men could be seen hurrying out of the front door. Woe betide any female student found with a man in her room out of hours!

At the end of each year there were university balls. These were very formal affairs, similar to modern sixth-year proms. For such an event, I needed an evening dress. Guess who arrived to whisk me off to the most expensive shop in town to buy whatever dress I liked? None other than Cousin Dorothy Buchanan!

She drove through with Mum and Elizabeth, her faithful dog Nigel accompanying her. He was even allowed in the shop, where I chose a beautiful Frank Usher, light-blue, brocade ball gown.

Around this time, I had taken a fancy to a medical student called David Dalrymple so I invited him to the ball as my partner. The 'dance programme' listed a wide variety of dances, a buffet 10.30 p.m. to midnight, and a cabaret from midnight until 12.30 a.m.

The lines of poetry from Longfellow on the inside of the dance card demonstrate how far females have travelled since 1963:

As unto the bow the cord is,
So unto the man is woman;
Though she bends him, she obeys him,
Though she draws him, yet she follows
Useless each without the other.

To the best of my knowledge, not a single female student remarked on their required subservience in this piece of poetry. It was just the way it was back then. Females were conditioned to get married and have children, while the males were expected to work and support them.

Beryl remembers the day her German lecturer arrived in the lecture theatre clutching a set of marked examination papers. He instructed the male students to accompany him to the room next door, where he returned their papers individually. Next he faced the female students and, without saying a single word—not even a 'Good Morning', he threw their exam scripts over the desks at the front, then disappeared. Some of the papers landed on the floor. The girls, desperate to know their marks, simply picked them up. *They didn't even complain.* Can you believe it? Fortunately this was the exception, not the norm.

I'm delighted to record that on one occasion Beryl and I wrote an angry letter to AIEN, the university newspaper. This was in response to a written comment from a male student suggesting that women who wore trousers looked 'underslept' and 'unwashed', reminding the readers that female students should dress as if for the office. We replied (and it was printed):

Surely it is obvious to the poorly informed writer of the article
that the majority of women students dress smartly and in such a way

as to ensure comfort. Taking into account the biting cold wind of St Andrews and the hazardous bicycle rides, it must surely be admitted that the average female student is even more smartly dressed than might reasonably be expected. The would-be fashion critic is obviously completely ignorant of his subject since ski pants are acknowledged in the most fashionable of circles to be stylish, chic and feminine.

We were very pleased with ourselves when this was printed. Just imagine—wearing *trousers* to lectures? How dreadful! But I suspect that student dress in St Andrews was not then (or perhaps even now) at the cutting edge of fashion.

One Friday morning in November 1963, Beryl and I went in for breakfast, to find two of our fellow American students sobbing uncontrollably. What a state they were in! When we asked what was wrong, they could barely speak for crying. I was more than a little surprised when I learned the reason—President Kennedy had been assassinated. This was awful, of course, but the outpouring of grief was extraordinary. I didn't really understand it. They hadn't known him personally so how could they possibly be so upset?

Meanwhile David and I, and John Hunter (David's flatmate and lifelong friend) spent a lot of time sitting in front of the fire in their flat, talking about everything and nothing, while David and I smoked incessantly. Poor John—he never complained and at the time of writing he is alive and well. Thankfully he survived the passive smoking we inflicted.

David's invitation to me to go out on our first proper date was accompanied by a warning. A refusal would mean I'd have to pay back all his cigarettes—the ones I'd smoked in the flat. I wanted to go anyway because I liked him but (as I told him many years later) he gave me no choice.

Our date was at Kate's restaurant in Market Street. According to David, he decided I was the one for him when I chose the cheapest dish on the menu—an omelette. Did his thrifty upbringing affect his choice of girlfriend? Or was it my charm, beauty and listening skills? Obviously the latter.

Before long, I was invited to his home in Ayr. The first time I was taken off-guard by the way his mum, Ella, hugged me warmly (she was clearly not from the west end of Glasgow). She also told me how lucky David was to have met me. Now there's a lesson for every future mother-in-law!

As a family, the Dalrymples frequently played bridge in the evening and it was there that I first learned the rudiments of the game. They were all good players, Ella even playing at Troon Bridge club.

I was so nervous at first that I used to twist and bend the cards in my sweaty fingers. More often than not David would play the hand for me. In the beginning, my favourite role was to take the dummy hand (for non-bridge players, that means you do nothing but watch).

Even with a grant, I was always broke at the end of a university term, so holiday jobs were the norm, especially if you wanted to go on holiday. The sixties were the era of job availability and I effortlessly found office work as a clerkess at Bilsland Bakeries, a big employer in Glasgow. It wouldn't be long before the work I did (transcribing figures from a horizontal to a vertical column) was defunct, replaced by a more efficient machine.

As soon as we could afford it, Christine, Caroline, Heather and I were on our way to our very first sunny holiday (or at least we hoped so) in Newquay. The boarding house had boasted a room (perfect), and roast dinners every evening (perfect), and it was within our budget (perfect). It turned out, however, not to be quite as *perfect* as expected.

Two extra beds had been put into the double room so that no fewer than four were jammed tightly together, *no* space between them. To get to our own sheets and pillows, we had to crawl over the other beds (there would have been more space in a tent). Our roast dinners comprised wafer-thin meat, sliced on a machine—not at all what we were accustomed to. Yet it never occurred to us to complain.

But the idyllic weather was a wonderful novelty, and the waves were ideal for bodyboard surfing—a new experience. On the very first day, we each spent most of our money on a small wooden surf board from a beach kiosk. And that was our holiday—sunbathing and surfing, and roast dinners and snacks from the kiosks. I was accustomed to beautiful but windy—occasionally sunny, but more often cold and wet—beaches, not a single soul in sight. And here we were on a hot busy beach, a small stroll to buy an ice cream or a hot dog. We loved every minute.

By the time we boarded the train home, we hadn't a penny between us and only one packet of polo mints to share on the journey. When the smart-looking lady in the corner of our carriage opened up her packed lunch, we fell silent and tried not to watch her hungrily.

If only we'd had debit or credit cards, cash points, bank transfers or an I-phone app! Sadly they hadn't been invented. Failing to manage your budget meant no cash. No cash meant no purchases—not even a sandwich. The smart lady didn't finish all her lunch. How we *longed* to ask her for her leftovers—but our courage failed us.

When we arrived home, I was broke again and set about finding paid work. Within a week (courtesy again of Aunt Isabel) I was off to Cheadle Hulme for three weeks as a surrogate nanny. Along with the cook, Mrs Shufflebotham (definitely not a Scottish name), I was charged with the care of three boys: Rupert, Clunie and Julian. Fortunately, I liked children and I enjoyed my new job.

My three wee charges were accustomed to a level of attention totally outwith my own experience, and yet in other ways they were neglected. They didn't seem to have any fun or any free play, though they were articulate and had clearly been taught how to behave. Polite and biddable, they'd no spontaneity or instinctive emotional responses.

When their Grandma came to visit, for example, they were instructed to shake hands and welcome her, and told what to say. It helped me understand why some socially and financially privileged people come across as formal and cold. Learned behaviour is a fascinating topic.

The holidays flew past and soon it was time for my third and final year at university. Mary Burton's parents picked me up at Colebrooke Terrace and for the very first time I arrived at St Andrews in style—in an actual car.

Tired now of residence rules and regulations, I was looking forward to sharing a one-bedroomed flat with Mary (from school) and Beryl, my very tidy friend from Durham. One of us would have to sleep in the sitting room because there was only room for two in the bedroom. Beryl was awarded the privilege (?) of sleeping on the sofa bed in the room where we entertained our main guests, namely David—now the love of my life—and Beryl's Roy when he travelled up from Durham.

Each week we put our cash on the hall table downstairs and our landlady confirmed our payment by a tick in her rent book. So simple!

It was essential to pass my exams—and I did. I ended up with an unexceptional MA, mainly in History. I now remember very few historical facts, and yet I strongly believe that the thought process acquired in studying for my degree has proved a life-long asset. It taught me how to evaluate people and events in the context of their time. What's more, I acquired a rational sense of perspective and balance—in short, learned how to see the big picture. Very few things in life are black and white (the only other subject I really enjoyed was Logic and Metaphysics).

And so ended my life at university.

As I headed back to Colebrooke Terrace for the next stage— now unofficially engaged to David—I decided to train as a teacher.

Chapter 25: Arnold Clark, a Boat Trip, Education & Some Weddings

Back home in my old room with its one-bar electric heater, I felt disorientated. I missed my flatmates. I missed the freedom and fun of university living. It was strange to be part of the family again. Jimmy and Elizabeth were at home and, of course, Granny and Mum. Mrs Kirk was there too in the mornings and Jimmy made her day when he ran her home in his latest purchase, a green MG convertible. Wherever you were going and at whatever time, a cooked breakfast was a must, and tea was invariably at 6.00 p.m. Nothing had changed much—except me.

Merchant seaman Jimmy, now fully qualified with his Extra-Master's Certificate, was finished with seafaring, had a shore job in Denholm's Shipping Company and was on the lookout for a wife —or at least a girlfriend. I suspect girls were something he thought about a lot during his years at sea with only males as companions. Apart from qualifying as a ship's captain and, like Dad, making amazing model vessels, he'd read widely during his long hours away from home, including every single Shakespeare play, and he even wanted to discuss them! Crikey, that was tricky—he was now so much better-read than me (*Love's Labour's Lost, Hamlet* and *A Midsummer Night's Dream* were the only three I knew).

My little sister Elizabeth had grown up too, and was now more interested in boys and clothes than walking poor old Bonzo, who still sat faithfully at the door waiting for her to come home from school. And Sandy was gone—to teach Science (but mainly rugby) at Merchiston Castle School in Edinburgh—a temporary post until he found one which used his BSc in Forestry. By this time he had met the love of his life, Sheila. Soon, like most of our contemporaries, they got married.

And what about my friends Angela, Christine, Heather, and Beryl? Without exception, they followed the customs of the time and within the next few years they married too. In fact, my own wedding was one of the last because David's medical course was so long. Now in his penultimate year of medicine, he visited Colebrooke Terrace most weekends.

Jimmy—delighted to have male company—always invited David to The Doublet, a pub frequented by a chap called Arnold, whose car showroom was next door. I remember Jimmy and David talking about this chap who, they said, 'was going places'. How right they were! In the sixties, Arnold went into finance, then car hire and soon he was buying up accident repair companies. He ended up as *the* Arnold Clark, Scottish billionaire and owner of a chain of motor dealerships, the biggest private business in the country.

I wasn't in the least interested in cars, but I *was* interested in Glasgow. David, Jimmy and I used to have heated arguments about the Glasgow shipbuilding industry and why it was failing.

Jimmy, with his knowledge of shipbuilding, would argue that union demarcation disputes and 400 different pay rates made the industry uncompetitive.

I counter-argued that the bosses were the problem, being mainly privately educated. They were too remote from their workers, too academic, I said, without practical knowledge and experience of shipbuilding.

David, on the other hand, thought our yards were too old-fashioned. They didn't—he pointed out—have modern factory systems, or up-to-date financial/marketing methods; with or without government intervention, they were doomed to failure. It was just a matter of time.

In fact, the decline of shipbuilding on the Clyde came about through a combination of all these factors so we were all correct. It was fortunate that the three of us could disagree without falling out. Whenever it was clear our views were irreconcilable, we had a cigarette and changed the subject.

This was the year that David and I formalised our engagement with a ring which I wear to this day, a beautiful blue zircon surrounded by diamond chips, paid for with money given to David by his mother from carefully saved cash. I'm not sure she expected him to spend it all on an engagement ring—but he did.

David's mum, like mine, was a widow. Her husband, John, had died of a heart attack a few years previously—suddenly and unexpectedly. When the families met for the first time, our two mothers quickly discovered they had a lot in common.

Meanwhile, David and my brother Jimmy talked about cars. David adored cars. He loved to talk about them, loved to get underneath the bonnet and see how their engines worked, and loved to get oily and dirty in the process. So did Jimmy!

David also enjoyed having someone around who could help him repair his ailing and ancient vehicle. (Cars were simpler in the sixties and you could often fix them yourself.)

David and I did talk about our wedding too—but since that was really my domain and he was willing to go along with whatever I wanted, there were no problems. Most bridegrooms at that time basically did what they were told. It was a perfectly satisfactory arrangement (things may have changed somewhat since then).

As to the cost, we were immensely fortunate. Granny Wilson was paying for the whole thing, including my wedding dress.

This was also the year Jimmy introduced David to sailing—a completely new, and perhaps not entirely welcome experience. Let me explain. Jimmy's pride and joy was his keelboat, Ruby, a Bermudan sloop kept in Dumbarton. During his quest for a girlfriend, Jimmy had met a girl the week before at a ceilidh in Loch Striven and wanted to see her again. He didn't have her phone number. Was he just expecting to bump into her, I wonder?

Apparently he'd warned her he would sail the eight miles to the head of the loch, anchor, row ashore and then find her. I've no idea how he planned to accomplish this (no mobile phones back then). Anyway, he needed a crew, and David and I were the chosen ones or—more likely—he couldn't find anyone else for the job.

When we arrived at the Ruby's anchorage in Dumbarton, Jimmy piled the sailing tackle into the tender, told David to get in, gave him the oars and pushed him off in the direction of the anchored Ruby. What neither Jimmy nor I knew was that David had never been in a rowing boat before.

In my youth, the Boatswain Badge was one of many that adorned my Girl Guide sleeve. I was very good at tying knots and quite a skilled oarswoman really, but Jimmy had never thought of asking *me* to row (I was a girl).

Trying to be helpful, Jimmy and I yelled instructions to David. I'm ashamed to say we laughed merrily at his struggle, although (to his credit) it didn't take him long to get the hang of it. Eventually he succeeded in off-loading the tackle and returning to shore to collect us. With the boat finally rigged and ready to go, we set off 'doon the watter' past Helensburgh, across to Kilgreggan, Dunoon, and round Toward Quay—and finally—Loch Striven.

Anchoring at the end of the loch was a memorable experience. The water was so deep that the anchor wouldn't hold and we had to search for a mooring in a bay which seemed very far away. For those who have never tried it, catching a mooring buoy requires considerable skill. The crew (in this case David) was expected to stretch out full length at the bow of the boat and—using the anchor hook—reach out and catch the buoy.

For sailors at that time, it was a matter of pride to the helm never to use the engine when performing this delicate operation. The end result for the crew, if things went wrong, was a dislocated shoulder or a dip in the water. After at least two attempts and a lot of bad language, our boat was finally attached to a buoy. We never did find the girl Jimmy was looking for—but David got a taste of sailing. I think he preferred golf.

✖

Meanwhile I had to get my teaching qualification—at that time a very easy course, or so it seemed to me. However, the cursory input on education, psychology and teaching methods, interspersed with three short, practical, on-the-job teaching assessments wasn't sufficient training for a teaching post, as I would soon discover.

Drama was also part of the course. It consisted of declaiming a text from the back of the lecture theatre. If the lecturer could hear you at the front, you passed. Perhaps there are *some* skills that can only be acquired by doing the job. (With the benefit of hindsight, I'd say the best vocational teaching involves both on- and off-the-job training, a combination of theory and practice.)

However, I was soon technically qualified to teach History. I could certainly write competent history essays—but that was no preparation for talking about historic events or getting young people interested in the topic. Nowadays, teachers can access film footage of more recent historic events. They can take pupils to historic sites and castles, and afterwards talk about the trips in the context of learning. No such luxuries back then. It was hard-going. I survived my teaching practice without too much difficulty but also without much glory.

Then there was the probationary teaching year in Queens Park Secondary School. I nearly stopped dead in my tracks when I first saw the Head Teacher. Mr Easson was a dead ringer for Alfred Hitchcock. As a new member of staff, I was given the classroom adjoining Mr Alfred-Hitchcock-Easson's office and he could hear every word I said.

This was undoubtedly a wise move from both his point of view and my own. I felt secure with him nearby and, being keen to show him I could teach, I prepared my lessons in much greater detail than I would have otherwise.

There was one small difficulty. Mr Easson insisted on the use of the Lochgelly tawse. It was standard practice, he said, and my pupils would be waiting to see if I could use it properly. He demonstrated how to raise my arm high above my head so that the leather strap could land a slap on a badly behaved pupil's hand with appropriate force. I spent one lunch time with another new teacher (Isabel Far-quharson) whacking the radiator in the staffroom, with one or two of our teaching colleagues commenting and giving advice.

As it turned out, I never needed to use the belt. On the one single occasion when it was required, Mr Easson stepped out from his little office and performed the task for me. Such a gentleman! I was very grateful. (The use of the belt in Scottish schools was not illegal until 1987 but it was mostly phased out in Glasgow in the early eighties.)

During my first teaching year, Queens Park Secondary was rehoused in a much larger building and became Tory Glen Comprehensive School. The old Junior and Senior Secondary School system (with entry determined by results in the Primary 7 qualifying exam) was abolished and replaced with the 'comprehensive' schooling system.

On my first morning in the new school, Mr Easson took me to my class to introduce me. Accustomed to the class falling silent the moment they saw him, he stood expectantly waiting for the usual hush.

And he waited.

And he waited.

Not a soul paid the slightest attention. I had no idea what to do either but eventually one of the kids noticed us standing there and shouted to the others, 'Shut up you lot! The geezer wants tae speak!'

At this, the class fell silent, ready to hear what the geezer had to say to them.

From that time on, Mr Easson, alias Mr Hitchcock, reluctantly learned new skills and acquired a less formal teaching style.

Me? I enjoyed teaching in Toryglen Comprehensive School but I wasn't there for long.

✠

In January 1968, David and I got married in Stevenson Memorial Church and moved to Whitehaven in Cumberland.

My wedding (or should I say *our* wedding?) was without doubt one of the best days of my life. It wasn't, however, without its stresses.

I recall sitting in the drawing room in Colebrooke Terrace with Jimmy who, in the absence of Dad, was just about to go to the church with me and give me away—when the phone rang. The incoming call was from a phone box and the news was not good. My trusty bridegroom was going to be late—a small matter of forgetting the wedding ring. John had jokingly asked David if he should hand over the ring to him for safe keeping, only to discover that David had left this essential piece of wedding equipment in his suitcase in the Burnbrae Hotel.

David explained all this on the phone to Jimmy, who had the sad task of telling me that my husband-to-be and his best man, flat-mate and lifelong friend, John Hunter—would be about fifteen minutes late. Jimmy pointed out, not unreasonably, that since I'd already waited nearly four years to get married, another quarter of an hour wasn't going to make much difference.

It meant, however, that the wedding guests sat in the church for a mysteriously long time, fidgeting and whispering and wondering what had happened and what to expect.

David's mother was furious when she heard what the boys were up to. She had to be calmed down. When David and John finally arrived, quickly followed by Jimmy and me, the atmosphere of relief and deferred excitement set the scene for the rest of the wedding feast.

And it was a brilliant day. To have all your friends and family in the one place at the one time—all there to wish you well and to have fun—what on earth could be better?

Chapter 26: Such Things Only Happen to Other People

Now officially Dr and Mrs Dalrymple, David and I set off for our first married home, a rented house in West Cumberland Hospital, Whitehaven. We were full of eager anticipation but also a little anxious about the unknown. Our old Austin A7 was packed to the gunnels with luggage and a few wedding presents, although most of the latter were safely stored in the attic of 6, Colebrooke Terrace, ready for the time when we'd own a house of our own.

In 1968, Whitehaven was one of the few hospitals with married accommodation for junior doctors, so we were lucky. We settled down quickly in the small complex of detached houses; we both had jobs to get on with. Within a short time we'd met our neighbours, some of whom were Indian, of different castes; others were from different parts of the UK. Two doors along lived David's sister Belle and her husband Dave. Our neighbour on the right was a lady called Barate Mukarje, whose Brahmin husband (a houseman like David) had gone home to his arranged marriage in India and returned with her—poor girl.

Barate desperately missed her family and was so lonely she used to sit on my doorstep waiting for me to return from Distington Secondary Modern School, where I was the only history teacher. Before she was married, she'd lived in a well-to-do home with lower-caste servants for menial work, spending most of her time gossiping with friends and sisters. But now in her new and cold little house, she was expected to make and light the fire, clean the place and make all the meals for her new husband—who was rarely there. Once I got to know her better and stopped her freezing to death by showing her how to set and light a coal fire, I persuaded her to talk to my pupils at school about her arranged marriage. What she told them shocked and surprised both me and the teenagers. She bluntly stated that an arranged marriage had a much better chance of success and longevity than western love marriages, since husbands and wives were chosen for their compatibility, similar values, shared traditions and were permitted to see a photo of each other and meet a couple of times before a decision had to be made. She even produced statistics to back up her argument. I can't say my teenage class agreed with her or were persuaded, although possibly it made them consider a point of view other than their own—which is, in my book, a form of real education.

The Indian caste system* also caused problems for David in the hospital. Barate's husband was from a higher caste than his boss, the Senior Registrar, and refused to communicate with him directly. He would only do so through David, the other doctors, and the nursing staff. What a nightmare!

David was kept extraordinarily busy. The NHS then, as now, extracted its pound of flesh. One Sunday—having been on call all weekend and having barely slept at all—he phoned to say he would be home in half an hour for something to eat.

Like the new and conscientious wife I was, I had mince and tatties cooked, plated and on the table as he came through the door. Hungry and tired, he sat down, took two mouthfuls—and his pager bleeped.

He lifted his knife and fork, then slammed them down so hard that the plate broke in two. There was my lovely mince—scattered all over the tablecloth! He swore loudly, left immediately and didn't return until late in the night.

Undoubtedly these were hard times for junior medics and 'constantly exhausted' is a true and accurate description of their state. I personally witnessed the long hours, the unaccustomed responsibility, difficult decision-making and problem-solving that were suddenly thrust upon a young, newly qualified, overworked and overtired doctor.

Our neighbours on the other side were Isabel and Malcolm and they had a new baby which would only fall asleep in a moving car. I knew nothing about babies and, to tell you the truth, neither did they. Isabel came from a large and wealthy Catholic family, and three of her brothers were at the exclusive Fort Augustus Abbey School (run by Benedictine Monks). It would be interesting now to get their take on their schooling.

Isabel was delightfully down to earth, and as a four (if ever our husbands managed to be off at the same time), we got on famously. We even spent a few days holiday together on the Isle of Wight. From Isabel I learned that it was possible to buy a *whole* fillet steak (her mother had had a family of seven and money to go with it, so this is what she'd always bought). I had to explain to her that normal people bought small, individual fillet steaks for a special treat, or—much more likely—a pound of mince.

David came to the end of his six-month contract in Whitehaven in July and, since the house went with the job, we had nowhere to live. We promptly rented a small cottage, while David worked as a locum GP—a sort of medical 'temping' to earn some money before his next House job, due to start in January. I really liked that little cottage. We were able to put some of our wedding presents in it and it felt homely—and it didn't smell of curry. Many of the rented hospital houses had been lived in by Indian doctors whose wives naturally cooked them mostly curry dishes. But in the sixties David and I had never tasted curry nor did we like it much but being polite we had to eat it when visiting his fellow Indian doctors. Despite the Hospital Trust cleaning the houses between tenants we were always very aware of the lingering curry aroma in most of the houses.

On 17 October, we were asleep in our pretty little cottage when the peaceful night was shattered by the shrilling of the phone. David answered it, as he always did.

Half asleep, I paid little attention, expecting to turn over and go back to my dreams. But it wasn't to be. I heard him say, 'We'll come right away.'

Too sleepy to note the 'we', I was surprised when he shouted to me to get dressed, pack a bag and get in the car—we had to get to Glasgow straight away. Seeing my questioning face and reluctance to move, he promised to explain it all when we were on our way, urging me to shift and get a move on. Still half asleep, I did what I was told, making a thermos of coffee for the long journey ahead.

By the time I was in the car, my mind was racing. What was going on? But I kept quiet because David, grim-faced and unusually silent, was concentrating on his driving. For almost an hour, neither of us said a word but eventually, he started to talk, the tears streaming down his face. It was the first time I'd ever seen him cry.

The phone call had been from Sandy, he told me. It was to tell us that my brother Jimmy, in his beloved Aston Martin DBII, had skidded on an oily patch on the Cardross Road and crashed into a wall as he drove home from his precious boat, the Ruby. There were no seat belts in those days. His head had gone straight through the windscreen.

As we drove, Jimmy was lying in the Intensive Care Unit in Killearn Hospital with little or no chance of recovery. In layman's terms, his brain was smashed to bits. In medical terms, he had 'brain stem damage', 'cerebral contusion' and 'closed head injury'.

Our journey through the dark, rainy night seemed interminable. We didn't talk much. We didn't really believe what was happening. Such things *don't* happen. Or at least they only happen to other people. That's what we all think—until it happens to us. We finally drew up outside 6, Colebrooke Terrace as the sun was beginning to lighten the sky. We could see Sandy and Mum standing anxiously at the window. There was no fresh news.

First thing in the morning, Sandy went to the hospital. Jimmy was dead.

That day we were all on auto-pilot, numb with shock and disbelief. It *couldn't* be true that we would never see Jimmy again. But it was, and death brings many practical tasks with it. This helped fill the dismal hours and days that followed. Sandy, who was only 27, grew up overnight as he made all the funeral arrangements and supported Mum, who decided she must have a new coat—she had worn her only other dark coat to Dad's funeral nine years before.

So two days later, she and I found ourselves waiting at the bus stop in Great Western Road next to Hubbards the Baker's, in the pouring rain. Water was coursing down the street (and, for that matter, down the back of my neck, but I didn't care). Mum's tweed coat was completely soaked. She stood there shivering, completely oblivious to everything around her.

The bus arrived and we climbed upstairs to find seats. All the passengers were acting normally. How dare they? At the back of the upper deck was an old man sitting by himself—and no wonder.

Coughing and spluttering and inhaling smoke from his Woodbine, he was making a nauseating job of getting the phlegm out of his lungs—but he was alive! A mum was struggling to light her fag and hang on to her wean at the same time, while two teenagers with bouffant, back-combed hair were actually *laughing*.

All of them were going about their daily lives as if nothing had happened. Which it hadn't—not for them—and in some part of my head I knew that. It was the strangest feeling watching the rest of the world, almost as if Mum and I were on another planet seeing everything from a huge distance away.

At Jimmy's funeral, Mum looked smart in her new coat. Possibly it helped her to feel a little better, but I doubt it. The number of people at a funeral is often inversely proportionate to the age of the dead person. Jimmy was only 29 when he died and so his funeral was packed, standing room only. The procedure after the service— where the family shake hands and speak to all the other mourners as they come out of the church in a long line—was a ghastly ordeal for us, an unnecessary burden for our grieving family. But it was the custom and practice of the time and so it had to happen.

The saddest and hardest days for my stricken mother came after the funeral. Life went on, but without Jimmy, her first-born. Sandy and I returned to our married life, leaving Mum, Elizabeth and Granny in the quietly dismal Colebrooke Terrace house, far too big, and packed full of empty Jimmy spaces.

In 1967, the Glasgow Academy School had written to the owners of 5-9, Colebrooke Terrace expressing an interest in buying the properties. Our neighbour Mrs Carson, at number seven, sold her house to them that same year, while Mrs Craig bequeathed number five to the school. Mum and Granny finally decided the time had come to sell up to the Glasgow Academy and move on. Mum now had money from Jimmy's insurance policy, and so she was—for the first time in her life—in a position to buy a house. Always be careful what you wish for.

⊠

By 1970, two years later, Mum was living in Park Circus in Ayr and commuting daily to her work in Glasgow. It was a house divided into two flats, the intention being to let one of them. Granny was living round the corner with her daughter Betty, and there was a lovely room for my little sister Elizabeth who was in Glasgow training to be a primary school teacher.

With minimal help from Sandy and me, Mum had cleared the contents of Colebrooke, disposing of all sorts of possessions. Dad's army trunk disappeared; Sandy's collection of lead soldiers was given to the children of Donnie Macrae, the Academy Head Janitor since 1960; my wedding dress went to Mrs O'Hara, the Academy head Cook and Supervisor since 1967; my red St Andrews gown was returned to Gordon (Jock) Carruthers, now a Senior Master.

Perhaps if Sandy and I had helped more, we might have hung onto some of the precious things that disappeared at that time. Jimmy had made models of two of the ships he served in. Sandy kept the MV Arisaig, but the other had a less auspicious fate. The Glasgow Academy Janitor, Donnie Macrae—keen to help Mum in whatever way he could—was in the middle of repairing Jimmy's model of the MV Clunepark. He laid it outside the door of his top floor school flat for the glue to dry. It disappeared and was never seen again. The Academy authorities refused to investigate it, fearing it would shed a bad light on the school, since one (or even a group) of the boys had obviously stolen it. Mum—too grief-stricken to make a big fuss—was enormously angry. But more than that—she was heartbroken. One of Jimmy's most precious possessions had been irrevocably and unfairly lost.

While all this was going on in Glasgow, I had made a momentous decision: to replace a life with a life. It wasn't long before I was expecting a baby. By mid-1969, we were leaving Whitehaven behind and on our way to David's new job, which was in Manchester. This time we were going to buy our first house, and we did—in Hale in Cheshire.

While we were house hunting, we lodged for a few weeks with Aunt Isabel in Timperley. She was absolutely delighted to have family visit *her* for a change, and showed me off to her friends, many of whom I had met over the years. I had acquired a maternal bump by then and wasn't much interested in anything else, except that and the new house.

My teaching work was a distant, but not unpleasant, memory.

Chapter 27: Childbirth Is Not A Walk In The Park

Our life was very different now. We had a mortgage, a house to furnish, a lawn to mow, and a baby on the way. David was working alternate weeks—as a demonstrator in physiology at Manchester University, and as an Anaesthetic Senior House Officer at MRI (Manchester Royal Infirmary). He had decided to specialise in anaesthetics and so any spare time he had was spent studying for his FFARCS (Fellow of the Faculty of Anaesthetics of the Royal College of Surgeons). This was an essential qualification if you wanted to be a Consultant Anaesthetist.

This year was very different socially from the year in Whitehaven. Fortunately our friends John and Hazel from our St Andrews days were in Manchester too, but we also attended university functions (sherry and polite chat), medical parties (too much alcohol and very rude jokes) and gatherings with our suburban neighbours (mortgages, house prices and naughty neighbour gossip). Without doubt, the medical functions were the wildest but the most fun.

Meanwhile my bump was growing and I had even taken up knitting to amuse myself, while David sat in front of the fire beside me with books, notes, bits of paper littered all over the floor, and the TV on (but neither of us paying much attention to it). David's way of learning was to explain things to me, but really to himself, and I would nod encouragingly, occasionally asking an irrelevant question. Endless cups of tea and ash trays full of David's cigarette butts completed the scene.

David had booked some time off for the week when the baby was due. But you know how inconsiderate babies can be. On the Monday morning—with no baby having put in an appearance—he returned to work. Two hours later (eight days after the due date) the baby decided to assert its presence. I felt a twinge. Ouch. I felt another twinge. *Ouch!*

I tried to call David—with the beginnings of panic, because he was nowhere to be found. I contacted maternity admissions next but they said they had no record of a 'Kirsteen Morag Dalrymple'. I asked them to check again and to continue to bleep Dr David Dalrymple. Genuinely anxious by this time, I phoned Aunt Isabel for moral support. 'I'm in labour,' I said, 'but I'm really hoping not to have the baby at home'.

Immediately after that, the hospital phoned back to say I was registered and they'd send an emergency ambulance right away. The siren blasted out as we sped through Manchester. If I hadn't been terrified and in acute pain, I might even have found it exciting.

Thankfully, David was waiting at the entrance to Admissions and I was rushed through to the maternity ward where … nothing happened. A fat midwife informed me that my labour pain wasn't painful, just a bit uncomfortable. I asked her if she'd ever had a baby. Her negative reply merely confirmed what I already thought of her.

I seem to remember saying something like, '*Pant-pant*, my arse. Get a DOCTOR—the baby is *stuck!*'

An anaesthetist arrived, knocked me out, the baby's head was turned round using a set of Kielland's forceps, and—hey presto!—I woke up to find myself being handed a perfect, beautiful 7 lbs 14 ozs wee girl. Our first child, Kirsty, had arrived.

But *how* did I wake up? To David slapping me hard on the cheek. Not having the greatest confidence in any of his colleagues, he wanted to make absolutely certain that I was coming round from the anaesthetic (or so he said). If sympathy is what you want, never ever marry a doctor.

After I came home from hospital, my mother (now a car owner) drove south from her new house in Ayr to help me. In those days, mothers knew best (they still do, really) and so she, remembering how well cared for she had been by Nurse de Rochefort when I was born, was determined I should have the same treatment. She thought our house was too cold for a new baby (although I can't imagine that Colebrooke Terrace would have been too cosy in 1944) and bought a baby's hot water bottle to put in Kirsty's cot to prevent her dying of hypothermia.

David promptly removed it, pointing out that hot water bottles can burst, baby Kirsty would never recover from a bad burn, and we had plenty of extra blankets. Nevertheless, although in the first few days I couldn't have managed without Mum, I felt a certain amount of relief when she finally returned to her job. David and I resumed our evenings in front of the telly, only now I had Kirsty to rock on my knee. Every so often, while I made a cup of tea, David would stop studying and take his turn at gently rocking her to sleep.

Shortly after Kirsty arrived, David had to go to London to sit his fellowship exams, so we arranged to stay with my old friend Angela. While David drove us south, I sat in the front seat nursing the baby. Despite Jimmy's fatal car accident the year before, it never occurred to either of us that this was an unsafe and a thoroughly stupid thing to do. Luckily we arrived safely. Angela and her husband Dave made us very welcome, and while 'daddy' did his exams, Kirsty, Angela and I socialised in Billericay.

A year before my own wedding, I'd been Angela's bridesmaid. After that, Angela had had to go back to Glasgow to nurse her mother and take care of her young sister Joyce. Life had played some rotten tricks on Angela, what with her dad dying young, her horrible TB treatment as a child, and then her mum being diagnosed with terminal cancer. But by the time we visited her in Billericay, the bad times were behind her—or so we thought. Her little sister Joyce was now in London training to be a Norland Nanny and Angela had returned to her job as a radiographer. It was good to meet up again and we talked incessantly over breakfast, lunch and tea.

But most importantly we had Kirsty to look after. The wee soul was crying and we didn't know why. What did we know about babies? Zilch. Angela asked a neighbour to come over for coffee and give us advice. The neighbour suggested she might be hungry so I supplemented her feeds with a bottle and she stopped crying quite so much. Another good lesson learned. When you don't know something, ask someone who does!

Seeing Kirsty must have made Angela broody. Nine months later, at home in Hale, David and I were tucking into mince and tatties yet again, with Kirsty blissfully asleep in her cot upstairs, when the phone rang with news of a birth. But that wasn't all—I have to write this quickly because what Angela told us is—even now over fifty years later—almost impossible to believe. Her husband Dave had just visited her in the hospital. He had refused to look at his new-born daughter, Suzie. Instead, he had informed Angela clearly, and without any emotion, that he wanted a divorce. He wanted *nothing* to do with his child. Not then, not ever. Can you believe it? What a dirty bastard he turned out to be!

Two days later David drove to the station in Manchester to pick up Angela and baby Suzie and brought them home to Hale. Not ready yet to talk about the future, Angela and I spent our days looking after our babies and making the dinner for David coming home. On one of those evenings, we had champagne on the table to celebrate his passing his exams. As I remember, David didn't drink the champagne, much preferring beer. So Angela and I, having being brought up not to waste anything, were compelled to finished off the bottle. Life was not entirely full of hardship.

As his one-year contract was approaching its end, David had been applying for Senior Registrar posts, one of which was in Glasgow. He was successful, as ever. Word soon arrived of a post for him as Senior Registrar in Anaesthetics in Glasgow Royal Infirmary starting February 1971. Crikey—no time to waste.

The house was sold, and our limited amount of furniture was despatched to storage until we found a new house. Leaving just in time for Christmas, Angela, David, Suzie, Kirsty and I crammed ourselves, plus essential baby stuff, into our still unreliable car. We headed for Mum's house in Ayr where there was plenty of room— even a flat for Angela until she was able to sort herself out.

Chapter 28: Fiona Is Born In Glasgow, 1971

Two days before Christmas, we arrived at 9, Park Circus, Ayr, and literally fell out of our old Ford Cortina. First out was Angela, still looking trim, not a hair out of place—holding baby Suzie, who was soundly and contentedly asleep. Next was me, trying not to drop my restless, energetic and wriggly ten-month-old baby Kirsty. Last was David, exhausted and desperately in need of a nicotine fix.

Angela and I had held our girls the whole journey, whether crying, sleeping or feeding—there was simply nowhere else to put them. The car was packed to the gunnels with our suitcases, winter boots and coats, baby stuff, Christmas presents from Altrincham market, and a kettle which couldn't go in the removal van because David always had to have a last-minute cup of tea. Tucked away in the boot was David's tool kit, just in case the car broke down, which thankfully it hadn't.

It was such a blessed relief to arrive, not just for us but for Mum as well. After Jimmy's tragic accident, she suffered acute anxiety about any of us travelling by car (no mobile phones in those days to let her know where we were and when we'd arrive). On holiday from her job at Kelvinside Academy, she had been very busy in her new two-flatted house. It now looked impressive, elegantly furnished with Granny Wilson's Victorian furniture from Colebrooke Terrace. She had also been busy knitting and when Angela went into her bedroom, there—lying on the bed—was a fine, two-ply baby shawl. This same hand-knitted shawl was passed from Angela to her daughter and then to *her* granddaughter, Maddie. Mum had knitted one for my baby Kirsty too but I didn't look after it quite so well: after its immersion in the hot tub washing machine, it emerged much reduced in size. Ah well! Easy come, easy go.

With two new babies, our Hogmanay that year in Ayr was very different from our young days. All we wanted to do was go to bed early and sleep—and we did. We made up for it on New Year's Day when we sat down to one of Mum's roast lamb dinners, joined by Auntie Dot and David's mum, Ella. Refreshed by a good night's sleep and surrounded by all his favourite women, David was in his element—the life and soul of the party. Even the gods were on our side that day—Kirsty and Suzie slept soundly through the meal.

But the next day might have been so different. Stewart and David had decided *not* to go to the Old Firm match in Ibrox. What a good decision that turned out to be! Heather and Stewart phoned to tell us about Glasgow's worst ever footballing disaster—sixty-six people dead, five of them children from Markinch in Fife, and more than two hundred others injured. The only two goals of the whole game had been scored in the final minutes, the first by Celtic. And then totally unexpectedly in the last few seconds, Rangers scored an equaliser. The combination of excitable fans, overcrowding and an accident on stairway 13, all contributed to this dreadful crush disaster as everyone tried to leave.

Thankfully, we were safely at home with Mum, where Angela and Suzie stayed on for some months. But as for us, we had to find a flat before David started his new job in Glasgow Royal Infirmary. And we did—a second floor flat in Partick—two up, with one of its two bedrooms used as a coal cellar. This provided us with yet another novel living experience. Kirsty got sore knees from crawling over cracked linoleum floors covered in coal dust and so she learned to walk very quickly—definitely a child prodigy.

As many people know, living with a baby upstairs in a tenement block (with no lift) is hard work. At the start of any planned outing, you have to carry the pram downstairs, leaving the wee one upstairs in a cot or a safe playpen. Of course, you need to make sure you have the door key safely in your pocket, in case the front door bangs shut behind you before you can sprint back up the stairs to get the baby. I learned this the hard way when I found myself outside the flat with Kirsty locked inside. A bad moment indeed! Fortunately we had given my neighbour, Mrs Campbell, a spare key—and Mrs Campbell was in.

We couldn't wait to buy our own house. When one came up in Austen Road, within the catchment area for Jordanhill School, we offered for it right away—and got it. It was good to be back in Glasgow and in many ways life resumed as if we'd never been away. Heather and I discovered that her first child was due in December, and my second in November, and her husband Stewart helped David rewire our new house. An electrician had to check it all out and the house was extraordinarily messy—but the wiring worked and we now had sockets everywhere. I was delighted. Never again would I have to contend with the Colebrooke Terrace one-bar, sizzling electric fires with their two-prong plugs gingerly inserted into two-pronged sockets.

And what happened to Angela? She lived with Mum until she successfully sorted out her divorce, and found somewhere to live down south. She was officially now a single parent and these were rare in 1971. Like so many people today, with no parental support and in full-time work, she struggled with childcare. But this was Angela, one of life's survivors, and she slowly succeeded in building a happy life for herself and her daughter Suzie.

In the winter months Heather and I joined a pottery class and trailed out every Tuesday evening to an art room at the top of Hyndland School. As was expected in the early seventies, we hid our unseemly maternity bumps under dresses loosely hanging from under the bust. Despite this, the pottery teacher *must* have noticed. Did he worry, I wonder?

On the penultimate night of the class, I phoned Heather to say I wouldn't be coming because I'd felt a slight twinge. So I cooked the tea and we ate it before David took me to Redlands Hospital. By 10.30 p.m. Fiona had arrived, another beautiful daughter, absolutely no bother this time. Perhaps a bit *too* quick, in fact—David barely had time for a quick pint with Stewart before he had to dash back to the maternity ward to see his new baby.

When I was still in theatre after the birth, the doctor asked me if there was anything more he could do for me. I replied that (after nine months' abstinence) I thought I deserved a cigarette. He erupted into a huge, infectious belly laugh. While I *did* clearly deserve one, he said, I would have to wait until I got to my room, as the combination of a fag and the oxygen would probably blow us all up. (Well, he did *ask*.)

Heather managed to complete her pottery mug before she had Karen in December.

Angela and Suzie came north to spend Christmas with us. Kirsty and Suzie were into everything, but Fiona (only four weeks old) would still sleep in her pram. Do I remember the parcels? Do I remember tinsel and a Christmas tree and fairy lights? None of these, I'm afraid.

What I remember is nappies. Buckets of nappies soaking in Napisan. Nappies on the radiators. Nappies on the fireguard. Nappies on the tiny pulley in the kitchen. Nappies on clothes airers in front of the fire. Even nappies hanging frozen, stiff as a board, outside on the washing line. These were the days before Pampers and tumble dryers. Such inventions are undoubtedly bad for the environment. But washing towelling nappies was no fun. In fact, it was hard work for new mums already short of sleep.

Christmas over, I settled into a daily routine. I would rush through the necessary boring chores and then—pushing the pram with Fiona asleep inside and Kirsty sitting on top, her wee legs dangling over the side—I'd meet with Heather and her new baby Karen. We drank coffee, smoked and chatted. It was good for us both to be able to share the worries and laughs that come with new babies and untrained husbands. We always sat too long and had to rush home to make the evening meal—because that was our job, part of the unwritten marriage contract for the 'stay at home' mums of the time. Some worked harder at it than we did.

One evening a week 'the girls' (Heather, Sheila and I) went swimming, while 'the boys' (David, Stewart and Ronnie) came to our house, drank beer and played darts. Kirsty would be asleep in her bed upstairs, but baby Fiona needed to be watched and her carrycot was carefully placed under the table when the darts match was taking place. If she cried, or was hungry, or needed her nappy changed, there were three unskilled, inexperienced and basically useless men to take care of her. David was a highly competitive darts player and could get very annoyed when he lost. But there was no doubt that these darts matches were intense and hugely enjoyable. And Fiona survived unscathed.

Shortly after this, Mum moved back to Glasgow to a large, four-bedroomed, ground-floor flat in Kelvin Drive, this time a five-minute walk from her work, rather than a tedious train and bus journey of over an hour. What was the point, after all, of her being in Ayr any longer? Granny Wilson had died in Ayr at the age of ninety-three, Mum's new Dalrymple granddaughters were in Jordanhill, and Elizabeth was due to get married in the summer of 1973.

Despite the aching absence of Jimmy, Mum hoped she'd be able to cope with living in Glasgow again. To avoid being alone, she invited a new, young, cheery first-year teacher from Kelvinside Academy School to lodge with her. But it was still hard. I don't think a mother—particularly a widowed mother—ever really gets over losing a child.

Chapter 29: We're All Jock Tamson's Bairns

The following summer, the bond between Heather, Stewart, David and me grew even stronger when we holidayed together in Dornoch. How we squashed four adults, three children, luggage and pencil golf club bags into the one car, I have no idea, but we did.

It wasn't the most comfortable journey we'd ever had. Ten minutes after leaving, at Anniesland Cross, Heather's little girl Karen, without any warning, decided to sick up her Weetabix breakfast. We cleaned up as best as we could, and carried on, now better prepared with a collection of sick bags to hand. Having paid for the holiday house and our first big family adventure, a bag of vomit wasn't going to stop us.

It certainly slowed us down though, because whenever Karen turned green, we had to break our journey. These sudden interruptions were only possible because we weren't travelling on a motorway. We had a pit stop on the way—friends of Heather and Stewart. Such a lovely couple! Their table was laden with home-baked scones, cakes, and every kind of salad and cold meat. Nothing was too much trouble. They entertained the children and helped clean up the car and us.

It was a holiday to remember for all sorts of reasons, not least because it included my little sister Elizabeth's wedding to Craig. David and I were able to drive down to Glasgow for the family wedding (Heather and Stewart baby-sat).

The holiday didn't last as long as we would have liked. David had to go back to work so we had to pack up. But there were other outings. For example, there was a visit to Ayr to see David's mother and his absolute favourite aunt—Dorothy—known to everyone as Auntie Dot. When we were there, we visited Christine, her husband John and their first child David, who was the same age as Karen and Fiona. Guess who was visiting them that same weekend? Heather and Stewart!

Christine, Heather and myself were all expecting another baby in the summer. We had a lot to talk about but we were so *not* amused by our three not very funny husbands running a bet on which of us would deliver first. Sitting on Christine's sofa, each of us managing a sizeable bump, we girls didn't find this in the least amusing. They wouldn't be laughing if *they* were pregnant, we told them. We left them to their merriment and went out for a coffee and a natter.

Back home in Glasgow, our future didn't turn out quite as planned—David and I still had one more move to go. Young as he was (only 30), David was appointed as a consultant in Anaesthetics and Intensive Care in Ninewells Hospital in Dundee. When this brand new state-of-the-art teaching hospital opened in 1974, it was the first of its kind in the UK, and the largest in the country (the story goes that some of the doctors used a bicycle to get round it). The close partnership established between Ninewells and the University of Dundee continues to this day.

So once again we put our house up for sale and, since it was in the catchment area for Jordanhill School, we sold it quickly. Sell first and buy later was our way of doing things so yet again we were homeless. Mum was still working and her house had a lodger, but her sister Auntie Helen came to the rescue and invited us to live with her in Whitegates, Cardross, a place with numerous good childhood memories for me. Auntie Helen thus found her peaceful life invaded by two small children, plus me and David. At weekends, if David wasn't working, we house-hunted in Fife and Angus. We had a very clear idea of what we wanted. Also it had to be near Ninewells because David would be on call. Sadly for him, a keen golfer, this ruled out Carnoustie and St Andrews.

My golfing husband had, as it happens, won the prestigious Denholm Golf Cup Trophy while working at Glasgow Royal Infirmary. I don't know which of us was more nervous at the presentation dinner—him or me. We were both much younger than the others and therefore well out of our comfort zone. David was an excellent communicator, but having to make an entertaining formal speech in front of all the big shots—most of them his hospital bosses—was a first for him. I'd listened to him rehearsing that speech so many times that I almost knew it by heart.

When I was in the cloakroom with the other wives before the dinner, they all seemed older, more confident and more sophisticated than me. They chatted comfortably while I stood alone like a lemon, knowing no one and feeling desperately anxious and self-conscious. But this was Glasgow, and one of the older ladies, beautifully groomed and clad in long, blue, brocade evening dress, clutch bag and evening gloves, with multiple diamond rings adorning her fingers, grabbed my arm. 'Excuse me dear, you're young and my eyesight isn't so good without my glasses. Can you have a look and see whether that's a pluke on my chin? If there is, would you dab it with this concealer?'

There was, and I did and it was the word *pluke* that relaxed me completely. I've often wondered if she said this deliberately to put me at ease. I'll never know but I learned a useful lesson, best described by a well-known Scottish saying, 'We're all Jock Tamson's Bairns'.

Chapter 30: Wormit—The First Few Years

We did find the house of our dreams. It was in a village called Wormit, on the banks of the Tay at the south end of the Tay Rail Bridge opposite Dundee. Most of the houses there had been built originally for the owners and managers of the Dundee jute factories. I hadn't wanted a place with steps, or one on a hill, because I would soon have a new baby; and David had wanted a garage. But when we saw 18, Hillpark Terrace, it was love at first sight. There was no garage, it was on a hill, there were steep steps up to the garden and a sloping path to the front door, but it had an amazing view of the river.

So we bought it. We moved in just one month before Catriona was born in July 1974. Mum yet again came to help out. Two small children and a baby visibly due weren't great assets to me when emptying boxes and crates and making up beds and cots. On our first visit to Wormit, we'd noticed there was no High Street as such, just a hairdresser, a post office, a garage and a corner shop. I think that was one of the reasons we chose it: it was entirely different from any other place we'd ever known. No more moving house for me. I'd had enough of change and we now had the rest of our lives to make our home perfect and make a life for ourselves and our children. We were finally settled—in the house of our dreams.

From the feature window on our lovely curved staircase, we could see Wormit Bay and the River Tay and, in the distance, the Perthshire and Angus hills. Standing at that window on a dark, windy winter's night, it wasn't difficult to picture the violent storm of 1895 when the original Tay Rail Bridge collapsed and no fewer than ninety-five passengers drowned.

But that was then, this was now. And summer 1974 was pretty frantic. Catriona was born in Dundee Royal Infirmary on 22 July. I was what was called an 'elderly prim'—in those days thirty was considered quite old to be having children. Fiona was two and Kirsty was now four. We had a new house and David's job was stressful and demanding. We badly needed a break.

Our plan for a 'stay-cation' wasn't really very sensible but it seemed to work. Heather and Stewart, plus Karen and Heather's new baby Anne (now six weeks old) came to stay with us on the banks of the Tay. We all shared the chores. I do wonder now, with the benefit of hindsight, if the daily 'happy hours' at 6.00 p.m. were a factor in my rose-tinted memory of that time. But the young fathers were there to entertain the older children, while Heather and I looked after our new babies. And there was a beach of sorts, and fields all around, and for anyone brought up in Glasgow, Wormit felt like the depths of the countryside.

Nevertheless, summer was soon over and so was the warmer weather. Brought up in cold Colebrooke Terrace, I wasn't accustomed to central heating but our new home was really cold—there were only two storage heaters to heat a four-bedroomed semi. In the mornings, I had to trail down in my dressing-gown to light the coal fire before I could feed baby Catriona, then get Fiona to Wormit Playgroup and Kirsty to Tayfield Nursery (in neighbouring Newport). Our first home improvement job was undoubtedly going to be the installation of gas central heating. What a joy it would be for the first time in my life to have a warm comfortable house!

We really needed to build a garage, too—but that had to wait. Right now, any work on the car had to be done in the street. More often than not, while tinkering under the bonnet, David would be summoned to Ninewells and—since no one likes a doctor with oily fingers and dirty nails—before he set off, he had to scrub his hands vigorously with swarfega, the first step in a prolonged hand-washing operation.

One morning I had dropped off Fiona at Wormit Playgroup and was walking up Bay Road, when I heard a voice calling from the other side of the road. 'Morag? Morag Wilson? Is that you?'

Looking across to find the owner of the voice, I recognised Pat Morton immediately, her hairstyle unchanged since our school days. She had thick, short, stubbly, brown hair. She was a big woman in every way—big-chested but not fat, with a big smile, a big heart and strong opinions. She was extremely capable, as well as practical, funny and occasionally sarcastic. As far as I know she never owned a lipstick and wasn't ever overly concerned about how she looked.

We certainly had a few years to catch up on since we were at school together in Glasgow; no shopping, cooking, washing or cleaning was going to get done that morning. We went to my house for coffee instead, so we could talk while Catriona dozed in her cot. We quickly discovered that our husbands were both consultants at Ninewells: Hugh was in Psychiatry, and Pat herself was a doctor working part-time in the Accident and Emergency unit of Dundee Royal Infirmary (DRI). We only just made it back to playgroup in time to pick up our children.

It was Pat and Hugh who later introduced us to Lis and Sandy Harvey. And it was Lis and Sandy who later persuaded David to buy a Graduate sailing dinghy. David had only sailed once before (in Jimmy's keel boat Ruby) but that didn't stop him inviting my brother-in-law Craig for a sail, and he—not knowing any better—accepted. Without life jackets and knowing virtually nothing about tides and winds, they set off from the Boating Club in Wormit on a choppy (but not gale-force) summer's day. For the two over-confident but inexperienced novices, it was a very wet learning experience. They gybed unsuccessfully three times and consequently capsized three times. They ended up hanging onto their overturned dinghy, with its mast pointing towards the bed of the sea. Fortunately a passing motor boat rescued them and towed them to Newport.

I was totally unaware of all this drama and hadn't even glanced out of the window to see how the intrepid sailors were faring. I just assumed they'd know what they were doing. In my family we knew all men could sail. Wrong! Since that occasion, I've never made the mistake of underestimating the unpredictability of wind and tide, nor of assuming a man automatically knows something—or knows better—simply because he's male.

A hot bath, a change of clothes and soon David had recovered with no serious after-effects. Our good friend and neighbour Sandy Harvey helped him recover the boat and return it—by land.

We had lots of visitors in our new house and the kids absolutely loved it when their grannies came to visit. When Ella (David's mum) arrived, the first thing he always asked her (jokingly) was, 'How long are you staying?' She took his question in good part but I really *did* want to know the answer, and such questions are always better coming from your son than your daughter-in-law. At some point early in our marriage, we'd agreed that difficult questions to our mothers should always be asked by their own child. This usually worked. I got on fine with Ella but I certainly didn't always agree with her opinions. She used to say to her friends that she always felt at home in Morag's house and able to make herself a cup of tea at any time. I took this as an accolade.

But there was never a dull moment when Ella and her sister Auntie Dot were around. David and his mum got on famously, they could talk about almost anything. As for Dot—whenever David was around, he would spend the whole time taking the mick out of her, and she loved every minute. Kirsty is the only one now who remembers much about her Granny Dalrymple, who—like David's Dad—had a heart condition. Four years after we moved into our new house, she died suddenly. We were all sad but busy too, and we dealt with it by being as welcoming as possible to David's Auntie Dot who was lonely and heartbroken.

My own mum was a great help when she came to visit, so I got a bit of a break. She could cook too, and we all enjoyed that, particularly David, who told her she was welcome any time. He had only one proviso—that she didn't hang her knickers on the washing line. Yes, he *was* cheeky. It was a joke but he had a point. 'Granny knickers' (and she did wear them) were huge baggy bloomers designed to cover both your corsets and the suspenders that held up your stockings. (About this time, tights were worn by younger women but not yet by their mothers.)

I don't think I would like to hear my mother's opinion of modern-day thongs....

Chapter 31: A Dreadful Shock For My Mother

Little did Mum know that—visit over—she was heading home to Glasgow for one of the most horrific experiences of her life. As she drew up in front of her flat, Elizabeth and Craig were standing outside watching for her. With no mobile phones to let them know when she was arriving, they'd been standing there patiently for hours, determined she shouldn't enter her flat alone. With good reason.

Earlier in the day, Elizabeth's friends, Alan and Lesley McFarlane, had been passing the flat when they noticed the curtains were shut. Concerned, they went into the close to find that the door had been jemmied. As they tentatively pushed it open, they heard the unmistakable sound of glass breaking as the intruders smashed the front window and leaped through it, leaving shattered glass everywhere as they legged it to the park opposite.

Terrified, Lesley and Alan stopped in their tracks and rattled the neighbour's door shouting to them to call the police. There they waited, until two policemen arrived and went in with them. In the hall was a suitcase and a bag filled with silverware and silver candlesticks. But this was nothing compared with the state of the rest of the house, which they viewed with horror. The dining room floor was a sea of broken glass—the remains of Granny Wilson's precious wedding crystal glasses. But there was worse to come.

The intruders had scrawled obscene graffiti on the walls and smashed sauce bottles everywhere so that the contents dribbled down the wall onto the floor and carpet. The beds had been used as urinals—and worse—and the soiled linen was scattered all over the place. As for Mum's lovely bathroom, excrement was everywhere—even smeared on the walls. Clothes, her personal belongings and the papers from her desk were scattered round the house, some of them ripped into pieces.

This was what was waiting for Mum when she arrived home.

She went in, ignoring everything else, and made straight for her papers, desperately hoping that her precious letters from Jimmy had not been destroyed. But they were gone for ever, never to be found. The mahogany baton—which had always been behind the door first in Colebrooke Terrace, then in Kelvin Drive—had vanished too. A few days later, the same three drug-hungry addicts used it to smash the head of a doctor who refused to give them what they demanded. This easily identifiable baton from Victorian times was one of the pieces of evidence that helped to convict them. Glasgow at that time had, and still has, a growing drugs problem. Mum had become one small but painful part of its collateral damage.

Elizabeth took Mum home with her to Edinburgh and brave Craig was given the terrifying task of sleeping in the flat until the door was mended. He confessed to being scared witless all night but the bad guys had moved on by this time and he survived.

After this appalling experience, Mum never returned to her flat. In fact, she never lived in Glasgow again, never visited Glasgow, and bought a house in St Andrews as soon as she could. However, she was still traumatised and feared every unfamiliar sound. One night some students terrified her by throwing beer cans into her garden. Her next move, a year later, was to Wormit—60, Crosshill Terrace, just along the road from me. At that time Wormit had no pubs and we all hoped and prayed that in time she would feel secure and safe in her own home.

Chapter 32: Two Happy Family Holidays End With Tragic News

David and I decided we shouldn't put off building a garage any longer (messing about with cars was his hobby and it saved money too). So when he got the chance to fund the project through a locum anaesthetic job (three weeks in Holland with a house for me and the kids), we jumped at it. We would take the car to Dover, cross by ferry and drive the rest of the way. David's skills as a motor mechanic had maintained our vehicles for years, so that summer when we set off for Dover to catch the ferry to Amsterdam, I was too busy packing for the family to worry about the car. This was David's department, not mine.

Just short of Manchester we heard a knocking noise. (Well David did—I didn't—but when he asked me to listen I thought I could hear something.) We stopped at the next garage and I waited with our three children in the garage forecourt, while David went with the mechanic into the workshop to find out the problem. After a long wait, the news was really bad (and I mean *really* bad)—the big end had gone and it would take at least a week to get the car on the road again. David's locum job was due to start in three days. Thank goodness for Aunt Isabel in Timperley! She came to rescue us and took us back to her house, where we repacked and reorganised ourselves to travel to Dover on the train. Within twenty-four hours we were on the ferry, and off to our Dutch destination, albeit without a car.

Believe me, all this was not as simple as it sounds. Catriona was two years old and not fully potty-trained. (This was the 1970s when there were no disposable nappies.) We ended up tying a piece of string to Catriona's potty and persuading her it was like her mummy's shoulder bag and she should carry it. As Kirsty and Fiona were really old (six and four) they had their own little bags, while David and I managed the rest. We only needed clothes, because everything else was provided for us (except, unfortunately, a car). When we arrived, we hired bicycles and this—other than the train—was our only form of transport all the time we were there. When David was at work, I had a bike with a seat at the front for Catriona and one at the back for Fiona. Kirsty had her own little bike. But this was Holland and there were flat cycle paths everywhere, and play-parks with swimming pools and child-friendly restaurants. I had never seen anything like them before. Amenities like these were completely new to me, brought up in the fifties in Glasgow.

$$\bowtie$$

Our next proper holiday in the summer of 78 was very different. It was not long since David's mum, Ella, had died, and we all needed a break. This time, we camped in the west coast of Scotland, the Mull of Kintyre. The amenities there were undoubtedly inferior to those in Holland, virtually non-existent, but the scenic backdrop to our tent was stunning—a view to remember for the rest of my life. There was a van which came round the campsite every morning, and the kids took turns to buy the breakfast.

The girls simply loved this holiday. Their dad was there all the time and he made it fun.

Our journey to the Kintyre peninsula was not without stress though. As our car roared up a very steep hill, it was making such a racket that it attracted the attention of a passing police car. How unlucky was that? When the police car signalled us to stop, the children, terrified, hid under their blankets, afraid they would be sent to prison. But fortunately, and unsurprisingly, we were let off with a warning and a suggestion that we should buy a new exhaust or else (and this was a joke, I think) we might be charged with 'disturbing the peace'.

Every day of this holiday, the kids had competitions with their dad, and their favourite was, 'Who could stand on their head longest?' Since David always won, it was his favourite too. Because he *did* like to win.

On the Friday morning of our camping week, we woke to the sound of heavy rain drumming on the canvas. Not a gentle pitter-patter, but big, noisy, ploppy drops—and we could hear the wind howling. When we ventured out, sheets of rain attacked us from all sides. A dreich day indeed. We packed up as best as we could, while water trickled down the back of our necks and the driving rain soaked every single thing we possessed. It was time to move on.

☒☒

We decided to finish our holiday by visiting Heather and Stewart in Glasgow. The thought of a house and a fire was like a magical dream, and the kids couldn't wait to see Karen and Anne again. Eventually we found a red phone box and phoned our friends to warn them we were on our way. I only had a few coins and Heather had just started to say something about some sad news from our friend Christine, when the money ran out and we got cut off.

With Christine at the forefront of my mind as we drove, I entertained David by telling him about Christine's lessons in the life skill of smoking, as well as some of our Hogmanay adventures. When we arrived, Christine and Heather's kids (Karen, Anne, Susan and

David) were eagerly awaiting our girls. Everything appeared normal, but where was Christine? The children, en masse, disappeared to the garden to play as Christine joined us. Only then did we hear what had happened. We couldn't believe it. No, it couldn't be true. Christine's husband, John, was—dead. What? Thirty-four years old, and Dad to David (seven years old) and Susan (only four)? How on earth could this have happened?

The circumstances were awful. An accident no one could ever have predicted—an unexpected fall from a great height. Heart-broken, Christine was suddenly a young widow. Reeling with shock, we carried on with the weekend, grateful to be diverted by our kids, the younger ones completely unaware of the tragedy in our midst.

As for me, I remembered Jimmy's sudden death all too well. I knew how hard it was for Christine. Still she coped, somehow concealing her anguish. And her anger too. *Why* had this happened to her? Her friends and her parents were there for her. Wee David and Susan needed her. So she kept going. One day at a time.

Back home I was well aware of how fortunate *I* was. Things were looking good. David (*my* David) was settled in his consultancy, even if working far too hard. We were financially secure. We had a dream house, three lively and lovely girls, good friends nearby, and Mum (now much happier) on hand for childcare. After Fiona's sixth birthday, we sat in the evening in our sitting room, warmed by our new gas central heating and cosy in front of the coal fire. David bounced Fiona and Catriona in his lap, as Kirsty and I cuddled beside him in front of the fire.

I felt a deep sense of contentment.

The only cloud on the horizon was minor concern about David's health. He'd been bothered by a bit of chest pain (nothing serious). On the advice of his doctor, he replaced cigarettes with a pipe. He was supposed to take Tinitrin tablets if he had chest pain but since his ECG results had been normal, I didn't really give this much thought.

He was fit and well. And after all, he was only thirty-four.

Chapter 33: The Year Begins Well

During the summer of 1978, I began to wonder if it was time for me to look for a wee part-time job. After all, my friends Lis and Pat were both working part-time. Mum was nearby and could watch the children if needed. Kirsty and Fiona were at school during the day, and Catriona had started nursery.

I scoured the newspapers and saw there was a part-time vacancy to teach something called 'Life and Social Skills' at a local college. I'd never heard of Life and Social Skills, but I acquired a book that explained them. Then I applied and before long was employed for three days a week as a part-time lecturer in Glenrothes & Buckhaven Technical College. Mum was delighted. Looking after my children around their school hours gave her a purpose. It also helped her meet people and integrate into Wormit life.

My first day in the new job was a venture into a completely unknown world. Local colleges in the seventies were all about apprenticeships and trade and vocational education, staffed in the main by men with extensive hands-on experience of the relevant trade (and sometimes an add-on teaching qualification). The teaching departments comprised Business Studies; Catering; Mechanical and Electrical Engineering; Welding; Mining; Special Needs; and General Education. I had joined General Education. I'd never been in a factory, hardly ever had a proper conversation with a tradesman, knew nothing about catering as a job, had certainly never been down a mine, and had never really worked in an office. Nor in my whole life had I ever come across a person with disabilities—in the sixties, disabled children were taught in special schools. Don't ask me how I got the job (perhaps no one else applied).

The people I met were very different from traditional school teachers and generally had more life experience. I was fascinated by the variety of staff in my department. Chrissie Duncan was my unofficial mentor. The daughter of a Fife miner (she described her father as one of the best-read people she'd ever known), Chrissie had left school at fifteen and acquired her degree through the Open University (OU). Then there was Brian Donald, who had been a baker to trade until one day (as he stood yet again at a bus stop at two in the morning) he'd decided to change his life style. He, too, had taken a degree through the OU.

The Head of Department, John Carder, came from the discipline and regulations of an RAF background. He liked to describe how he once reacted with great speed and urgency to a memo in red ink from the College Principal, only to discover that in the world of Further Education, red ink simply meant the Principal had a red pen in his hand when he wrote it. Everybody's favourite was Stuart Eglin, my line manager, although we didn't call them that then. But more about Stewart later.

I clearly had a lot of learning to do. The study of Latin, History, Logic and Metaphysics at the University of St Andrews wasn't going to be too useful—but never underestimate the value of a general, non-vocational, university education. It had given me the confidence, the curiosity and the underpinning skills to acquire new skills and knowledge—an absolute essential, particularly in the ever-changing modern world of 1978. My job was simply to help unemployed youngsters on government training schemes to acquire some confidence and basic skills if they were needed. After a while, I was allowed to take apprentices for forty-five minutes for general education. That was fun.

My mentor, Chrissie, advised me to forget everything I'd ever learned during my teacher training. Instead, I was to take a copy of the *Mail* or the *Sun* into the classroom and say something like, 'I think Maggie Thatcher will make a good Prime Minister...' and wait. A lively uproar and/or discussion would follow.

She was right. It did. And it was stimulating and interesting too, and I'm sure I learned more than they did. I learned that the police weren't always the kindly, fair, honest bobbies I'd been brought up to believe in, that the world was skewed in favour of those who spoke 'nice', didn't live in a council house and drove decent cars.

The only rule I tried to apply was that there are at least two sides to every issue. These apprentices had been brought up by their mothers to respect women, and I think female lecturers had an easier time than our male colleagues. Our students could all swear like troopers but they kept it for their mates and the workplace. Perhaps I was lucky, but I developed a great respect for the apprentices in the first years of college teaching.

1976: Kirsty, Fiona & Catriona in Holland enjoying their very first rainstorm
←

1977: Mum comes to live along the road from me at 60, Crosshill Terrace
→

←
Summer 1978: Catriona & Fiona outside the tent during a family holiday in the Mull of Kintyre

Children from left to right: Kirsty, Karen, Fiona, Anne, Catriona. Behind them Heather & Stewart & an empty chair—David is sorely missed
→

← I finally have a garage built at 18, HIllpark Terrace but too late for David to use. In front of the garage door, left to right: Fiona, Karen

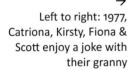

→ Left to right: 1977, Catriona, Kirsty, Fiona & Scott enjoy a joke with their granny

Friends and family rally round—we visit Sandy & Sheila in Meopham & take all six of our children to London; from left to right: Neil, Fiona, Sheona, Scott, Catriona, Kirsty →

Angela, taken when we visit her in Brighton 1979 →

Holidaying in one of my most favourite places—Tighnabruaich; Heather on the left with daughter Anne. I have Catriona on my lap, Susan beside me ↓

I meet a lovely chap called John ↓

← 1982 John & I get married ↓

John is so very proud of both his daughters, Amanda & Jane

1984, he takes Jane down the aisle
←

John's daughter Jane with husband Sandy.
→

John makes a go-kart for my girls

A summer & winter view from the garden of 11 Northview Terrace, Wormit ↓

Sailing & camping on the uninhabited island of Inchtavannah on Loch Lomond: left to right Catriona & two of Sandy's children, Sheona and Neil
←

Girls *can* sail: Kirsty & Fiona selected for British Sailing Squad training 1985
↓

Kirsty and Fiona Dalrymple—selected for British Sailing Squad Training at Rutland Water in England.

Recognition for five Wormit youngsters

WORMIT BOATING Club which has excellent sailing facilities at Woodhaven pier has always been considered one of the best family clubs in the district and as such has always given encouragement and training to youngsters keen to take up sailing.

This effort by the members has recently been rewarded as five young Wormit members, Kirsty and Fiona Dalrymple, Chris Harvey, Ken Drury and Donald Barclay were selected for special training at last winter at the Scottish Sailing Centre at Largo.

Of these five Kirsty (age 15) and Fiona (age 17) were selected for British Sailing Squad Training of Rutland Water in England and the next hurdle is the 420 Youth National and Ladies Qualifiers in Weymouth at the end of May.

Kirsty and Fiona are presently Scottish Ladies Sailing Champions

By HELMSMAN

and if they qualify at Weymouth they could go on to represent Britain at the World Championships in Majorca.

Wormit

Student wins 'Blue'. — Sailing enthusiast Fiona Dalrymple of Northview Terrace, has achieved the highest honour possible for a student sportswoman. She has been awarded a Blue for sailing. Fiona is captain of Glasgow University sailing team and captain of the Scottish Sailing Team. In order to qualify for a Blue, candidates must achieve success both with the university. Fiona is a winner of Scottish league and championships and was second in the British Students Championships. She also won the Scottish Ladies Championships twice. The award, given in the form of a certificate, was presented at a dinner and

- 239 -

Christmas Day over?

1990s, a sailing holiday in Greece: left to right: Pat, Angela, me & John ←

← John & me in the Harveys boat

I learn to ski (sort of) →

Skiers left to right: Lis, Sandy, Fiona, me, John↓

My favourite part of skiing ↓

Slaggan Bay: John & I love wild camping

Granny Wilson & I enjoy Catriona's graduation in Aberdeen 1996 →

John giving away Kirsty 1998 ↓

John giving away Fiona, 2000 →

John giving away Catriona, 2002 →

↑Me at Kirsty's wedding

← No one can believe the sad news & John's brothers & sisters all come to see him; left to right: Eddie, Eileen, Frank, Mike, Pat, Ged, Anne, Brian, Mary & Cath; John is seated because too weak to stand

→

Left to right: Jamie, Stuart, Katie, Jane's children, John's grandchildren, 1991

Kirsty's daughter Jenny (& her new umbrella) catches the drips from the leaking roof in my new house
↓

↑ Fiona's son Cam is born in Southampton 2004 & I retire and move to Dalgety Bay

← Kirsty's daughter, Annabel, & Catriona's son, James love their trip to Cairnie Fruit Farm

Chapter 34: Everything Changes

I'd been in my new college job for nearly four months when I woke up one Sunday, the day after Fiona's birthday, to the sound of David disappearing very early for Ninewells—another emergency, I guessed. I didn't pay much attention. With no noise from the children's rooms, I wanted to catch a little more shut-eye, a precious commodity when your kids are young. I must have gone back to sleep because it was quite late when I slowly and reluctantly decided to get out of bed.

I'd just started to make breakfast when the phone went. I assumed it was for David. He'd left hours before, so I ignored it. It kept ringing and ringing. Annoyed, I went to answer. Right enough, it was a call from the hospital.

'Yes this is his wife,' I said. 'But I'm sorry my husband isn't here. He left quite a while ago. You'll probably find him in the Intensive Care Unit.'

The voice kept talking. I had difficulty understanding. 'Sorry? You want *me* to come to the hospital? I don't understand. Are you telling me that my husband is a *patient*?'

I started to listen more carefully, unable to believe what I was hearing. I had to repeat it to make sure I had it right. David had collapsed? And had been taken to theatre? And I had to come across straight away?

I put the receiver down and froze, staring at the phone. In the background I could hear the girls talking to each other. They were feeding their dollies their breakfast, sticky Weetabix landing everywhere. 'Mu-um—' Their voices somehow galvanised me into action.

I phoned Pat. I phoned my mother. In practically no time, Hugh Morton (Pat's husband and David's friend) was at the door, keys in hand, ready to drive me to the hospital. Trying to keep calm so the kids wouldn't suspect something was wrong, we chatted to them until Mum arrived. As we left, they waved a cheery goodbye.

I've no idea what Hugh and I talked about—if anything—on the way to Ninewells but when we arrived, a person in a white coat was waiting for us. I assume he was a doctor. But even the fact that a doctor was waiting at Reception failed to alert me to the gravity of the situation.

There was no small talk. He simply showed us a seat in a waiting room and told us someone would be with us shortly.

Can you believe we sat for twenty minutes in a bleak hospital room? Was David alive? I can't remember whether we sat in silence or chatted. Somehow I still wasn't overly concerned. Even when you *know* something terrible is happening, your brain refuses to process it.

Someone opened the door and stopped. I think it was the consultant, Mr Walker. He just stood there. He was ashen. He almost blurted out the news—as if he himself couldn't believe it. 'Mrs Dalrymple?'

'Yes?'

'As I told you earlier,' he said, 'David collapsed in the ward this morning—a heart attack followed by cardiac arrest. We rushed him to theatre where—despite all our expertise and equipment—we've been unable to resuscitate him. I am so very sorry'.

I asked for a phone and called Mum. Curtly, and without emotion, I told her David was dead, he had died in theatre. What else was there to say? I didn't even cry. All I could think of was getting

- 244 -

home to my children. And that's precisely what we did. Ninewells could do no more for us.

Hugh and I drove home in complete silence. There was nothing to be said. He offered to come in—but I wanted to be alone with my girls and my mother.

Once inside, I went onto autopilot, keeping busy, trying not to think. But I knew—somewhere in my head—that David would never come home again. His girls would never really know their dad.

It was 26 November, 1978. Kirsty was eight, Fiona seven, and Catriona four years old. Kirsty remembers that time. Here's her account in her own words:

> The night before Dad died, I remember as fun. It was Fiona's birthday and I'm not sure where we'd been but it was a Saturday. Dad had been at work and we'd been with Mum. In the evening we were all in the sitting room and Dad had Fiona and Catriona on his knee and was bouncing them up and down. Everyone was laughing and in a good mood.
>
> The morning he died started like any other morning. The first point I realised something was wrong was when Mr Morton came to pick Mum up to take her to the hospital. I could sense something was wrong by the urgent way he ushered her into his car and the grave look on his face.
>
> The next memory I have is Granny taking the call to tell us Dad had died. As far as I remember, she told us right after she put the phone down. We were in the sitting room and I was standing between the piano and the back of the settee.
>
> I'm not sure whether Granny was just very good at putting on a brave face and holding everything together or whether she was already expecting the worst, but the way she took the phone call was as if she was expecting it and the person she

spoke to just confirmed what she already knew. After we heard the news, I've no idea of how much time passed but my next memory is standing alone in the dining room shivering and unable to cry but knowing something terrible had happened.

Mum must have arrived home at some point. The only detail I remember is Granny hugging Mum. My memory then goes to Granny making a meal which I assume was lunch. I've no idea what she was cooking but I clearly remember standing beside her at the cooker and saying to her that it would have been a lot worse if Mum had died. Granny didn't answer.

My next memory is of Mum taking a box of tissues and her phone book and asking me to sit beside her while she told people. There are only two phone calls I remember from that afternoon—the first was to John Hunter who wasn't in, so it was Hazel she spoke to. I also remember her phoning Mrs Drury (my friend Kim's mum) to ask her to let the teachers at school know what had happened.

At some point much later, Uncle Sandy arrived. I have a vivid memory of Mum cuddling us all on the landing that evening before she put us to bed and promising she would do her best to make sure we could carry on living in the same house. I think that was the point when it became real for me.

I went into my own bed in my own room first and then Mum moved me to the other bed in Fiona's room so we could keep each other company. Fiona had the room with the jungle wallpaper.

Although Mum said I didn't have to go to school the next day, I didn't want to be different or anyone to make a fuss, so I opted to go.

When I arrived, I remember feeling very strange. I recall one girl telling everyone in the lockers that she knew something but her mum had told her not to tell anyone. I knew she was talking about me.

During the morning the teacher (Mrs Scott) called me over and told me she knew what had happened and I wasn't to worry about doing my homework. When she said this, I remember thinking I would make sure that I definitely did my homework. During lunch and break I was kept inside with Kim and two other boys to do jobs in the classroom. At the time I didn't think this was anything out of the ordinary. Now I can see that this was for my benefit.

At some point before the funeral, Mum must have gone shopping because I remember her buying a long grey coat and I remember her coming home and telling me that Dad's death had been all over the billboards in Dundee. Once she'd explained what billboards were, I remember thinking he must have been important.

I wasn't aware of the funeral being on until someone brought me home from school for lunch and there were lots of people I knew in the house. I remember Mrs Sutherland (Laura's mum, my best friend in Glasgow) and Mum trying to persuade me not to go back to school, to stay and speak to people. But I thought I would get into trouble, so I went back to my class.

The evening of the funeral, I remember Mum sitting me down and reading what the Minister had said about my Dad. The only bit that's stuck with me is something about his age being the same as Jesus when he died. She also described the funeral and told me there'd been lots of people there and some of them had to stand because there weren't enough seats. This made me proud.

Fiona (a year younger) remembers repeatedly trying to tell her friend Jane at school what had happened. Jane wouldn't believe her and thought she was joking. Fiona got more and more upset, and angry too. Then a teacher intervened and confirmed it was true. Catriona, only four at the time, has no memory of her dad at all.

My brother Sandy (only thirty-seven himself), made all the funeral arrangements for me. I was unable to function properly. I was—and am still—grateful for his help. After all, it was only nine years since he'd had to organise everything when Jimmy died.

How did David's funeral go? I survived it. Someone gave me a pill. I don't know what was in it but it must have helped because I spoke to everyone and managed to hold it together. Until I was finally on my own and could cry.

I went back to my job in college soon after that. It occupied my mind. It was easier than staying at home because I didn't want to make my girls sad.

Besides when I wasn't working, neighbours either crossed the road to avoid me (because they didn't know what to say) or came across to console me wearing their sorrowful faces. Both behaviours were well-meaning, if unhelpful.

Local friends rallied round, but for them, too, life went on. They had husbands and children to look after and jobs to go to.

Chapter 35: Family & Friends

That first Christmas was hard for all of us. Special occasions are particularly heartbreaking—the first Christmas, first birthday, first wedding anniversary. But it's the *little* things that unexpectedly knock you for six.

A letter addressed to David, for example. At that time, and for a long time afterwards, all letters were automatically addressed to the male householder, and I was plagued with these for years. Or it might be a particular song on the radio. Or the sight of a mum and dad together, enjoying their children.

For me, the first big hurdle was Christmas. How were we to get through it? My mother tended to treat me like an invalid. She tried to do everything for me. I didn't want that though, and she had other grandchildren to see and enjoy.

I decided to invite David's Auntie Dot for Christmas. A single lady, she'd lost both her sister, David's Mum, and her beloved nephew David in the same year. I knew she missed David almost as much as we did and would be acutely aware of the big empty space in our house.

Santa brought a kitten that year and the children were thrilled. They'd always wanted a cat but David had been allergic to them. My loyal Wormit friend Pat Morton crept along with the cat basket at midnight, knocking quietly at the back door so as not to wake anyone. Along with Auntie Dot, she and I shared a wee dram and exchanged Christmas greetings.

The Christmas tree was a disaster, though. I'd popped into the local shop in Newport when I saw the trees heaped high outside. I chose one too big for me to lift—a stupid mistake. 'Perhaps your husband could pick it up?' suggested the shop-keeper. I burst into tears and said my husband had died. The poor chap didn't know what to do. I could come back later with a car and collect it, he said—no offer to deliver.

Our good neighbour Sandy Harvey brought the tree to our door the very next day, but it still had to be put in the pot and decorated. It stood like the leaning tower of Pisa all through the festive season with no lights. Still, the kids didn't care and had great fun decorating it with no supervision or advice. They were truly creative and very messy. As for Dot, I'm not sure she even noticed we *had* a tree. Our new kitten pulled all the decorations off the branches anyway.

As a Christmas treat for the children, Dot and I decided to take them to the cinema in St Andrews. They were very excited as we climbed into what had been David's car. We were rolling along famously, had passed Leuchars and were only a few miles from our destination when the engine cut out. What *on earth* was I to do? In the dark? In the rain? With three children and Auntie Dot? Even if I'd been a member of the AA, I couldn't have contacted them because there were no mobile phones.

I went outside in the rain, opened the bonnet and stared inside. I had absolutely no idea what to do next. I must have looked pretty pathetic. Despite this, a few vehicles roared past mercilessly. Finally a couple stopped. The wife got out while her husband sat in the car. 'Can we help?' she asked. I explained the situation. She opened the car door and gave her husband his instructions.

He was to ferry me, Dot and the children to the New Cinema in North Street immediately, because we were not to miss the beginning of the film. Then he was to arrange for my car to be picked up and taken to a garage, find out when the film finished, pick us up and take us home to Wormit. And that was exactly what happened. We had planned to go for fish and chips afterwards but not wanting to chance my arm, I didn't mention that.

To this day, I have no idea who she was. But what a wonderful experience for me and the children to meet with this amazing kindness from such a good Samaritan. Wormit was a small place. Perhaps she knew all about our tragedy? I've often wondered.

Back at work I was telling Chrissie Duncan, my unofficial mentor, all about the incident when she interrupted. 'Can you afford a new car?' she said. I said I could—and before I knew what was happening, she was on the phone. Then she ushered me to my vehicle and told me to drive to Lambert's Garage in Leven, where I made the necessary purchase. The following day she and I used our lunchtime break to pick up my brand-new, blue Volkswagen Polo. No more break-downs for me.

Even so, driving in winter terrified me. On one occasion, I was returning from work in Leven over the hill to Cupar in freezing fog. I couldn't see where I was going. Terrified of ending up in a ditch, I stopped the car and sat in some sort of layby wondering what to do next. After a while I saw headlights and I followed that poor driver, headlights on, all the way to town.

When I finally arrived home, ready to burst into tears, Mum called out as she heard me open the door. 'Is that you?' she said. 'There's a light bulb gone in the bathroom. Will you sort it when you've got a minute?'

And—as all working mums know—your children save up their daytime disasters for sympathy when you return. By the time I'd listened to them, I had little time to feel sorry for myself. I was supposed to feel grateful that I had a convenient granny on hand to make the meal. But I didn't. I felt tired and angry. What was more, if any more neighbours told me how lucky I was to have my mother to look after the children, I was going to punch their lights out.

Underneath this muddle of emotions, however, I knew the neighbours were right. I never had to worry about my girls. Mum loved them as much as I did.

✖

Hogmanay was the next big hurdle. As the girls and I brought in the New Year, along with neighbours and friends, I found myself looking forward to a very different future from the one I'd envisaged a year ago. On the plus side, the children were fine and healthy, my mother was there to help, and I had a widow's pension, a house and a job.

But the downside was having sole responsibility for absolutely everything. The car, the house, the garden, the bills, the children. It was all weighing me down. I knew I'd survive—I had no choice—but I felt as if overnight I'd aged a hundred years. Fun? What was that again? I was desperately lonely.

Initially weekends were dire. They had always been our family time and we badly missed a dad being around. We were used to his periodic absence on Saturdays or Sundays, but even during busy on-call weekends, he'd always been home at night. My family and friends stepped in to support me, cheer me up, invite me out and help me through what was the worst of times.

✖

That first David-less summer we went to Orkney. I'd always wanted to visit Skara Brae, so Hugh and Pat encouraged me and bought me a book about the islands. Kim's dad, an engineer, re-fitted the car to take our bikes. I booked accommodation for us in Stromness Hotel and off we went on our adventure.

We were excited as we boarded the ferry to Scrabster, and I was hoping to get a glimpse of the Old Man of Hoy. The crossing was only supposed to be a couple of hours and no one had mentioned that the Pentland Firth could be rough.

Ten minutes into our journey, with the boat (and my stomach) heaving as I tried to hang on to Catriona, I had to put her down and rush to the toilets to vomit—copiously and continually. The kids couldn't be allowed to roam round the ferry on their own, so Kirsty and Fiona had the job of entertaining Catriona in their seats. She, meanwhile, complained constantly about being hungry. It wasn't exactly enjoyable, nor the best start to the holiday—and it was another thirty years before I finally saw the Old Man of Hoy.

It was a huge relief to dock at Stromness, and finally reach the luxury of a hotel. That holiday was probably not one of my better ideas. The children were too young, it rained a lot and I was too raw—too recently bereaved. However, I do remember we all enjoyed playing Knockout Whist in the hotel lounge—even Catriona (who celebrated her fifth birthday while we were there). As I remember, she even sometimes won, but that would certainly be disputed by her sisters.

Christine, Heather, Stewart and their kids came to visit us in Wormit that summer as well, which cheered us up. We had daily outings to Pittenweem or Tentsmuir beach, the latter favoured for goosebumps from the bitter cold swim in the sea, followed by chittery bites and games of rounders and football to get circulation going again.

Occasionally if the weather was really bad, we hired Madras School swimming pool and we mums would race each other. Heather mostly won, but my children could cheer the loudest because there were three of them. Stewart, not a swimmer, managed the cheerleaders.

We also visited my brother Sandy and Sheila that summer, in sunny Meopham in Kent. We adults decided to take our combined children (six in all) to see some of London's attractions. When Sandy and Sheila nipped away for a minute during the visit to Madame Tussaud's, I was left with all six kids, threatening them with dire consequences if any of them dared move. That was when a woman came up to me and said, 'Such lovely children! Twins or triplets or both?' They did look very alike—but triplets? *Really*? Sandy and Sheila returned to reclaim their children and the woman, looking sheepish, made a quick exit.

Angela wasn't going to be left out so when we visited her, she took us to Brighton beach where there was an amazing play-park. But that wasn't all there was! As we walked along the prom back to the car, the kids couldn't believe their eyes. What were they seeing? Men and women playing ball on the beach with no clothes on. A nudist beach. That was so much more exciting than the play-park.

And so with the help of family and friends, Kirsty, Fiona, Catriona and I somehow survived—and lived to tell the tale.

Chapter 36: Picking Up The Pieces

At work, I soon had a full-time, permanent teaching post. As a single parent with three young children, I was treated as an equal to the male applicants. I was no longer a middle-class wife looking for a part-time job to fit in with the children, and secure a little financial independence. Although such female staff were undoubtedly valued, it was somehow different being a full-time bread-winner. Today's modern women take this in their stride, I'm sure, but it's hard work. Equality comes at a price.

I was still a bit of a wimp about driving to work in the bad weather. Previously David had been the main driver. To top that I had had four attempts at driving my test, and Jimmy my brother had died in a car accident. But this problem solved itself when a new chap started at the college. He lived in Wormit and when he offered to share the driving and always drive if the weather was bad, I had no hesitation in accepting his offer. Given that he was also tall, dark and good looking, it wasn't a hard decision to make. His name was Bill Shearer and he has become a much-valued life-long friend.

It was a bonus for me that no one at work had known David. Work colleagues didn't talk much about their families. I managed for longer and longer spells to forget about my loss while my mind was distracted by other things. At breaks and lunchtime, we discussed anything and everything else—the MP Willie Hamilton's views on royalty, Callaghan's Labour government, the upcoming Scottish Devolution Bill and, of course, our students.

And we talked to and with our students. This was our job—to give craft and technician trainees three-quarters of an hour in their college day to consider the events and issues of our time. In other words, to think for themselves. Most of them were day-release from full-time apprenticeships with time-served journeymen who had already started this process, sharing their opinions on everything from sex, marriage and politics. Today's young people—unlike the apprentices back then—have fewer opportunities to mix and learn from older adults in a work situation (a great loss both to young-sters and to society and to their elders).

Our students didn't place a high value on the non-examinable 'general education' we offered. They participated, nevertheless, and seemed to quite enjoy it. One young man told me that no-one had ever asked his opinion before—he'd only been taught what to do and how to do it.

One morning I entered my classroom in Buckhaven to be met with a row of grinning faces. There, in the middle of the mining apprentices, was a lad with his hair cut into the biggest Mohican I had ever seen. I knew they were waiting for my reaction.

'Morning boys,' I said. 'There's something different about you today, Tam, but I can't work out what it is.'

A hush descended over the classroom as we waited for his reply.

Tam piped up, 'Ah've git new boots oan miss. Dae ye like them?'

The class fell about laughing. And so did I, a proper laugh—the first since David had died.

The General Education Department was expanding rapidly, not least because we were involved in YOP schemes (the Youth Opportunity Programme). This had been introduced by Jim Callaghan's Labour government and later expanded by Margaret Thatcher's Tory regime into the YTS (Youth Training Scheme). To meet the needs of those programmes and others, our department grew arms and legs. We acquired new subject areas and new staff with a range of diverse skills.

We were also involved in a course for non-academic school kids where our 'Industrial Institute' employed them for a four-week period, treating them like real employees. There was a range of simulated occupations e.g. office work, mechanical engineering welding, joinery and catering. They had to clock in and out, and follow all work rules. They really liked it—but what they *didn't* like was the forty-five minutes of General Education where they had to sit in a classroom, just like school.

I was worried about what to do when it came to my turn with this group of youngsters (their reputation had preceded them) so I asked my boss Stewart Eglin for advice. This was at a time before 'political correctness' was invented and Stewart knew that, more than anything, I needed to learn to laugh again.

With a serious voice and a grave expression, he said, 'Well, Morag, my advice—and this is based on personal experience—is to go to the butcher's and buy a bone, like you would for your dog if you had one. Then find a long stick and sharpen the point. Start by smiling a welcome as your students arrive—but make sure you stand at the door. Once they're all inside, throw the stick—meaty bone speared at the end—into the classroom, quickly shut and lock the door, then go for a fag in the staff room. When forty-five minutes are up, open the door and if any of them are alive, let them out.'

It took me a minute to register that he was yet again taking the mick—but in a magical way, laughing released the tension, and the worry. He followed it up by suggesting I show them an excellent film demonstrating the dangerous effects of smoking. He assured me this would go down a treat. Since at that time practically *every*one smoked, including me (but not my colleague Kay Morrison, an early pioneer of the non-smoking campaign), it was definitely a case of 'do what I say not what I do'.

✄

Just before Christmas 1979 I was afraid I might get the sack for taking the day off to attend a funeral. But for me, it was Hobson's choice i.e. *no* option at all. I had to go. It was another tragedy for my widowed friend Christine, even more unexpected than the last. It had been so good throughout the year to have her to talk to, a widow of the same age as myself. We spent many hours chatting on the phone about our children, about how difficult life was, how much it had changed and all the horrible things we had to deal with. Christine was also grateful for the support of Heather and Stewart round the corner in Kelvindale. But then something else happened.

Christine's son, wee David (seven years old), had a fall in the playground and hit his head. He had slight concussion, so was sent to Yorkhill Hospital where they decided to keep him in as a precaution. He was there for a couple of days. Each day Christine expected him home. But then his blood pressure suddenly crashed and with a suspected bleed on the brain, he was rushed to the Southern General.

Christine was summoned and Heather went with her. They were concerned, of course, but not unduly worried. They knew he was in the best possible place—the ICU (Intensive Care Unit).

Wee David was awake when they arrived but he was attached to a life support machine, slipping in and out of consciousness. The doctor suggested they go and get something to eat, they might be there for a while. When they returned, they sat in the relatives' room, waiting to be allowed back in. Then Heather heard that most terrifying of sounds: a long, continuous bleat from the life support system. As a physiotherapist familiar with hospital procedures, she knew what had happened. She could visualise the long flat line on the monitor. David had died.

Somehow Heather got Christine back to her mum's house and called her GP, who came immediately and gave her a sedative. David's Christmas presents were all wrapped up ready for him (poor Heather had the job of disposing of them). She also had to tell the shocking news to his school teacher, who burst into tears and ran out of the room. It was a dreadful, dreadful time, and for many years afterwards Christine hated Christmas with a vengeance. Wouldn't you feel the same? How she managed to survive it all is truly astounding. I have the greatest admiration for her.

Festive period over, Christine came to stay with us in Wormit. It was a safe place where no one knew her, we were both widows and no one asked awkward questions, and Susan—wee David's little sister—had my three girls to play with. We went to the ice pond at the foot of the hill and Susan simply kept throwing stones and cracking the ice. We all did. We were both angry and sad.

Children process grief in their own way. During the visit, Susan ate practically nothing, but always—after every meal—she repeated the same words: 'Thank you for a lovely breakfast/ lunch/ dinner, Morag'. Each time she said it, I had to swallow a great lump in my throat.

In her own home there was a particular chair in front of the TV that she and David had always fought over. For a long time after his death, Susan refused to sit on it. When Christine finally summed up courage to visit the school, the teacher showed her Susan's paintings. None of them had any colour. Each one was black and white. But life went on year by year, as it inevitably does, and Susan's paintings began, bit by bit, to gather colours.

I returned to work the day after the funeral and my unexplained absence was never mentioned. I didn't get the sack. Of all the numerous funerals I have been to, wee David's was by far the worst. The memory of that tiny coffin will haunt me to my dying days.

Heather and Stewart's home was always open for Christine and Susan—by day or night; night or day—and for many years. That's true Glasgow friendship for you. It's a friendship which continues to this day.

As for me—wee David's death made me count my blessings.

Chapter 37: God Works In Mysterious Ways

Even before David died, for me sailing was always a problem. Whenever it was windy I was frankly scared. But it's the wind that makes the boat move, and if it isn't windy, the sailing's either cancelled or the boat goes backwards.

Somehow, from somewhere, I had summoned up enough courage over time to learn to sail in gentle winds. Most of our family had duly become active members of Wormit Boating Club. Our friend Sandy Harvey sailed a 'Graduate' and it was he who persuaded first David, then Pat's husband Hugh, and next a chap called John—a newcomer to the area—to buy Graduate sailing dinghies. This way there would be a Graduate class and we could all sail against each other.

But the 'best laid plans gang aft agley'. David had died, and although I kept his dinghy, I soon changed it for a Mirror, which I believed was easier to sail. I didn't actually go out in the boat much, but I kept in touch with the Club. The newest member of our Graduate sailing group, John, was preoccupied with caring for his wife Lucy, who had been diagnosed with terminal cancer. After some sad months Lucy, too, died.

Every year Wormit Boating Club had an Annual Dance and one day Lis Harvey arrived at my door to ask if I'd mind if a recently widowed chap joined our table. It was no other than John from the sailing club. I said of course I didn't mind, and so he and I were seated opposite each other. With so much in common—both of us single parents, recently bereaved, and with mutual friends Liz and Sandy—we had a lot to talk about. Once you add to the equation that John was a superb ballroom dancer, you can see why I was interested. I invited him to call round any time. And he did call. But on the first occasion, circumstances worked against him.

The idiot chose to arrive on Hallowe'en, and hadn't thought to wonder why so many children were wandering about the street in fancy dress. I was, and am, a serious Hallowe'ener. When John arrived unexpectedly, I invited him in to a kitchen filled with children. My mother's brass jeely pan, filled with *Irn Bru*, was bubbling away on the stove, scones covered in treacle were hanging from the pulley, and in the middle of the floor there was a bucket, surrounded by children dooking for apples.

Was I looking my best? Well, the answer has to be: I hope not. When I answered the door, I had on my head a witch's hat with knotted black hair on each side, my face was concealed by a grotesque mask, and I was wearing my black graduation gown over my tracksuit. Despite my looks, John continued to visit, helping me with various jobs around the house and—bless him (having heard my sad Christmas-tree story)—bringing a beautiful pine Christmas tree hand-picked from Tayfield Estate in Newport. He even sorted out the fairy lights.

I definitely fancied him and he definitely fancied me, and we got on like a house on fire when there were just the two of us. I couldn't believe my luck that such an attractive guy had walked right into my life. I knew what I wanted. But did he?

Neither of us was good at articulating how we felt about the other. What was more, we came with 'baggage' (a modern term that I dislike intensely) and from very different backgrounds. John was one of seven children from a practising Roman Catholic family in Manchester. He'd known his first wife Lucy since primary school. Both were clever and since they excelled academically, they were awarded scholarships to Catholic grammar schools. John's late wife Lucy, like my husband David, had been the story-teller and the communicator in any social gathering. And I was a Protestant Glaswegian brought up in sectarian Glasgow

New relationships don't come with any sort of guarantee. You can't just walk into the easy, long-term, comfortable connection you've had with a long-term spouse. John and I were most at ease with more recent friends—for example the Mortons, the Harveys and the Winches in Wormit. Unlike David, John would never have told my mother not to hang her knickers on the line—but then my mother treated John in a different way from David. She was disapproving, cold, stiff and formal. She seemed to resent his presence.

For a while it was like hovering between two lives, the old and the new. When holiday time came around, I rented a house for a couple of summers in my favourite place, Tighnabruaich, and invited various combinations of old and new friends and family. John visited for a short while, towing my boat for me and meeting for the first time some of my friends from my life with David.

The children enjoyed it best when Heather, Stewart and Christine and their girls were there. There was a continuous game of Canasta, and a daily treat was when Stewart took various combinations of girls to the local hostelry for a packet of crisps (and a pint or two for him). The journey there and back was fun and full of nonsense, one of the highlights of their holiday.

Back at school afterwards, the kids were always asked to write about the most exciting events. For them, it was the excitement of watching a coffin being carried off the Waverley Paddle Steamer, a car going on fire in the main street of Tighnabruaich, and a stray dog that attached itself to Heather, who repeatedly took it to the police station (but somehow it kept coming back to our door). And yet John *still* hadn't asked me to marry him. I knew he really liked me. He knew it was what I wanted. He had shown in all sorts of ways that he cared for me. But he hadn't made a formal commitment. Perhaps after all, it wasn't going to be a fairy story with a happy ending.

My life was going on as usual in every other way. There was my full-time job and the children, old friends and family to consider. College was demanding and there were new educational initiatives to contend with. Old syllabuses were converted into forty-hour units called 'modules', while the General Education Department continued to diversify and expand. Change, change and change was the name of the game.

Within the Wilson family, another kind of change and source of conflict was taking place, upsetting my mother and making her even more disapproving of my remarrying (if John ever got around to asking me). My Dad's wealthy sister Betty had died, leaving her estate to be divided between me, my mother, Sandy and Elizabeth. But Betty's second husband successfully contested the will. Guy was granted his legal rights and we were no longer the main beneficiaries. The lesson to be learned, according to my mother? Don't ever marry more than once!

Meanwhile, what was going on in John's head? Was he having second thoughts? As a metallurgist, he had a managerial position in Delta's of Dundee: they made copper pipes for gas fittings. He secretly knew, however, that the firm was about to fold and he was going to be made redundant. With his two girls, Amanda and Jane, at university, he had no intention of becoming a financial burden to me.

So he said nothing about the future but tried in his own way to resolve the problem. His solution was to retrain as a maths teacher at Dundee College of Education. Aware that maths teachers were in short supply, he knew he'd be assured of a permanent pensioned post with Dundee Council. When (and only when) he had qualified and been offered a permanent post at St Saviours High School in Dundee, did he actually propose.

I was delighted and accepted immediately. I knew without a doubt this was what I wanted. Soon afterwards we told my girls the news. This is what John said to them, word for word:

'I think you know already that because your mum and I want to be together, we're going to get married. We've found a house in Newport with six bedrooms. So there'll be a room for each of you—Kirsty, Fiona and Catriona, and Amanda and Jane [his own two girls] too. But it's not all good news,' he went on, pulling a long face. 'Poor me, I'm the only one who'll have to make a sacrifice. I'll have to share a room with your mum.'

Unlike me, my mother wasn't in the least delighted. And when I sold some of the beautiful (but very large) mahogany furniture from Colebrooke Terrace, she was horrified. We'd decided to use John and Lucy's Ercol furnishings—much more suitable for a modern, sprawling Canadian-type house. I understood Mum was going to miss us as near neighbours but we were only moving about three miles away, and Catriona was still going to her Granny's after school.

Mum's real problem was that John was a Catholic. Having been brought up in sectarian Glasgow, she didn't trust Catholics. She'd been brought up to believe that if Catholics did bad things, they could confess to the priest and it was automatically okay—

they could do whatever they liked. She was also anticipating that I would 'turn' (the Glasgow term for converting from Protestant to Catholic, or vice versa). The children would duly become indoctrinated, she thought. And of course Catholics didn't believe in contraception. At the age of 38, therefore, I was bound to end up with lots more children. *Really?*

To add insult to injury, she was appalled by the fact that once I remarried, I'd no longer be entitled to my NHS widow's pension. This was true—but I *would* still be entitled to the pension for my children as long as they remained in full-time education *and* I had the salary from my college post. And John, too, would have a salary

At first Mum couldn't see John as a person. All she could see was a Catholic. John didn't know what to say to her and she had nothing to say to John. It was definitely uncomfortable and to manage this, we all concentrated on the children.

When John and I both sold our houses quickly, we decided to marry earlier than planned since our new house was there waiting. Guess what conclusion Mum came to about our bringing the wedding forward? What was the only possible reason for marrying a Catholic sooner than planned?

John *did* have a strong Roman Catholic faith. But it was personal and private and I learned to respect it, not least because it made him what he was—a good man, husband and father. The only time his religion was observable was when the kids asked where he was on a Sunday morning. I had no religious beliefs and he knew this. The only time I myself went to church was on Christmas Eve—the Watchnight Carol Service.

And on one other occasion, of course. On 20 November 1982, John and I were married. Was it the first time my mother had ever been in a Catholic church? Possibly. Nevertheless, she did turn up and Sandy did give me away. As for me, I would have married John in a barn or a registry office, but I knew it was important to him to have the Church's blessing. And so we made our vows in Newport Catholic Church. All I had to do was show my christening certificate, although we both had to have a talk with the priest before the wedding.

I had previously been married for ten years, and John for twenty. We reckoned we probably knew a bit more about marriage than the priest. But what was the first thing he said? 'No one is an expert on marriage least of all me.'

I warmed to him after that. Whether his little talk did us any good or not, I don't know, but it certainly didn't do us any harm. 'Love' and 'compromise' are the only two words I remember.

On the actual day of the wedding, it was freezing cold both outside and inside the church, and afterwards my family, John's family and our Wormit friends gathered back at our new house. We were both working full-time, so our honeymoon was very short indeed. We both had to be back at work on Monday morning.

✂

None of our five children liked the Newport house. Possibly my youngest, Catriona—who had no memory of David—was the exception. John worked hard with his new family. He cooked the evening meal, made a go-cart for Catriona, and in winter when the first snow arrived, he helped the girls make an impressive igloo with individual ice bricks. His own kids, Jane (20) and Amanda (23), were young adults and mainly did their own thing.

My middle daughter, Fiona, partly coped with the change by persuading us to finance a pony in Carnoustie. For Kirsty, my oldest, and a teenager, the change was undoubtedly more difficult. Besides, the house was really too big. We needed a gong to alert everyone when dinner was ready. If our kids were dropped off by school friends, they insisted on being left at the foot of the road because their home was so embarrassingly huge they didn't want their friends to see where they lived.

Within three years of our marriage, both John's girls had got married too. Our Newport house was now *definitely* too big and since my three children missed Wormit and their friends (as did I) we decided to sell up and move back—to 11, Northview Terrace.

Which was to be our home for the next twenty years. It was one of the best decisions I ever made. And John only wanted what was best for all of us.

Chapter 38: Glenrothes College Expands

But it wasn't all plain sailing (pun intended). John and I still had full-time jobs. I enjoyed mine, but John hated every minute of his experience at St Saviours. He liked the staff but wasn't so keen on the teaching. He said it was the hardest job he had ever done and he admitted he wasn't cut out for working with teenagers. His Mancunian accent probably didn't endear him to Dundee kids. But he needed to work.

A saving grace, in the form of Sandy Harvey, came up with a totally different kind of opening for him. John became an assistant to Sandy who, as an educational adviser, reviewed resources (and particularly software) for use in schools. John settled happily into Sandy's smoke-filled, messy, untidy office for most of the rest of his working life.

However, my job was more demanding than his. It was unbelievable how many changes had been made in the further education sector since I'd first started at Glenrothes and Buckhaven Technical College. There were to be many more over the next decades, a process that continues to this day. But back then in the early eighties, our courses were directly connected with the growing unemployment figure, a result of the decline of the mining industry, increased automation, and falling profits as global markets overtook the UK in manufacturing.

Many of our former day-release mining students came back to college to retrain, some of them in what we called TOPS courses (Training Opportunity Scheme). Our department's job was to improve their communication skills. Can you imagine what it must have felt like for these guys who had worked in the real world and earned a living wage to be back in the classroom? They wanted new jobs but it was hard for them—and for us.

One of my favourite students explained that during the first year after his pit closed, he'd stayed at home to 'mind the bairns' while his wife worked. He moaned long and hard about his wife's lack of appreciation for his domestic efforts. But his particular skill, and the one I appreciated most, was that he could make the whole class laugh.

'Ah couldnae dae a thing richt. Whaun the wife cam hame, whitever ah'd dun, it wis wrang—an honestly ah'd reely tried. Ah couldnae mak the beds richt, the mince wis too watery, it hadnae enuff onions, the kitchen flair wis sticky, there wis crumbs an beer stains oan the carpet—and mair often than no ah'd forgot tae pit oan the washin.'

And his last word on the subject?

'And whaun we went tae bed at nicht *she* wis (sorry, Miss) too f*****g tired!'

Meanwhile, the YTS (Youth Training Scheme) students arrived at the college, some for a short burst of general and vocational training, others on day-release from work placements. They were young people with little, if any, experience in the workplace, and this was their chance to get into some kind of employment—provided things went well. It was a first step.

Their opinion of the experience depended on their employer, the quality of the training and whether or not there was a job at the end of it. Some were positive about the scheme, while others labelled it as 'cheap' or 'slave labour'—and in many cases there was some truth in that. But what was the alternative? The YTS scheme was abandoned in 1989.

In 2021, it looks like the current government is about to bring in a similar scheme, but the snag is the same. Although education is rarely wasted, you can train all you like but—if there are no real jobs at the end—what happens next? In the fifties, sixties and seventies, with full employment, and tried and tested apprenticeships, young people learned from adults and were gradually able to become financially independent, move on in life and bring up their families. How can young people turn into adults without jobs, without financial independence, without mixing and mingling with adults in an adult world? Rant over! There's no simple solution, politically, constitutionally, or economically.

In college developments, we learned to apply the business principle of SWOT, an analysis carried out according to Strengths, Weaknesses, Opportunities and Threats. Every new bit of legislation was examined in this way. Unlike schools, we didn't have a ready-made cohort of students every year to teach. To survive, we had to attract students by providing courses with government or European funding; or funded by specific government contracts; or to meet employers' explicit needs; or to fill a gap in school education; or to meet probable future needs in line with economic trends. This is what we tried to do—and so, over thirty years, the college I'd joined back in 1977 became almost unrecognisable.

By 1989, our General Education Department, under the leadership of John Carder, had blossomed, encompassing a huge variety of diverse skills and subjects and a large number of staff. It wasn't easily manageable and so it was restructured and divided into three sections—definitely a more logical and practical arrangement.

I became Section Head of all the bits and pieces that were left after Communication & Media, and Catering became two sections in their own right. I found myself in charge of Physical Education, Community Care, Fashion, Art, Information Technology and—for some reason—Maths. Each subject area was, at this stage, quite small. I knew little or nothing about any of these subjects. Did it matter? Not really. Within the section, there were hard working, professional, knowledgeable and innovative specialist staff, a joy to work with. And as we grew, we employed more like them.

It soon became clear that my job was twofold. Internally, my task was to fight for accommodation and a fair share of the re-sources. Externally, I was primed to grab every opportunity for growing new relevant courses and attracting funding. It wasn't long before we acquired another building in Flemington Road (renamed the Community Access Centre) as a base for our expanding social, health and childcare courses. Many of our students were what were called 'adult returners', clever and able people who hadn't done well at school or had left early, and now were seizing the opportunity to get qualifications.

The Flemington Road building was long, with a stair at either end. One day as I left, I met a dejected female student, a motherly looking woman. She was sitting on the stairs, tears streaming down her face. What was wrong? She told me she'd been working at a computer all morning to write an essay. She'd been using Ms Word but had forgotten to save her document before she switched off the machine. So she'd lost the lot (no automatic data-save in those days).

As we stood outside the building puffing away on our fags, she told me about the many hurdles that she—like so many of our adult returners—had gone through to get to this stage. We agreed that (compared to what she had endured already) two hours of lost essay were merely a blip. When she returned to her class the next day, her concerned tutor, Gordon Scrimgeour, was waiting to help her. I would be surprised if she ever again forgot to save her work.

Another morning, on the same staircase, who should I pass but Henry McLeish, exiting discreetly through the back stairway. Henry was Labour MP for Central Fife from 1987 to 2001 and, in response to a request from staff member Esther Higgins, he'd been talking to one of her classes about community involvement. He hadn't come for a photo shoot, to talk to the Principal, to win votes, or to make money—he came because he cared about the students and his local community. A busy man, he simply slipped into the building, talked to the students and left quietly. He and Esther had wisely ignored the time-consuming, burdensome and bureaucratic protocol devised by management for visiting speakers.

Under the able leadership of senior lecturer Christine Mathers, the Care part of the section grew very fast. Finding accommodation for so many students was a constant challenge and a full-time occupation. Much of my time was spent writing reports to the college Principal, proving through quantitative data our urgent need for more and better classrooms. But I was fighting against custom and practice, as well as the remaining male bastions of privilege.

The college's purpose-built accommodation—the Centre for Industrial Studies—was the Principal's darling. It had been designed for income-generating Management courses, where students and staff wore suits and considered themselves superior. But the demand for such courses had fallen, as a result of which many of the CIS rooms were unused.

I argued that my Section could fill these rooms with students. Mike Stones, the Assistant Principal in charge of accommodation, bravely decided to go ahead without the Principal's permission. He annexed the most suitable (unused) room in the building for my section to use. It was going to be a Life Sciences Learner Centre.

Teaching her students in the right environment was care lecturer Evelyn Jardine's priority. She was over the moon at hearing she was to have her own room, and she moved in, lock, stock and barrel, bringing (as well as her unquenchable enthusiasm) two life-sized skeletons, and both a child-sized and adult-sized 'Resusci Annie'. She covered the walls with anatomical charts and the shelves with biology and health-care books. Filed alphabetically in cabinets were the self-learning resource materials available for the different levels of National Certificate modules and Higher National units to be taught. She was very pleased with the result. It was almost too good to be true.

And yes—it *was* too good to be true. Late on Friday. Tom Burness, the Principal, happened, by sheer chance, to pass through his precious Centre for Industrial Studies and what did he see? A full-sized skeleton positioned at the entrance to his favourite Conference Room (placing it there was definitely an error of judgment). To say he was angry was the understatement of the year. Mike Stones, who was with him at the time, fielded the brunt of this displeasure, and our apoplectic Principal ordered him to have the room returned to its original state by Monday.

Evelyn, the college janitor and myself spent a hectically busy Saturday removing all our stuff from the room. But it wasn't all bad news. When the Assistant Principal finally managed to get a word in, he pointed out to the Principal that large numbers of health-care students would be arriving on Monday morning. Where were they to go? Should he perhaps send them to the Principal's Office? And so it was that we were finally, and officially, allocated not the

Conference room—not yet—but another spacious room in the Industrial Studies Building. And as everyone knows, great oaks from little acorns grow.

Over time, the whole of the Centre of Industrial Studies building became the Centre for Health and Social Care.

Result!

Chapter 39: The TGIF Wormit Pals*

At this time, John and myself, Lis and Sandy, Pat, Dave and Jan used to meet every Friday in the Wormit pub for a TGIF (Thank God It's Friday) drink or two. On one occasion we started to talk about old age and retirement plans. Fuelled by a little whisky, we came up with this brilliant entrepreneurial plan: we would buy our own Old Folks Home. I would organise staff training; Sandy would take care of technology; John would do any DIY; Lis (a speech therapist) was in charge of communications; Jan (a home economics teacher) would see to the housekeeping; Dave (Jan's husband) would sort out finance; and Pat (a doctor) would be the health manager.

What a wonderful thing it is *not* to be able to see into the future. We could have run that home, too. But sadly it didn't work out as planned. Although none of us was near retirement, my life with John was changing. I had an increasingly demanding work commitment. John's daughters were grown-up and married. And my own three girls were—on the whole—independent: Fiona and Kirsty (now graduates) were frequently working abroad; Catriona was at university. Finally, John and I could have some child-free holidays.

Up to that time, John and I had always agreed—or perhaps more accurately John had agreed with *me*—that since I worked full-time all week, our weekends and holidays would always include the children (dedicated 'me' time for parents is a fairly modern invention). But now our kids were up and away, so we started to go skiing with Sandy and Lis, and Jan and Dave (Lis's youngest child, Bob, and our youngest, Catriona, sometimes joined us). We also sailed in the

Harveys' Keel Boat but—best of all—John and I went on camping adventures by ourselves. Unlike the Girl Guides, this was camping with a difference: we had money in our pockets and we could book into a hotel if the weather was unforgiving.

On one of our camping trips, I took John to see the little croft in Sheigra, north of Kinlochbervie, where I had holidayed as a child, not long after Dad had died. At least it was my intention to take John there. We never actually found the croft but the weather was glorious—a bit breezy perhaps, the sun so bright I had to rummage in the kit bag for my sunglasses. And swimming and camping on the shores of Sandwood Loch was an unforgettable experience for us both. Not another soul in sight for miles around and light until after midnight.

All I could remember from my childhood were soggy wet jam sandwiches, and my mother—like Ma Broon in the *Sunday Post*—boiling the kettle of water on the camp fire. In such barren countryside, it had been hard for us kids to find wood for kindling, and when we did, it fell into two categories: damp and sodden. But on this sun-baked trip decades later, it was utterly magic. John thought so too. Brought up in a city, like me, he loved the freedom of the open countryside and the lochs.

Our next camping spot was Slaggan Bay, near Aultbea where we cooked fish on an open fire. Well, John did. Just in case you're wondering—no, we didn't catch the fish. We bought them uncooked from a pub nearby.

After our meal, we sat looking out on to the loch late in the evening. Even I, unartistic as I was, could appreciate the sunset, the sky changing in an instant from red to purple. As we snuggled in the tent, we could hear the gentle lapping of the waves against the shore and smell the smoke from the embers of our little fire. I fully understand the attraction of what is now called 'wild camping'. But this was the west of Scotland and the weather the next morning was less than idyllic.

Inside our two-man tent, we were cosy and warm, but outside was a completely different matter. This was no gentle pitter-patter of rain—it was bucketing. Remembering the daily cups of tea made for me at home by John, my Girl Guide training came to my aid. I wrapped myself in my waterproof sailing jacket and ventured out to make tea and toast on our little gas stove. I returned to a hero's welcome.

We stayed in the tent until the rain finally stopped. Then we promptly headed straight for the nearest decent hotel. As John signed us in, I crept past Reception with the soaking wet tent crammed into a holdall. We stretched it out to dry across the bedroom, went downstairs for lunch and—hey presto—when we returned, the canvas was almost dry.

We had other good holidays too. They included skiing with Lis and Sandy while visiting our grown-up children Chris and Fiona in Meribel. Then there was the one at Mark Warner Sailing School in Greece where Kirsty had worked. In fact, it was the thought of our kids in the sun while we were enduring a dreich Saturday at Wormit Boating Club that made John, Pat and I book that sailing holiday in sunny Greece. And since my Glasgow friend Angela (who'd never sailed in her life) fancied a sailing holiday too, she joined us, sharing a room with Pat. Which is how John found himself going on holiday with three women! The other holiday members of our Mark Warner Sailing Group were clearly curious as to how we four were connected. Having no desire to share her own or Pat's personal story with strangers, Angela explained, in response to an unwanted (and somewhat tactless) enquiry, that we had all been married to John and I was his current wife. No one asked us any more questions. In fact, no one spoke to *any* of us much after that. John strutted about with folk looking on and wondering....

But it was a great holiday. We laughed a lot and we certainly experienced sailing in warm water. Unlike Wormit, it was, if anything, *too* hot: we had to hide in the shade much of the time. However, John learned to windsurf (badly), Pat and I learned to sail single-handed dinghies (badly), and Angela discovered she didn't really like sailing at all (cruising on a large ship drinking cocktails was more her style).

These were good years and, over time, traditions evolved. John loved everything about Christmas, for example, and his enthusiasm was infectious. Thoughtful—but not necessarily expensive—presents were carefully and lovingly wrapped and hidden.

One Christmas morning, I unwrapped one of my gifts. It was a box of Thornton's chocolates. I don't specially like them (I prefer Cadbury's) but I thanked John and put the box aside. Amanda and Jane kept telling me to *open the box*—in fact they insisted. Why? Did they want one? John was grinning. What was this all about?

To keep everyone happy, I removed the cellophane. *Open the lid Morag!* Inside the box? One of the chocolates had been replaced by a pair of gold earrings with a pearl in the middle. The following Christmas, and each and every year after that, I knew to open my box of chocolates.

On Christmas Eve, John used to go to mass in St Andrews with his daughter Jane, returning in time for a wee dram before he accompanied me and Pat to the Watchnight Carol Service in Wormit. While John was at mass, I—and anyone else who was around—peeled the tatties, prepared the sprouts and set the Christmas table. The girls (except Catriona who was too young) spent the evening getting hammered in Wormit pub. Sometimes the pub-goers—in various stages of inebriation—arrived at the Watchnight Service too. But fortunately they rarely made it!

John loved his Christmas tree and spent hours decorating it, while we lounged on the sofa, doing what we were good at—namely, giving advice. As for cooking the seasonal turkey, that was John's job. I'm not sure I've ever cooked one myself to this day. Jane made our Christmas pudding and our Christmas cake, which was finished off and 'fed' regularly with brandy by John. The booze-drenched Christmas cake was never really appreciated by my hung-over student children, but John loved it.

On Christmas mornings, after putting the turkey in the oven and opening our presents, we would head to Jane and Sandy Milne's in St Andrews, where there would be champagne, delicious nibbles, good chat and, of course, the grandchildren, Jamie, Katie and Stuart, who were beside themselves with excitement. Home again, we relaxed. Sometimes Mum, sometimes Aunt Isabel—sometimes both—would join us. Occasionally, we spent the whole day at my brother Sandy's* in Milnathort.

I felt immensely fortunate. Once again I was able to enjoy stable, happy, family years.

Chapter 40: Educational Legislation & Its Effects

From 1993 onwards, my college job became harder and harder, with little reward, not much fun and almost no job satisfaction. To compound matters, at the beginning of April 1993, the legal status of all colleges changed. This was as a result of the Further and Higher Education Act (Scotland) 1992. All forty-five Scottish colleges were now to be run by Boards of Management. These boards would become employers owning and maintaining college property, agreeing staff pay and conditions, and balancing the books. Previously, colleges, like schools, had been funded and governed by local education authorities.

The changes required were complex, demanding new skills, constant ongoing staff development, and huge advances in management systems for the collection of student data. A funding formula had to be established which reflected the cost of each course type and the type of student enrolled. A new computerised management information system was set up to collect this information, and a formula for capital funding was laid down. Overnight, management terminology and focus changed. The agendas of our meetings, once filled with student-oriented or teaching-related topics, now listed Student Registration, Staffing Levels, Computerised Time Tabling, Room Usage, Performance Indicators, Development Plans, Health and Safety, and Quality Control.

In fact, there was a *total* culture shift. Numerous staff in every part of the college gave unstintingly of their time to make this work. Technology advanced on all fronts. I particularly remember Helen Beaton (in her own way a pioneer) almost single-handedly compiling teaching and assessment materials for four Levels of

Communication and putting them on a CD for every member of the teaching team. A huge, complex and time-consuming task.

In order to be funded, the college had to write a 'development plan' predicting how many SUMS (Student Units of Measurement, equivalent to 40 hours of learning) each faculty would earn the following year. Yes—the college had been restructured again, this time into 'faculties'! I found myself responsible for Communication, Creative Arts (including Fashion), Media and Music Technology—all lumped together. Once again I knew nothing much about any of these subject areas, but each one had a Senior Lecturer with curricular responsibility, and each course had a 'programme tutor', although these tutors no longer had responsibility for recruitment. It was reckoned to be quicker, more efficient and undoubtedly cheaper to have an Admission system staffed by non-teaching administrators.

Predictably, the programme tutors now felt they had responsibility without control, because they hadn't selected their students. But these—like so many other changes—were necessary in the light of the ratio of SUMS to teaching staff. If this sounds like meaningless algebra to you, that's more or less how it struck many of our staff. Nevertheless, this was a Scottish Government initiative. There was no going back.

Further education staff and management worked incredibly long hours to implement the new systems effectively. The college, with the help of a successful application for capital funding, became 'fit for purpose'. European funding allowed us to build a wonderful new restaurant, the 'Rotunda', and the Creative Arts facilities in Southfield acquired some state-of-the art equipment. For the first time, a practical and efficient process was applied to the delivery and despatch of goods. But there was a cost, and the price was high. What the college lost was the goodwill and team support of many of the staff. Face with the increased emphasis on computerised systems and inflexible administrative procedures, they no longer felt valued.

Each faculty's income was to be determined by how many SUMS were predicted and delivered. Development plans are commonplace now in many organisations, but I was absolutely horrified that I was expected to produce a plan for the faculty which stated exactly how many SUMS we'd deliver the following year. How were we to *know* how many students we would recruit, how many would remain, how many would complete the course and achieve? The best we could possibly manage was an educated guess.

Since staffing was dependent on these units of measure, however, we had to get it right. There was a strict ratio of SUMS to teaching staff, which in effect meant that if one member of staff had fewer students, another had to have more. (Unfortunately, sessions online to several classes at once weren't in vogue back then.)

The new ways took their toll on most of us, including me. To add to my stress, in December 1994 Aunt Isabel, now 89, who had supported our Wilson family in so many ways when we were young, was in need of some help herself. She had been admitted to Whyteman's Brae Hospital, Kirkcaldy and in my already busy timetable, I struggled to fit in a hospital visit either at lunchtime or at the end of the day.

When I *did* turn up beside her bed, bearing straggly flowers grabbed at the petrol station, she was so pleased to see me that it was all worth it. Six weeks later, she died peacefully and painlessly in Roxburgh House in Dundee. Hospices certainly know how to treat their dying patients *and* their visitors. The drinks trolley came round each evening with a much-appreciated wee sherry for the patient and her visitors! Somehow it made the whole melancholy experience more bearable, more civilised.

The next few years were a heady (and very busy) mixture of highs and lows. The highs included Catriona's graduation in Law, Fiona's qualifying as a Maths teacher and Kirsty now practising as an Oncology graduate nurse in Manchester.

Another high was undoubtedly Kirsty and Richard's wedding in October 1998, which was planned for the end of the sailing season and to fit in with my college holidays. In his father-of-the-bride speech, John started by saying, 'Although Kirsty is actually my step-daughter and has been for sixteen years, I'm privileged and honoured to be taking the place of her late father, David Dalrymple.'

At this point, John was overcome with emotion himself and there was hardly a dry eye in the house—but they were happy, not sad, tears. Kirsty looked radiant and it was a brilliant day. John had now taken Jane, then Amanda, and now Kirsty down the aisle. Would there be more weddings in the future?

But despite all these lovely occasions, I was not feeling great. At home I had been bursting into tears for no good reason. I was brittle and irritable, yawning continuously and feeling tired from morning to night. I found it impossible to talk about anything personal, even to John. Headaches were sometimes so bad that I had to stop the car, open the door and vomit on the road on my way home.

Was this really me? Morag? I was one of life's survivors, wasn't I? My coping mechanisms had carried me through a lifetime of ups and downs. What had gone wrong? No one guessed how I was feeling, and I hid it well, thinking it was a blip. Like so many other folk, I simply expected each day to feel better.

And I kept going. My college work had eased, and this helped. I was lucky in having committed, hardworking staff. June Smith, together with the other promoted members of staff, was mainly managing the Faculty, while I was absorbed in fund-raising. In our new college world, faculty heads often had to look for a variety of ways to draw in money to keep good staff in work. Some of us applied for European funding, an excessively tortuous and complex process, while others looked to other income streams. I was fortunate that an opportunity arose for me to attract income, and it was an area that I knew something about.

Tony Blair's Labour government had come into power on May 2nd 1997 and in their first budget they announced a range of proposals designed to help people back to work. This was known as their 'Welfare to Work' programme and was to be financed from money raised from the windfall tax on the now privatised utilities like electricity, gas etc. The 'New Deal for Young People' was part of this programme, and private employers, voluntary organisations and public sector bodies were all invited to tender contracts for its delivery. I was given my own laptop and complete freedom to get on with our tender. At that time—and I suspect for ever afterwards—sourcing additional income was always encouraged by our directors.

I really needed my laptop because contract applications had to be completed on line. What a pity I could neither work the machine properly, nor word-process with any skill or speed! With the help of college technicians and Hazel Shepherd, our forthright but very competent departmental assistant, my computing skills rapidly improved. Soon we were awarded a 'Gateway to Work' contract, plus a share of the New Deal for Young People.

This meant I was able to take on non-teaching staff (the first were Doreen Ovens and Shaun McAllister) to organise and oversee the delivery of programmes running intermittently throughout the year, with starting dates determined by the length of time 'clients' had been unemployed. This didn't happen by itself; it took its toll. But it worked, and the resulting income generation reduced the pressure on staffing if we failed to meet our SUM targets.

Nevertheless, after Kirsty's wedding, I decided to speak to Caroline Henderson, our Human Resources Manager about my job. Not about my feelings of exhaustion, but about the financial consequences for my pension if I went part-time (I was one of the fortunate females who only had to work until I was sixty).

I really wanted to relinquish the faculty-head part of my job and concentrate only on the New Deal contracts and programmes. This would give me satisfying responsibility but also control, and freedom to make decisions. Best of all, I'd decide my own holiday dates.

The advice from Human Resources was not unexpected: if I wanted to receive a reasonable pension, I'd have to continue full-time a little longer and work part-time for the last three years. But they agreed to begin the process.

Meanwhile, another major sadness was looming large. Lis, the love of Sandy's life, and my sailing, skiing, bridge and TGIF pal, had terminal cancer. So much for our plans for our group running an Old Folks Home together! On Hogmanay, Sandy invited us all to share his signature dish, shepherd's pie. We sat round the table and the meal was served up, then Sandy disappeared to deliver a minuscule portion to Lis. He quickly returned. She was fast asleep.

After our meal, we moved into the sitting room and Sandy poured our drinks, ready for the bells at midnight. He disappeared again. This time, when he returned, he was carrying what seemed like a small bundle. But it was Lis—now a frail, tiny, stick-like creature.

Sandy settled her in her favourite armchair and she was smiling, although her teeth now seemed far too big for her mouth. Her morphine pump was working its wonders and she wasn't in pain. Since she was too weak to hold a glass, Sandy gave her a specially prepared, tiny, sherry ice cube to suck.

Her voice was faint, and we strained to hear what she was saying—but for that short time, here was the old Lis, entertaining as ever and still with plenty to say, while her husband Sandy for once was too sad to be opinionated. She gave instructions that we were all—immediately after her death—to accompany Sandy and their family on a ski holiday. And we did....

Lis died on the second day of January.

On the ninth, John and I, and Jan and David set off on the night sleeper from Leuchars to London. Then we boarded the train to Moutiers and caught the bus to Courcheval, where we were met by Sandy.

This proved to be my last skiing trip. I badly missed my friend Lis. A much better skier than I was, she had led me down gentle green and blue slopes. It was a whole different experience skiing with Sandy, Dave and John (renamed by their children Foggy, Clegg and Compo from the TV series *Last of the Summer Wine*). Truth to tell, it was not the best holiday I've had. All the same, I hope it helped the Harveys start to process the inexpressible grief of losing Lis.

And so it was that in the last ten years of the twentieth century I had experienced the best of times and the worst of times.

What was the new millennium going to bring?

Chapter 41: The Millennium

That moment when the twentieth century turned into the twenty-first was celebrated throughout Scotland. There were parades, rock and pop bands, huge firework displays and—as always, at midnight—a wee dram or two and drunken renderings of Auld Lang Syne.

The new century promised much for me. For starters, Kirsty's first baby (my first grandchild) was due in February, while Fiona's wedding was planned for August. And perhaps I would finally be able to reduce my working hours and still get a reasonable pension.

The birth of Alistair David on February 24 was an unexpectedly overwhelming event. My daughter Kirsty, who was living hundreds of miles away in England, had to have an emergency caesarean section. I won't forget the heart-stopping relief when I realised both she and the baby were okay. But he was born on a Thursday in Stockport and I was still working in Glenrothes.

The baby was two days old by the time I made it to Kirsty's and held him for the first time. The intense rush of emotions really surprised me. Kirsty had some recovering to do and I wanted to be there to help her. Was I one of the first grannies to work from home on line, I wonder? The New Deal from Work funds had given me my own laptop and I had bought myself a modem. This was initially so I could complete contract applications at home in the evening (their successful completion was the be-all and end-all of my job).

So each time I set off to Glossop I was armed with my laptop and my modem. I have a feeling I had to plug the modem into the phone socket but I can't really remember now. Anyway it worked well enough and the contract applications were done in time—just!

I could always phone Hazel or the helpful technical support guys if I was stuck. I found learning the correct words to describe the tech problem was very difficult. Patience and simple communication to help them understand me and other 'non-tecky idiots' must have been an essential part of their training.

But some weeks later, baby Alistair was back in hospital with a fever, a rash, his skin inflamed and red, and blisters beginning to appear. He'd developed staphylococcal scalded skin infection and urgently needed antibiotics. I can still hear his plaintive cries as the young paediatrician repeatedly tried and failed to insert a cannula into his tiny veins. After at least six unsuccessful attempts, my son-in-law Richard was unable to bear it. 'Stop! There must be another way!' he protested.

Which is why we found ourselves at home administering oral antibiotics every four hours with the tiniest syringe you've ever seen. As an amateur with a syringe, I once (honestly only once) nearly choked him. Richard and I suffered a heart-sinking moment of abject terror as we watched a choking, spluttering, gasping baby fight to catch a breath. But there is a God. Somehow, little Alistair finally swallowed, coughed and started to cry—the most welcome sound I've ever heard. Kirsty was asleep, and so this was (until now) the best kept secret ever.

Kirsty and Richard's decision in March to move from Glossop to Scotland saw me and John travelling south yet again to help them with their removal. John was driving. He always drove on long journeys and listened to the cricket (my least favourite thing). I was half asleep when I heard his urgent voice from the driver's seat. 'I'm going to get us killed,' he said. 'You'll have to take the wheel right now before I fall asleep.'

What? This just wasn't like him. Also he had stopped on the M6 slipway, so I promptly changed seats and he immediately fell asleep. He seemed fine when he woke up nearly two hours later but he agreed to see the GP when we got home. As it transpired, his blood count was very low and he was referred to Ninewells for tests. He confessed to me that he could no longer manage to cycle up the steep Mount Stuart Road either. But why? Was it old age? After all, he was sixty-six. There were more tests and regular blood checks but still no diagnosis or treatment—other than for anaemia—so life settled down again.

Then there was an unexpected call in the middle of the night. It was bad news, as such calls tend to be. My mother had had a stroke and it soon became apparent that despite the best efforts of family and home carers, she could no longer live on her own in her sheltered flat. On 12 July, she was admitted to St Serfs Care Home in Newport—a sad time for us all.

That was a definite low point, but to Fiona's delight her granny recovered enough to attend her wedding on 12th August. June and July were busy with choosing the bride's dress and our outfits, the venue, the invitations and all the other preparations that accompany a good wedding. This wasn't made any easier by the fact that Fiona was teaching in Southampton at the time. The reception was to be in St Andrews, the home of golf, and one of the few Scottish places that our guests from the south of England had heard of. For most of Paul's Southampton relations, this visit to Scotland was a first.

All the planning paid off. It was a brilliant wedding and reception—Scottish ceilidh mixed in with disco and ballroom dancing. There was no problem persuading the guests to dance: they were up for every number on a crowded floor. John and I decided we must be getting old because we had to sit down for a rest every so often. This was now the fourth time that John had taken a daughter down the aisle. Would Catriona be next?

I was still at work all day and every day, but since John was now retired, he was able to be there for my mother. He sorted out her house (which was up for sale) and drove her to Ninewells for her various appointments.

But he, too, had investigative hospital visits. Eventually they came up with a diagnosis—a tumour in his colon and he would need a partial colonectomy. We were both surprised. John was so healthy, young-looking and fit, and had such a healthy appetite. It seems strange now but I don't remember either of us being particularly worried. We regarded it as a blip, a temporary hiccup.

John was mostly concerned about recovering in time for Christmas dinner and after that for the summer sailing season. I was simply very busy. They *did* discover a cancerous tumour but they were able to assure us it had been completely removed.

When I visited him in hospital after work, I could see immediately he was a favourite with the female nurses. Despite having two daughters, three stepdaughters and a wife, he was enjoying the unaccustomed female attention, and the banter. That was John.

Whatever post-operative medicine he was on, it must have made him hungry. When I picked him up from the hospital, he wanted to stop in Tesco's to buy some things he had in mind for his tea. We came out with six tins of cullen skink soup, garlic bread, prawn cocktail, and two venison steaks. And here was I thinking I might make him some scrambled egg, custard or toast! Perhaps that healthy appetite did him good because he recovered in time to cook the turkey for Christmas as usual. Soon he seemed to be back to his former self.

The year 2000 had been an eventful one. Surely 2001 would be calmer—at least until my part-time contract was finalised. I was still unusually weary, falling asleep every night in the chair. I longed to stay at home for at least part of the week. There seemed to be so many demands on my time.

Chapter 42: My Past Returns To Haunt Me

When John returned to hospital for his check-up after Christmas, he was advised to have one course of chemotherapy (six treatments). This was as a precaution, the tumour having been successfully and completely removed. During February, March and April, he had two treatments every month.

The timing of these sessions suited him perfectly because he had found a new passion, a lady-love named Aurora, a keel boat belonging to his widowed pal Sandy. Without a doubt there was life after chemo.

Sailing adventures were awaiting the three elderly adolescents, Compo (John), Clegg (David) and Foggy (Sandy). Before this, John and I and Lis and Sandy had sailed together. But now Lis was gone, Jan didn't like sailing, and I was away at work. The three retired 'boys', after their lifetime of responsibility, savoured their bachelor freedom and had some wonderful trips round the Western Isles, and once as far away as Ireland. Each day's sailing was topped in the evening by a mooring in tranquil surroundings, a dram or two and a highly competitive, fiercely fought game of Scrabble. All three of them loved Scrabble.

John and I were very independent of one another at this stage of our lives. I was absorbed in work and work and work and the children and my new grandchild. I don't remember certain key phrases even being in my vocabulary back then. I mean things like 'work/life balance' and 'quality of life'—not to mention 'mental health'.

And yet I should have known better. In earlier years I had shown struggling mature students with families how to draw Hopson and Scally Life Skill Pie Charts, which compare percentages of time spent variously on maintenance (washing, cooking etc.), paid work, college studies, recreation, family, and partner time. Believe me, those charts led to very many lively and interesting discussions, *especially* in mixed classes (I'll say no more).

At work, my main focus and interest was still concentrated on setting up more New Deal contract applications which underpinned the 'Gateway to Work' provision. These Gateway courses began every month and ran throughout the year. I was also responsible for pre-tender briefings relating to 25+ New Deal, and also Core Skills. I was definitely stressed.

As the New Deal for young people expanded, we employed (in addition to Shaun and Doreen) two more project officers—not teachers because teachers didn't work during school holidays. The 'officers', paid less than teaching staff, were chosen for their ability to organise, liaise with other organisations, develop self-confidence in New Deal clients and above all help them find a job. The college got significantly more money from the Government if our clients not only found jobs but also stayed in them for a reasonable length of time.

Most of our clients didn't choose or want to be unemployed. Few were lazy; many lacked self confidence. For some, it was uneconomical to take on a job unless they earned above a certain amount. Lack of transport was a major issue for them, particularly for out-of-town evening and night-shift work in small hotels.

To combat this, a scheme was devised. A local garage offered special terms on used cars to New Deal applicants taking on out-of-town hotel jobs. This encouraged our clients to stay in the job to pay off the car, even if it wasn't ideal. The college was able to offer them vocational training, too, if required.

Childcare was also often a major problem for the male applicants whose wives were in very low-paid jobs with shifts outside school hours. Others had creative ideas—like the three young men whose ambition was to set up a Bee Gees tribute band. With the help of the college Music Technology staff, they made a CD to promote their music, earn money and come off benefits.

Attending meetings, both within the College and with our external partners, was horribly time-consuming (I learned to keep my head down when they asked for volunteers). What kind of meetings? Financial Management, ESF (European Social Funding), Evening Provision, Open Days, Faculty Heads, PAL (Flexible Learning), Voluntary Sector Conferences, Community Learning, ICT Capital Bids, New Deal Steering Group, Room Surveys, Development Planning, Marketing, Core Skills Profiling, New Deal Dissemination of Good Practice, Staff Appraisal (SQMS), Quality Audits, Principal's briefings—and so it went on. And on. And on.

No wonder teaching staff grew disillusioned. They cared about their students and simply wanted to teach them but now they were asked to do numerous other tasks as well. I don't know what I would have done without June Smith, who was landed with the unpleasant job of passing on the latest item of news, whatever it happened to be.

It was a time of pressure and change, and in the workplace, few people relish change, however inevitable and necessary.

But things were looking up for me personally. On May 14, 2001—three years before my retirement date in 2004—I finally became a part-time member of staff. I was in charge of New Deal contracts, responsible for contracting and delivery, but nothing else. What a relief! But I was working for the college whenever I was needed. A double-edged sword for sure, but at least I could plan, and control my life better to include home commitments.

By July, John had succeeded in finding a buyer for my mother's flat. Funds were now finally available to pay for the St Serf's Care Home.

And soon, more happy family occasions came along. Kirsty was expecting her second child in January 2002, and Catriona and Keith announced their engagement and intention to get married in October 2002 (after the end of the sailing season).

And if I planned my work well, I'd have time to enjoy them. There was a lingering concern though. I was *still* feeling tired, losing weight and I had an annoying cough. Like so many of us do, I'd been ignoring it, on the assumption it would go away.

But it stubbornly refused to disappear. I hadn't smoked in a long time. All the same, a nagging voice in my head kept reminding me my father had died of lung cancer.

My loyal doctor friend Pat persuaded me to pay a visit to my GP. He had no hesitation in sending me almost immediately to the chest clinic. Now *that* was scary.

Very soon after this, I received a letter inviting me come in and discuss the results of my chest X-ray with my doctor. This was even more unnerving. I chose to go to the appointment alone, leaving John, Pat, my mother and the girls sitting in the garden to await the news.

'I am really sorry to have to tell you, Mrs Ridings—', announced my doctor (this was it: I was going to die) '—that I'm 99% sure you have TB. When it's confirmed—after a small biopsy—you must take at least six months' leave from work.'

The poor doctor was a bit confused at my reply.

'*Yessss!*'

What better news could he possibly have given me? I wasn't *allowed* to go to work for at least six months and I had a curable disease. *So* much better than lung cancer.

When I got home, I walked straight past the anxious faces assembled at the kitchen table, saying nothing, and brought out a bottle of fizzy stuff. They looked confused not knowing what—or if—they were celebrating. Only when we were all sitting down with a glass of champagne did I tell them the diagnosis.

But how on earth had I developed TB? I had no idea. My consultant thought that my Glasgow upbringing had come back to haunt me. It was likely that I'd had latent TB since childhood. Because I was now so run down, my immune system was ineffective—hence the onset of the active disease. My treatment, unlike Angela's in the fifties, was simple. Each day I had to take antibiotics—big round tablets, the size of an old penny or a modern two-pound coin, almost impossible to swallow without gagging. Aaargh!

On and off, I did feel unwell enough to take to my bed, but by and large I was reasonably okay. Each day I grew stronger and better—more like my old self. Soon they told me I wasn't even infectious. Nevertheless, my GP insisted I continue to rest.

Since I was officially off work, I could babysit Alistair. Mum was brought along from St Serf's Care Home to see her first great-grandchild, and I witnessed first-hand the natural ability of small children to sense the frailty of those around them. I saw it as soon as I called them both through for lunch. Alistair—a wobbly toddler of twenty months—was instinctively aware of Mum's unsteadiness.

He gently held her hand as they wobbled together into the kitchen. It brought tears to my eyes (and still does when I think about it).

John was very good at collecting and returning Mum to St Serf's but he was also really busy during his retirement years as the family property manager. When the girls were at university, we had bought flats for them. During their student days, the rents of their flatmates helped to pay the mortgages. Our plan was ultimately to own these properties outright and use the rent to augment John's pension. (Most of his thirty-five years of employment was in the English private sector, in some cases in non-transferable pension schemes much less generous than Scottish public sector pensions.)

By John's retirement year, the mortgages for the flats were almost paid up. Still, he was occupied with repairs, rents, change of tenants, tax returns and everything else that goes along with the letting business. Happily, he was able to squeeze in his sailing, his lunches with Amanda, his grandchildren, his bowling and his financial management of the Catholic Church funds.

I had very little to do with the priests when they very occasionally came to the house to discuss church business, but there's one I remember clearly. Gaunt and scrawny, Father Campbell was a chain-smoker and a recovered alcoholic from Glasgow (a rare phenomenon). He was not greatly admired by his parishioners, including John. But I enjoyed his self-deprecating humour and always took the time to make him a cup of tea and listen to his chat.

On one occasion at a church 'do' in the pub (the Catholic Church allows a drink on its social occasions), I even found myself dancing with him. One, two—*hop*; one, two—*hop*. I recognised the steps.

'The Locarno?' I ventured.

'Yes,' he chuckled, coughing at the same time. His frequent

cough reminded me uncomfortably of the smokers on the top of the bus in Glasgow in the fifties. We both agreed perhaps better not to mention where he learned to dance. That was probably my sole communication with a priest during my marriage to John.

There was more welcome news at the end of the year. Fiona and Paul were expecting their first child in July. With Kirsty's second baby due in January, and Catriona's wedding in October, the following year was going to be a good one. Best of all, I would have time to enjoy it all. By the time I was eventually allowed to go back to work, I would be officially part-time—with flexible holidays.

Chapter 43: Babies, Weddings & Eye Problems

Kirsty's second child, Jenny Louise Higgins, was born in St John's Hospital, Livingston, on January 26, 2002. I was in Dalgety Bay looking after Alistair while Kirsty was in hospital, but on the day she was due home, Scotland was battered by storms. Hurricane-force winds, flood warnings and power cuts caused widespread disruption. I was stuck in Dalgety Bay taking all the crisis phone calls, while John was busy sorting my broken-down car.

The day got worse when Catriona's fiancé Keith was admitted to St Margaret's Hospital in Dunfermline with suspected appendicitis and ended up in theatre having emergency colonic surgery. Fortunately, he lived to tell the tale and has been fine ever since. But at the critical time Catriona was still in Edinburgh. In desperation, she jumped onto the very last train allowed across the Forth Rail Bridge. She phoned me during her journey and, with memories of the Tay Bridge disaster in my mind, I listened as she described the carriage rocking and swaying in the wind. Her last words—before our mobile connection was lost—were that the train had 'stopped half-way across the bridge'.

Then silence.

I visualised the train toppling from a broken bridge into the stormy River Forth below.

But at that very moment I heard two-year-old Alistair shrieking for help as he tried to drag his tractor downstairs. The image of the collapsing bridge vanished as I grabbed Alistair and his tractor just before they toppled head-first. Another emergency visit to hospital wasn't going to help anyone!

Much *much* later, or so it seemed to me, Catriona phoned to say she'd arrived safely at the hospital and Keith was going to be fine. Ten minutes after that, Richard, Kirsty and baby Jenny arrived home after a difficult drive via Kincardine to avoid the Forth Bridge. The relief of having them all safely back in Fife was indescribable. Surely there could be no more shocks in store.

I didn't have much room in my head for work. Correction. I didn't have *any* room in my head for work. Fortunately my GP, still concerned that I was underweight and not fully fit, insisted on signing me off work for a bit longer. I didn't put up any resistance, though financially it wasn't good. I was now on half pay on the part-time contract that had started two months before my unexpected TB diagnosis.

We were also having problems with our flat rental business. One tenant wasn't paying her rent and John was stressed out from dealing with the charity, *Shelter*, and the associated landlord and tenant legislation. It was an anxious time. After protracted negotiations with all parties, an agreement would be reached, the rental cheque would arrive and ... it would bounce, just like the last time. Back to the drawing board.

The additional paperwork was a burden because John's eyes, never good at the best of times, were giving him trouble. Four months later, he finally managed to serve our drug-addicted tenant a legal notice to quit. This allowed her forty days to find other accommodation and every possible supporting agency was informed. By this time, we'd both decided that being a landlord brought too many moral dilemmas. Ignorance is bliss!

And John's eyes were *still* not right. The Ophthalmology Department could find no reason for his occasional vision problems, so he was referred for an MRI scan, presumably to check for abnormal tissues in his body after his colonoscopy. The scan showed nothing untoward, thank goodness.

At the end of March we headed to Southampton to see Fiona and Paul. While there, we managed to shop for a new pram for Fiona's baby, due in July. We also enjoyed a barbecue with Paul's parents, Doreen and Victor, and fitted in a visit to Petersfield to visit Angela, her daughter Suzie and grand-daughter Maddie. We enjoyed the trip hugely. Boarding our plane for Scotland on Saturday, 30 March we heard the news that the Queen Mother had died—at the age of 101.

Once back home, John was sent to Ninewells for an EEG to see if it was something in the brain that was affecting his eyes. They found nothing. John celebrated with a visit to Loch Creran to help Sandy prepare 'Aurora' for their next sailing adventure. He returned home just in time to welcome Heather and Stewart visiting us before our Glasgow Girls' lunch in St Andrews.

Despite all the positive test results, our GP continued to be concerned about John's periodically defective vision. He insisted that John had his bloods checked regularly. Which he duly did, always a little apprehensively.

But—relief! The blood test came back okay, which was the all-clear for another Compo, Clegg and Foggy sailing trip at the end of May. This was to be their longest trip yet, sailing for ten days, a total of 273 miles. They had a great time.

Then in June, John and I attended Angela's daughter's wedding. Angela was a single parent so there was no father to give away the bride. But without hesitation Angela took on this role herself. She gave Suzie away *and* made her own 'mother of the bride' speech. I was enormously impressed. The bride and groom had written their own vows to include their child Maddie. At the time, all this was highly unconventional (not so much now, perhaps). I found it meaningful and moving—and we were treated like royalty throughout.

The following day, we visited Fiona and Paul. We'd flown to Gatwick and hired a car. That meant I had to drive because John's vision was too unreliable. Scared witless by the busy, fast-moving traffic, I gritted my teeth, put the car into gear and headed for my daughter's lovely new house in Southampton. It was well worth it because we saw Fiona, visited Paul's parents, Doreen and Victor, and even managed to take the ferry to the Isle of Wight for lunch.

For me, this was the first of many visits to Fiona and Paul's. It turned out differently for John.

Chapter 44: Stunned

When we got back home, John was clearly unwell. Dr Hepworth sent him for an endoscopy. Once more, it showed nothing that might explain what was going on.

Determined to get to the bottom of all this, our next visit was to a consultant neurologist. We needed the different specialties to work together, we told him. We were thoroughly weary of the uncertainty and lack of diagnosis, the ongoing health concerns. He agreed. He sent John for yet another MRI scan.

The result was utterly unexpected. Impossible to believe. Can tumours grow so quickly? Apparently—yes. John had terminal cancer. There were small secondaries in his lung *and* in his brain.

The first thing he said was, 'How long have I got? My daughter's wedding's planned for October.'

The consultant's reply was non-specific, but it told us all we needed to know: 'If I were you, I wouldn't put anything off. Do what you can, when you can. The brain tumour may make your behaviour unpredictable.'

We walked hand in hand across the forecourt of Ninewells Hospital. Stunned by the news, I saw an acquaintance approaching, a big smile on her face. I blanked her completely. We carried on walking, grim-faced, towards the exit. Somehow we made it to the car.

Back home, we faced the appalling task of telling everyone the news. John phoned Amanda and Jane and his siblings in Manchester. I did the same for my family. No one could take it in. It couldn't be true. Surely there was something could be done?

But there wasn't.

The next day I phoned work and was granted unpaid, indefinite compassionate leave.

John and I took a decision: we would make the most of the time he had left. But first things first: some plans had to be changed. The wedding was planned for October. Should the date be changed?

According to Keith and Catriona, bringing the wedding forward would be easy. Catriona phoned the venue (Murrayshall House Hotel in Perth) and fixed a new date: Sunday 18 August. Keith's parents phoned guests and sent out revised wedding invitations. The bridesmaids rearranged the flowers. The groom sorted out the cars. Sutherlands, the hairdressers in Newport, agreed to open their salon on the Sunday for the hair styling and make-up. All that remained was to buy the outfits, including the bride's dress, and my own.

Four days after his diagnosis, John's sisters left home at some ungodly hour and drove up from Manchester to see him, bringing their own hamper of tasty delicacies. They knew their brother well and how much he liked his food. A heartbroken Amanda arrived too—she loved her Dad deeply—and they went for a walk and a talk together. It was a beautiful sunny afternoon. We all sat in the garden enjoying a cheery family catch-up and blether. It was well-nigh impossible to believe what lay ahead.

Meanwhile, Fiona, almost due to give birth in Southampton, was coping with the shock of the news without the closeness and support of her own inner family. John and I decided to take the train south to see her. We were picked up from the station by a heavily pregnant daughter. Only two days later, on 28 July, Thomas John Bragg arrived at 8.30 a.m., weighing 8 lbs 15 ozs. Fiona and Paul were elated, thrilled to bits with their strong healthy boy.

But Fiona was sad too, watching John fighting back his tears as he held Thomas for what he thought might well be the first and last time.

Once back in Scotland, we still had wedding shopping to do. We set out for a day in Perth. Kirsty and I went looking for our wedding hats, while Catriona disappeared with John on a secret mission. This turned out to be an anniversary gift for me in preparation for our twentieth wedding anniversary on November 20.

But I could tell there was something troubling my youngest daughter. And there was. John was determined to give her away at her wedding but she was worried about the 'Father of the Bride' bit. There was no telling how the brain tumour would affect him, although he desperately wanted to make a speech and was already working on it. With the greatest skill and tact, and without even hinting that he might have difficulty on the day, Catriona successfully persuaded him to print out his words for all to read. The speech was to be put beside the menu at each setting on the wedding table. All he then had to do was to say the Grace before the meal, which would be easy. Problem solved.

There was one more challenge for all of us. This was to be a wedding, not a wake, so our sorrows had to be kept at bay.

And it certainly *was* a wonderful wedding. I don't think you would find anyone to disagree. Both families, though inwardly so very sad, hid their feelings well. We celebrated a happy event happily. The smile never left Catriona's face—nor John's. Thanks to good planning, he was well enough to enjoy things. Catriona and Keith's wide circle of friends played a large part in this too.

✕✕✕

After the excitement of a wedding, there's usually a bit of a downer, but our visitors kept on coming. John's daughter Jane arrived for lunch with her kids, and grandson Stuart persuaded John to mend the blue go-cart for little Alistair. By the end of the day, with the help of Richard and Keith, John the grandfather had done the trick.

But of course John and I needed time together too. Our Aberdeen flat needed some attention and so we headed there for a couple of nights. We decided to visit some old haunts for the last time. Findhorn first, but it was too quiet. We made for Grantown-on-Spey and enjoyed the luxury of a couple of nights in the Grant Arms Hotel.

Over dinner we were hesitant at first to talk about 'what next'. As we ate our starters, we shared good memories. After a glass of wine, however, our tongues loosened and John made it clear that while he didn't want to die just yet, he wasn't afraid. He genuinely believed in life after death.

Throughout our nineteen years of marriage this was the nearest we ever got to having a religious discussion. I didn't share his beliefs, I said, but I did think that how we live our lives affects those who come next. I might even have pointed out that *despite* him being a devout Catholic (and that *was* a Proddy joke I thoroughly enjoyed), he had made my life and my children's lives worth living after David died. And not just that either. He had made us happy.

John reminded me of our agreement, many years back, for his ashes to be scattered with those of Lucy, his first wife. He knew I had no problem with this. To me, ashes are simply ashes—the dead person lives on through the memories they leave behind. Just as well really—we might have been an awkward threesome in heaven!

We went on to cheerier topics after that, and the next morning we set off for Aviemore where we were lucky enough to see a cavalcade of Harley Davidsons driving along the main street. Not only that: we stopped at the House of Bruar for a hearty lunch. John's palliative care medicines were undoubtedly increasing his appetite and enjoyment of tasty food. But day by day his strength was diminishing.

Home again, we babysat Alistair and Jenny, and Alistair played with water most of the day, his project being to clean (?) our kitchen window. There was water everywhere inside and out. At first he refused to join us for lunch but when I said it was a *window-cleaner's* lunch, he was right there.

The following day John's sailing friends David Winch and Terry Doughty helped him realise one of his last wishes—to visit the Falkirk Wheel.

Each day he grew more frail. Soon—sooner than we had expected—his legs were too weak to support his body. But the special bed, the wheelchair, the hoist, and the rest of the assistance (including the carers) weren't available instantly. What was I to do? The GP and (on the advice of Kirsty) the Macmillan charity, were doing their best to put all the help we needed in place as quickly as possible, but it was going to take time.

John wasn't ready yet for his children to see him helpless and dependent, I knew that instinctively. At a loss, I phoned my childhood radiographer friend Angela in Sussex. She'd been moving patients for thirty years, she would know what to do. Over the phone she gave me some useful practical advice. The very next morning about 10.00 a.m., I heard the door-bell ring. Guess who was standing there? Angela, of course—as elegant as ever and, as usual, not a hair out of place. 'What goes around comes around,' she announced. She was clearly remembering the time when David and I helped her after Suzie's birth back in 1970. She stayed with us until Catriona and Keith returned from their honeymoon. But before she returned to East Grinstead, she gave them their instructions. Their job was to help with the night care.

In fact, all five of our girls were there at various times to assist. Everyone played their part. Kirsty was on unpaid maternity leave with Jenny, now about seven months old. Jenny became known as our 'cuddle bundle': she was handed around (as in 'pass the parcel') to whichever one of us was having a wobbly moment.

The support at this time was amazing: from care staff, medics, friends and family. Towards the end, John's sister Mary from Manchester arrived. She sat with him through the last long nights.

We approached the final weekend in September sensing it would be his last. Catriona had an application for promotion due in on the Monday. But if things went as expected, she wouldn't be there that day. She had to ask her boss to complete her reference on the Friday. She got visibly upset when she tried to explain why, but he happily completed the reference, and his remarks were very complimentary. On the train home she read what he'd written and burst into tears. A kind lady sitting opposite offered help. Catriona explained through her tears that her dad was dying and her boss had said lovely things about her—it was just all too much.

On the last night, Jane, Kirsty and I sat talking in the sitting room not far from where John lay. The priest had been and done his bit, a cross was now resting on John's chest and he was sleeping peacefully and pain-free, his bed facing the window, through which, if he opened his eyes, he could see the Tay Rail Bridge.

Every so often we checked to see how he was. Was he listening to our chat? Could he hear it?

Just after 1.00 a.m. Catriona, asleep upstairs, woke up and came downstairs, bringing with her more tea and more biscuits on a tray.

Kirsty, our qualified nurse, checked the invalid every so often and at about 4.00 a.m. she suggested we call our GP, Dr Hepworth.

At 5.30 a.m. on September 29, 2002, at the age of 67, John was pronounced dead.

At 58, I was a widow for the second time.

Chapter 45: Living On My Own

E veryone copes with bereavement in their own way. But where do you start? When you lose the person at the centre of your life, how on earth do you survive?

John had had a 'good death' (if there *is* such a thing) but although this was a consolation—of a kind—it didn't help me in my task of carrying on. My strategy was to try to think as little as I could about what might have been. It made me too sad. I tried to train my head to think about the here and now and—believe me—there was plenty of here and now to contend with.

For a start, there was endless paperwork to be completed. On every official document, the 'Mr & Mrs' had to be replaced by 'Mrs' only. From experience, I knew how vital it was to understand and take control of my own affairs. But actually doing that was a painful and emotional experience. Customer Service Departments (at that time anyway) were still profoundly inadequate when it came to dealing with the bereaved.

I had to telephone utility companies, insurance companies, and others. If only I could have just completed an online form. I had to explain to each and every organisation that John was dead—how hard it is to say that word aloud to a stranger!

Despite family support, and my adorable grand-children, it was a desperately lonely period. The first time I was widowed I'd had young children to distract me, my widowed friend Christine to empathise, and the support of family and close friends all round me. This time, I was living alone for the first time in my life— without an abundance of friends near at hand, with the exception of Pat, my loyal Wormit pal and Jan and David. I was eating alone, sleeping alone, watching the telly alone. I was talking aloud to myself instead of John.

Then there was the practical side of things. John had changed light bulbs, emptied the hoover, mended anything broken, cut the grass, lifted anything heavy, and done most of the cooking. He had also looked after the rented flats and the paperwork. My children helped whenever they could but they had busy lives with stressful jobs and young children.

There were other social adjustments I had to make too. I learned the hard way that as a widow, I was relegated to a second-class status by some (but definitely not all) my married friends. Filling in time, they would phone me when their husband was out, to see how I was and then—in the middle of a conversation—a husband would come back and the chat would be abruptly terminated. Had I been boring them? I was left feeling even worse after that kind of 'cheering me up' phone call.

I was invited to loads of lunches but somehow as a single person—not half of a couple—the invitations to meals in the evening were rare. What I also found out was that some couples were easy and enjoyable company together, whereas with others it was somehow only possible to talk to one of them at once, but not both at the same time. In the old days with John, he would have chatted to one, while I spoke to the other.

I returned to work very soon after John died and it was good to be back. I had the job I'd planned before the onset of my TB and was now able to manage my work and my childcare commitments.

After a day's work, as so many times before, I would arrive home at the gate of Northview Terrace and step out of my wee blue Fiesta into the gloomy dark street.

Why on earth hadn't I turned on the outside light? Why hadn't I got myself some sensor lights? Never heard of them.

What should I do? Struggle down the steps in the dark, open the door, switch on the lights—then nip back up to collect my mountain of paperwork?

In the pitch dark, one hand on the rail, step by step, I felt my way down the twenty-five steps to the back door. Standing outside, I searched for the small house key I knew was in my bag. I'd definitely put it there that morning when I left.

As I rummaged, I felt the mass of wet, knotted tissues, the purse given to me by Amanda, a lipstick and some blusher (essential items to make me look healthier) and of course my spectacle case. I finally found the key right at the bottom of the bag.

I had no key ring. No wonder the small key was difficult to find. *Why* didn't I have a key ring? The answer was simple. Since we'd moved back to Northview Terrace, John—or my mother, or the children—had always been there to welcome me home.

But not any more.

Inside the house, the silence was deafening. I turned on the lights, the TV, the radio, the kettle. At least the AGA range kept the kitchen warm.

As I sat watching the TV and eating my dinner from a tray on my lap, I wondered how in such a short space of time it had come to this. Living alone in a large brick built Victorian house? *Me*? I finally understood why my mother had sold Colebrooke terrace after Jimmy died.

And where *was* my mother? While we had all been looking after John, my sister Elizabeth and brother Sandy (both recently retired) had been supporting Mum as well. Her health had deteriorated and

St Serf's Care Home was no longer able to look after her. It was a difficult time. Her last days were spent in Duncreggan Nursing Home in Newport. When I visited her, she was adamant that she'd 'had enough'. She was tired of living and wanted to die. I understood. There comes a time when the quality of life is such that it is a kindness to let someone go.

On 23 September, 2003, a year after John's death, and a year before my retirement, Mum finally passed away. She was 87. She had survived the war and early widowhood and lived her whole life for her family. She'd lived long enough to see her children settled and all her grandchildren achieve university degrees (one of her treasured moments was attending Catriona's graduation in Law in Aberdeen). She had also desperately wanted to leave her children an inheritance, but this didn't happen. She was appalled that her house had to be sold to pay for her care.

The absence of legacy had further ramifications. When John and I had bought the house in Aberdeen for Catriona as a student, we had funded it by the combination of a mortgage and a loan. The loan was from Mum—£25,000. This, when she died, was to be deducted from my share of her inheritance. But in the event there *was* no inheritance, so after her death I had to pay the sum back into her estate. I did this by selling the Aberdeen property; I couldn't manage that house and its mortgage without John anyway.

Mum's engagement ring was bequeathed to me but after her death, her fingers were bare. No ring. It had vanished, never to be seen again. Where? And why? And when? Did it disappear in one of the homes? Or the hospital? Was it stolen, or lost?

To this day I've no idea. Coping with grandchildren, my job, selling the Aberdeen house, I hadn't the energy, the time or the inclination to pursue the matter. And in the big scheme of things, although it was upsetting, jewellery—even the kind we value for personal reasons—is not what makes the world go round.

At some point when I was rushing between college work in Glenrothes, babysitting in Dalgety Bay, then home to the empty house in Wormit, I took a big decision.

I would sell Northview Terrace in Wormit and buy a house in Dalgety Bay. It was where two of my married children now lived.

This was one of my best moves, one that would lead to some very happy years. Perhaps I had learned an important life skill—to look forward and not back.

Chapter 46: Granny Morag

For the first time in my life, I chose a house just for me. I listened to loads of wise and sensible advice, and nodded in agreement. Then I bought exactly the house I wanted—a four-bedroomed bungalow close to Dalgety Bay Sailing Club, opposite a little sandy beach where there were a few boats anchored, and within walking distance of the shops, the train station, the local schools, and my grandchildren. Perfect!

Certainly it might have been better if the roof hadn't leaked. But, hey-ho—not every house has everything you want. When the grandchildren arrived in the morning on a rainy day, they would fetch the yellow bucket unasked and place it in the middle of the sitting-room floor to catch the drips.

Fortunately I'd sold the house in Wormit fairly easily and could afford to make changes to my new property. What I did was simply adapt the house to suit my lifestyle as a childminder, a widow and single lady. After knocking down the wall between cooking and dining area and replacing it with an 'island', my kitchen was open-plan with an easily moppable floor. I could now talk to everyone as I prepared food and keep an eye on the kids at the same time.

From the dining area, two steps led into a very large sitting-room with a huge gallery window. This room was home to a forty-year-old, re-upholstered suite, originally from John and Lucy's first house. The suite comprised a four-seater settee along with three matching armchairs, each with removable arm and seat cushions. This was to be the scene of many a den, battle area, maze, hospital, school and/or a theatre with my old sheets, towels and dust sheets frequently completing the picture. The foot-stool was often reserved for the winner, or the leader, or the loser, or the patient—depending on the game.

In the other, smaller, front room, I built a wall of shelves for my books, and a desk for my laptop at the sea-view window. My wall of books was a bit of a bluff because I never read any of them—or very few anyway. Redundant items (like silver and brass, delicate china-tea-sets and fragile ornaments, some paintings, fancy wedding hats, elegant clothes and anything else I was unlikely to need) were abandoned in storage boxes in the partially floored attic.

There was a permanent step-ladder leading to the attic from the laundry room. On his first visit to my house, Alistair, now aged four, immediately climbed up the ladder to see what was in the attic. His eyes lit up with sheer, unadulterated joy.

'If you have a naughty step, can I sit on this ladder, Granny?' he asked, anticipating the forbidden delights of exploring my attic, box after box.

'Sorry, I don't do naughty steps,' I said. 'I just cut off your head instead—' (waggling the plastic cutlass he had abandoned at the foot of the stepladder) '—that's what that orange bucket is for—to catch the head, and the *blood*.'

Kids like blood—the idea of it anyway. Also that was the end of that non-PC conversation.

The new house came with a spearmint-toothpaste-coloured bath. It was a corner whirlpool bath, and a child's delight—they adored it. For the 'sleep-over' bedroom, I began by putting John's collection of shells on the shelf. From there, it grew into what the kids always called The Dolphin Room.

One of my secret joys in the morning was listening to the cars driving past on their way to work. While I certainly missed friends from the college, I never for one minute missed the responsibilities. Perhaps you have to work full-time for nearly thirty years to really appreciate retirement. Still, I will never regret those decades of employment. I learned and experienced so much and met such a variety of talented and amazing people, both students and staff. And for the most part I enjoyed it, but—I was very, *very* glad when it came to an end.

And now I discovered something else about myself: I really liked and enjoyed small children (well, my grandchildren anyway) and possibly had a child's brain myself. To see the world through children's eyes was a privilege. A child's joy at the simplest of things was infectious —splashing and jumping in muddy puddles, hiding round corners, giggling at nothing at all, and best of all making a mess. Children and mess simply go together, like a horse and cart or strawberries and cream.

As every mother knows, one small child and a biscuit can ruin an hour's hoovering. Wanton destruction was definitely a crime but in my house mess was another matter, so long as it was tidied up (sort of) afterwards. Splodgy painting and cutting supposedly develop creativity. Perhaps so. But isn't the thing that children really love about it ... the mess?

What about hand- or finger-painting? Great fun, but horrendously messy. All parents and grandparents remember the moment when a child asks you to guess what their painting is, and you have that sinking feeling. You have absolutely no idea.

Jenny, for example, once painted a face covered in dots. 'What do you think it is?' she demanded.

'A lady with spots? With measles? With chicken pox?'

'None of these, silly. It's piercings.' And she was *five*.

For me, it was always about the fun of the process, about the experience, and not about the end product. Like work, there were bad days as well as good, but these were relatively rare. Some days we would simply don our coats and go out for an aimless walk, perhaps along the shore or in the woods or on the beach. On our way, 'I spy' competitions were popular. Sometimes it was numbers on gates, or dogs or funny-shaped clouds or stones of a certain shape or size. It mattered not.

Again, it was a learning curve for me. Each child was unique, seeing something completely different in his or her own way.

Many of my assumptions about small human beings were proved wrong. I thought *all* children enjoyed baking cakes. Wrong! Did they instinctively know *I* didn't really enjoy baking either?

'Do I *have* to stir the mixture, Granny?'

'No, I don't want to lick the spoon. Can I go now?'

Yet they would play games of their own making for hours, the rules developing and changing constantly and often inspired by a story book or a TV programme.

On one occasion they played a game of 'going to work'. They knew to pick up a laptop, put on their coat and go out the door towards the car—but then they were stuck. They had absolutely no idea what to do next!

Within two years of arriving in Dalgety Bay I had acquired three more grandchildren. Fiona's second son (Cameron) was born in Winchester in October 2004. Catriona's first son (James) followed four months later in Dunfermline in January 2005, and, Kirsty's third child (Annabel) put in an appearance in June of the same year in Livingston. Last—but certainly not least—there was David (a brother for James) two years later in April 2007.

It was a busy time. All the young parents had to work if the couples wanted to buy a house, which they did. So—depending on their ages—the care was shared between parents, nursery and school provision, a childminder and me.

It was so very different from my time when most women stayed at home at least until the children went to school. When I had my children in the seventies, husbands were only allowed a mortgage of two and a half times their salary, and there was tax relief on mortgages, plus family allowance paid directly to the mother.

As we know all too well, nothing stays the same. Times have changed and house prices at the time of writing are astronomically high for first-time buyers. But I no longer worked for the college and was more than delighted to be an unpaid child-carer. In fact, this was my top priority for the next few years. It's something I enjoyed and something I'll never regret. Perhaps it would have been different if John had been alive. That, I can't know.

I was, however, only available for child care Mondays to Thursdays. I kept Fridays and weekends free for myself and for some visits to Southampton to see Thomas and Cameron, from whom I used to get an amazing welcome.

I used to travel by plane, arriving late Thursday night, and wake up very early in the morning to find two wee boys standing by my bed patiently waiting for me to open my eyes and read them their favourite story. In later years, the Monopoly board or the Rummikub set awaited me. They were football-mad (still are) and when they were very young I was instructed to stand in front of the tiny football net in the garden while they practised kicking goals. They were also good on health and safety: 'Cross your hands in front of your willy, Granny, in case the football hits it.'

I did as I was told, of course, but couldn't wait to tell their mum that I didn't think they'd met any baby *girls* yet.

A 'granny walk' became a useful threat in later years. One weekend while Fiona and Paul had some time off, I took the boys for a ramble. They were sturdy and healthy and loved walking but I got lost and the light was fading. I'd forgotten I was in the south of England. The boys had complete trust in me (they know better now) but they did wonder why it was getting so dark. To be fair, the boys were great walkers, strong and resilient. They didn't whinge or moan. But their pace was getting slower and slower, and so was mine, and I was rapidly running out of stories and diversionary tactics.

I finally arrived back at the house with two exhausted children, having had to ask for directions from strangers—several times. Thomas and Cameron, trained *not* to speak to strangers, were horrified. They were very glad to stagger into their warm home. After the rainy expedition, the two little angels ate heartily and slept soundly. But from that time on, a 'granny walk' became a byword in the Bragg household for an undesirable experience.

Back home in Dalgety Bay, none of my new acquaintances knew my name. I was simply Granny Morag. It was so much better than being labelled as 'the woman with two dead husbands'. I enjoyed quality time with my girls too. I loved to hear about their jobs and—like most mothers and daughters—we shared the children's concerns and achievements.

These were good years for me, although certain aspects were hard. With each grandchild, I worried about the first days at school or nursery, not to mention the days they came home crying because they'd fallen out with their best friend. They seemed to enjoy the learning though, and that was good. If they had homework (mainly reading), it was always easy and enjoyable.

I pored endlessly over catalogues for children's books. The grandchildren, without exception, loved the Mr Men series (is that now sexist, I wonder?). *Mr Tickle, Mr Rude* and *Mr Impossible* were top favourites. The very thought of shouting 'Big Nose!' at a grown-up filled them with glee. And *Mr Impossible* doing extraordinary feats, like jumping over a house, appealed to them enormously.

We had favourite films, *Bambi* being one of them. The bigger boys—the fierce pirates, the tough rugby players and the footballers— always hid behind the sofa when Bambi's mum died. So brave! And they would use Bambi's mum's advice to Bambi—to *me*: 'If you've got nuthin nice to say, then don't say nuthin at all.'

Swimming was another favourite pastime. I'd taken them all to swimming lessons: that was the boring bit. I love swimming and had joined the Health Club of the Keavil House Hotel in Dunfermline, just because of their swimming pool. I sometimes took the children there.

Once I forgot that Annabel still needed armbands. Fortunately Jenny noticed and Annabel lived to tell the tale. I did enjoy playing in a swimming pool and so did they. But I definitely wasn't keen on the game where Alistair stood on the bottom of the pool with his friend Jonathan standing on his shoulders. The object? To see how long they could stay under the water. Scary!

I undoubtedly enjoyed the childminding part of my life. But what about the rest? How difficult was it for me as a widow in a new place? Did my social life improve?

That was quite another matter.

Chapter 47: Social Life In Dalgety Bay

I now lived opposite Dalgety Bay Sailing Club, so you might think I'd have continued to sail. But for a long time I had been either too busy or too ill to sail, and when I left Wormit after John's death I lost all interest. However, I did join the sailing club in Dalgety Bay as a social member and made good use of the clubhouse. I decided I'd much rather swim in a swimming pool than capsize in the River Forth or Tay—a decision I've never regretted.

It was through this shared interest in swimming that I met Fiona McLaughlin, who lived a few doors away. She was also a member of Keovil Swimming Pool and sometimes we would chum each other there. Her dad, unlike mine, had played a pivotal role in her life. A lawyer herself, she had worked in his family law firm. After his death she missed him and, like me, she now lived alone. Friends already, we had no inkling that an escapade we were to share would make that friendship even firmer.

Next door to Fiona lived an elderly, single widower, who had already entertained her to dinner and now she was expected to return the invitation. An interesting and likeable character, yet a very proper lady, Fiona wasn't comfortable with having a single gentleman over for a meal and so she invited me along too. I wasn't exactly overwhelmed with dinner invitations at that time. I was delighted to accept.

On the night of the event, I arrived a little late (thanks to my childminding duties) and found our well-oiled, eloquent, and chatty neighbour sitting on the sofa relishing his pre-dinner drinks. During the starter course, we heard about the tragedy of his late wife and his various successful businesses. By the main course he was entertaining us with his flying experiences. During dessert, we heard about his frugal ways, buying bread at the end of the day in Tesco's and freezing it. In short, we listened to his life story.

At the end of the meal, we transferred him to Fiona's lounge and left him there while we tidied away the dishes and made the coffee. Returning with the tray of coffee cups, we noticed he'd dozed off. Fiona and I took the opportunity to chat away to each other since we'd barely spoken a word all evening, just listened and listened and listened. Yawn. No doubt he would soon wake up. But come midnight, he was still well and truly asleep. We repeatedly tried to waken him—and failed. We checked his pulse and (thank goodness) he was definitely still alive and breathing

As there was absolutely no way Fiona—a respectable unmarried lady—would allow him to wake up in her house the next day, we had to get him home somehow. I volunteered to search his pocket for his house keys, and found them. One on either side, our arms around his waist to keep him reasonably upright, we dragged him to his front door, his feet trailing along behind him,

What next? We couldn't just dump him inside. As all our houses were similar, we knew exactly where the master bedroom was. Still dragging him along, we upended him on to his bed, removed his shoes and loosened his tie. A worried Fiona suggested we stopped at that, and I agreed. We left him propped up on the pillows and with considerable relief escaped to our own homes. What did we do with the key? We left it beside his bed and left the door unlocked.

The following morning, Fiona had a phone call from him. Clearly he remembered nothing of what had happened. He had called to thank her for a lovely evening and to tell her that ('silly me') he had even forgotten to lock his front door! He's dead now so I can tell the story. For a long time, it was one of our best kept secrets, one we wisely decided not to share with other neighbours. The moral is, folks: beware the combination of alcohol and elderly gentlemen.

In the old days, another of my hobbies had been social bridge. During my first marriage, David and I played with Sandy and Lis Harvey, our Wormit friends. After David's death, I had taught John how to play and we often played as partners—again with Sandy and Lis, and sometimes Jan and David. But now I had no partner. Nor did I know anyone who played. What about joining a bridge club? My neighbour Trixie, though not a bridge player herself, kindly arranged for me to partner the guy who ran the local club (his usual partner was on holiday).

Blissfully ignorant of what skills I might require in an actual bridge club (other than bridge), I cheerfully turned up on the night. After all, I had played on and off for forty years. How hard could it be? When I arrived, there were eight card tables arranged round a bleak hall, and four strange, green boxes sitting on each one. My kind and friendly partner, known as 'the Director', ushered me to an empty table and walked round the room, allocating each table three boards, with a pack of cards divided into thirteen for each person.

Shortly after that, he rang a little bell. Without a word, the players started to play. Not a sound. Hardly anyone spoke. My partner now had time to communicate with me (softly). What bidding system did I use?

'Culbertson, I think,' said I, not ever really having given it a name before.

'I play Acol,' he said.

This meant absolutely nothing to me. After some boards had been played and everyone moved round, we joined one of the bridge pairs and started to play the next set of boards.

No one said, 'hello' or 'good evening', or smiled a welcome, and they talked across me to each other using unfamiliar terms like 'transfers' and 'weak twos'. What? The only transfers I knew were soaked in water and stuck to your hand. The only twos I'd ever heard of were the terrible-toddler kind.

Nerves made my fingers into thumbs. As for the green bidding box—I just couldn't work out how to use it properly. If I managed to get the correct bid *out* of the box, I couldn't get the wretched bidding cards back *in*. How could I possibly concentrate on playing bridge at the same time?

As for bidding, common sense went out the window, and my new—and definitely temporary—partner was probably bordering on despair. If I could, I would apologise to him right now.

At each table we moved to, I could feel the irritation and impatience of the opposite pair. With the exception of my partner, 'kindness' and 'tolerance' were concepts totally alien to that particular group of players on that particular evening. There wasn't even a cup of tea!

'How did you get on?' asked Trixie next day. 'Are you going back?'

'I'd rather stick pins in my eyes,' I said.

I'm happy to say this wasn't the end of my bridge escapades. My next door neighbour Lynn Vrolik and I devised a cunning plan. We would ask Fiona and Linda Arnott to join us—and we would teach ourselves Acol! Bidding boxes and four copies of Ron Klinger's *Basic Acol Bridge* were duly purchased.

We never looked back. Every week we met and practised our Acol—and more importantly, we thoroughly enjoyed our social bridge evenings.

Golf was something else I'd always wanted to take up. It surely couldn't be that hard, once you had the time to practise? I'd tried a few times before but never got very far. My sister Elizabeth (now known as Liz) wanted to start too, and she lived near me in South Queensferry. So we decided to learn to play golf together but—oh—we were so *bad*. Not an ounce of natural talent between us.

When Liz stopped trying, which was quite frequently, she would pick up the ball, put it in her back pocket, pat it twice, call it an ASDA shot (remember that advert?) and walk on to the next tee.

We frequently—no, mostly—duffed it. If somehow we connected the ball and the club, we thinned, sliced or hooked it. Even if we hit it, we still had to pitch it on to the green and then putt it into the very small hole frequently placed just behind a bunker. It was all unbelievably difficult.

I found it hard to believe that some folk took only three or four shots to get the stupid ball in the hole. Those who think golf is a good walk wasted may have a point.

But in reality, it is—without a doubt—the hardest game in the world to learn. Like life, the more you know, the less you know. Each time I thought I'd mastered a particular golf skill, it simply vanished the next time I played.

My sister Liz gave up the game, possibly wisely, but I was more stubborn and continued to play, initially without much success or even enjoyment.

One day, while I was chatting to Eric Dey, the electrician who was rewiring my new kitchen, I mentioned—by way of small talk—that I'd joined Aberdour Golf Club, and had been given the highest handicap (at that time 36).

His eyes lit up. Would I like to be his partner in the Walter Bald Mixed Cup?

Well, by that time I knew enough about golf to realise that my handicap of 36 was the attraction—not my charm, looks or golf ability. However, since I had nothing to lose and nobody to play with anyway, I agreed.

Somehow he and I got through to the final. When the day came round, each time I played a bad shot (which—poor man—I did frequently) I simply declared, 'Sorry, you can't have the strokes *and* good golf!'

Surprisingly and unbelievably, we won. (He was a very good golfer.) We collected the Walter Bald Trophy at Aberdour Annual Awards Evening. Nothing ventured, nothing gained.

I wasn't too excited about the win. It was all down to Eric really—although quite a few of my putts managed to make their way into the hole on the green when it mattered. In the semi-final, though ,we had played a couple I hadn't met before: Linda and Jo Arnott. I recognised a kindred spirit in Linda and from that time on, I had a congenial golf buddy in Aberdour.

In this way, hobbies and interests helped me to make new friends, and life began to improve—or so I hoped. But what was I going to do about holidays? They can be a real problem when you aren't one of a pair.

Cardboard boxes are ok but watching *Ben 10* is much more fun
Left: Kirsty, Thomas, Ali; right (left to right) James, Thomas, Cam, David ↓

Watching *Bambi*, a very
scary film
→
Left to right: Ali, Annabel,
Jenny, James, Thomas

An important Granny job is to teach
grandchildren to drink cocktails
↓

Harry Potter visits 40, The Wynd →

2007, Botswana holiday, Ngepi Camp: the bush hut with no door ←

June, a great reader, oblivious to snakes, lizards, crocodiles and hippos ↓

No mirrors for these children who are excited at seeing themselves on my phone ↓

I am actually petrified here, having just watched a crocodile a couple of metres away slither into the water → (George to the left, June far right, me in the middle)

June & I took calculators, batteries and footballs to Matsitama School ←

Etosha: National Wide Life Safari Park

Should anyone ask if there's any sex in this book, the answer is YES →

2012, I move to Lathro Park in Kinross, Annabel standing in my doorway →

↑
'Sickie' days: James on the day my car broke down

Annabel enjoying some cosseting →

2014, hot tub at
Christmas time in
my garden
←

On our way to
Kinross Golf Club for
a family meal →

2019, enjoying the Fire Pit at
Gateside Barn in Fossoway
←

Hide 'n seek on a
Northumberland holiday—
David, the youngest, has the
best hiding place
→

←At Beamish—little do they
know I travelled to school on a
Glasgow tram

A present from children
& grandchildren on my
seventieth birthday
→

Old school pals →
for over 60 years go to
the races in Buccleuch
Arms, Kelso; from left
to right: Diane Stewart
(Muir), me, Elizabeth
Dickie, Elizabeth Moore
(Dalziel), Heather
Mackinnon (Craig), Pat
Paterson(Gammie),
Jean O'Callaghan
(Lindsay), Pat Allison
(Whitton), Sheila
McIntyre (McVey)

→
This is one of Tom's happy
memories when he came
to stay with me. From left
to right: TJ, Lucas &Tom,
winners of the Fife Schools
Football Cup. *Yessss!*

Beryl &I finally learn about the Romans
← ↓

↑ With my new SNISO friends, I just love the thermal pool at the Secret Lagoon in Iceland, 2019; from left to right: Jean, Morag M, Laura, me & Jean, sub-editor of this book

Family walks when they were finally permitted during lockdown
← ↓

← 2021: Heather, Christine & I sail doon the Clyde on the Waverley to revisit my favourite place Tighnabruaich

Beryl & I visit Madeira, 2021 →

Kinross, 2022, dinner & wine in the Kirklands Hotel with my three favourite people ←

← Milnathort 2021 Catriona & Keith's barbecue hut: male members of the family; left to right: James, me, Cam, David, Keith, Richard, Ali

Happy Golfers at Kinross Golf Club: left to right me, Betty Brannan, Alison Morrison, Rena Duncan →

← 2022, Kirklands Hotel, Kinross Catriona's birthday cocktails: left side of table front to back: Susan, Kirsty, Emma, Fiona; right side: me, Catriona, Jenny

Chapter 48: A Year of the Unexpected

The year started with my neighbours Lynn, Thom and I celebrating Hogmanay at the Sailing Club across the road. Since all three of us were relatively new to the district and everyone else appeared to be lifelong friends, we resorted to 'the drink' to get us through. I can't tell you much about the evening. I'm not sure what *they* remember.

What I do remember vividly is what had happened only two weeks later. On January 14—a Sunday—I had a call from my brother Sandy. His middle son Scott, a BSc (Hons) graduate in Genetics at Glasgow University, had died during the night. It was totally unexpected. Scott was only thirty-four years old. Results of the post mortem showed he'd died of natural causes (pulmonary oedema precipitated by underlying heart problems).

Losing a child is the worst thing that can happen to you. Sandy and his wife Sheila were incredibly brave. Sandy spoke movingly about Scott at the funeral. He even managed to make us smile through our tears with one-line quotes from Spike Milligan, Scott's favourite comedian. Scott's two siblings, Neil and Sheona, and his partner, Tia Hastie, were for a long time inconsolable. But shared grief can—and, in this case, did—create lasting bonds. Since his death Tia has been a source of strength and support to Sheona's children (Scott's nephews and niece).

Birth and death are part of the natural cycle of life, and good news often follows bad. Four months later, on Sunday April 15, Catriona (my youngest daughter) had her second boy, weighing in at 7 lbs 15 ozs. He was to be called David, after the father she never really knew who (like her cousin Scott) had died at 34. The baby's middle name would be Alexander after my own father, who died when I was fourteen. Baby David was my seventh grandchild, and yet the feeling of wonder and relief was just as strong with each new arrival.

Catriona decided to take a year off work to look after her two wee boys. When she returned to her job as a Crown Office Fiscal with responsibility for staff, she was asked how confident she felt after a year at home with children.

'I've had the best training ever,' she said. 'I've coped with a new baby, and the Terrible Twos. What more experience do I need?'

I agreed wholeheartedly.

With Catriona at home for a year and Kirsty working part-time, we spent a lot of our time visiting each other. I also visited Fiona's new house in Eastleigh, and nipped down to look after Cameron while she went for an interview.

Life was hectic for the girls and their families and I helped as much as I could. I tried not to think how much better it could have been if John had only been alive.

Then something unexpected happened. It was something that would never have occurred if I hadn't been a widow. An email arrived from my old friend Janette, my St Andrews' University Wardlaw Wing room-mate. She, like me, had met and married a fellow St Andrews student. For forty years, they had lived in Canada while Neil grew his successful business and Janette looked after the home and their two children and in her spare time trained as a stockbroker. We had kept in touch on and off and had met up a few times when she visited Scotland.

But life can change fast. Janette was recently divorced, and angry with her husband's decision to leave her for another woman.

Here, out of the blue, was an email from her inviting me to visit in Toronto in July. Should I go?

I had never been on a long-haul flight, with or without a companion, although by now I had flown solo to Southampton many times. Until recently, my holidays had been activity-type events, camping, skiing, sailing or family holidays with children, sea and sand. The question was—would I *enjoy* a trip to Canada? I knew Janette was fun (or used to be) and we were both now single again so why not? Was I up for an unknown adventure?

Yes I was! I decided to break the bank and go Business Class to soften the experience of travelling alone for such a long journey. What a wonderful experience the flight turned out to be, starting with being ushered first onto the plane to seat 1A and offered a drink while a hostess took care of my jacket and hand-luggage. A delicious three-course meal with wine was served in flight and I can remember having fillet steak, one of my favourites. I watched the film *Mrs Doubtfire* for the first time, fell asleep and before I knew it, the plane was landing in Toronto.

I was first off the plane as well, but Janette wasn't there to meet me.

Fifteen minutes later, there was still no sign of her.

An hour later all the other passengers had gone and I was sitting outside the airport with one sole companion—my big suitcase. I discovered that my cell phone didn't work in Canada, and asked this chap who had just joined me on the bench if I might borrow his. Without any hesitation at all, he replied, 'No!'

Hmmpph! I was rapidly going off Canada and Canadians, and decided to lug my big suitcase into the airport and look for help. Thank goodness they spoke English at least. I saw a sign saying

'Customer Services', and headed straight for it. They phoned Janette, she answered and I was able to speak to her. 'Where are you?' I demanded. (Note lack of expletives: the Customer Service staff were listening.)

It transpired she had misread the time of arrival in my email as 18.40 not 16.40. What a numpty!

I treated myself to a coffee and very soon a two-seater Mercedes sports car arrived to pick me up. The image was spoiled just a little when Janette emerged from the car leaning on a stick (she'd had a hip operation not long before).

It wasn't a very practical car either—I could barely get my suitcase in the back, but it felt good as we sped along the Canadian highways to her townhouse in Thornhill.

From then on, it was a holiday unlike any I'd ever had. No responsibility for me. We simply talked and talked—we had forty years to catch up on. Food, even breakfast, simply happened when we felt like it. I didn't much like her breakfast offerings, so we headed for *The Three Coins* for as much coffee and tea and water as we wanted while choosing from a menu chalked in large letters on a board. The walls were covered with pictures of Marilyn Monroe.

As we listened to Elvis booming 'Jailhouse Rock' from the juke box, I was transported back to the fifties, to the Café de la Paix in Hillhead in Glasgow when Heather, Angela, Christine and I sat there after the Girl Guides on a Friday night drinking coke and smoking cigarettes.

The morning passed quickly as we listened to the Beatles, and even Bill Haley and the Comets while we got stuck into eggs, bacon, pancakes, maple syrup and fries. Now *that's* what I call a breakfast experience!

I stayed for two weeks and in that time saw some interesting parts of Ontario, including Markdale, the winter home of John's Wormit sailing buddy, Sandy Harvey. After Lis died, he lived in Canada in the winter but in the summer months he returned to Scotland to his family, his old friends and the other great love of his life, his keelboat Aurora. Since he wasn't in residence himself, he'd arranged for us to have the keys and we stayed in his house for a couple of nights while we explored the Bruce Peninsula, Hope Bay, Lion's Head, the Sauble Falls and, of course, Tobermory.

I was amazed by the frequency of familiar Scottish town names in Canada, and the diversity of churches. The history of settlers from Scotland was round every corner. Each time we visited a gift shop or a craft shop, I always had the children at the back of my mind and I spent hours choosing little gifts I thought would interest them.

We also decided we should leave a thank-you gift for Sandy. I knew he liked Harvey's Bristol Cream Sherry and so of course I had a bottle of that for him, but when we spotted two little wooden dollies, our eyes lit up. Great minds thinking alike and grinning from ear to ear, we bought them and before our departure carefully laid them on Sandy's bed with a note, 'Thank you for having us!' This made us cackle all the way to Niagara-on-the-Lake, and hopefully it cheered Sandy up when he arrived home to his Lis-less house.

Niagara-on-the-Lake was an interesting little town, not as well-known as it probably should be because it was there that the first anti-slavery legislation in the British Empire was passed. We even got chatted up when we went for lunch but decided that Janette's Mercedes was probably the real attraction.

When we visited Toronto, I commented on the fact that everyone was walking about with a coffee in one hand. Why?

Janette didn't answer, just guided me into the nearest Starbucks and asked me what *kind* of coffee I wanted. Wicked woman! She knew perfectly well that in 2007 I didn't know there were different kinds. We held the queue up for ages while I hummed and hawed, not having a clue what to choose. I settled for a black coffee with cold milk. I had never heard of an 'Americano'.

It was with mixed feelings that I finally boarded the plane home. I knew I would miss Janette's fun company but I also knew I'd missed my family dreadfully. The good news was that all three of my daughters were going on holiday with their families to Marbella in October, each with their own apartment but in the same block. And I was going with them.

In fact, I shared Catriona and Keith's apartment, so that I could help with David, only six months old at the time. I had a continual stream of small visitors (which naturally had nothing to do with my secret drawer full of sweets, tricks, cards and mysteries). Most of my time was spent swimming with various grandchildren in the indoor swimming pool, or pushing David in his pram to lull him to sleep. Apart from a sickness bug attacking various members of our group at different times (almost inevitable when there are seven children), we had a great time.

When it rained, we visited a safari park. When the sun shone, there was Villacana and Puerto Banus, where we watched the rich at play with their designer gear and luxury yachts.

Annabel, two at the time, will probably not remember the new blue size four Crocs which she wore day and night throughout the two weeks. The three older ones (Ali, Jenny and Thomas) were old enough to join in the kids' football and Thomas won the award for scoring most goals. Although Jenny didn't like football and wouldn't play, she knew the name of everyone there, and Ali (two years older but failing to score any goals at all) was awarded 'Man of the Match' by the diplomatic Kids Holiday Rep. Cameron and James, both nearly three, played happily in the sand.

We hadn't been home long when another amazing email invitation arrived for me. When I read it, I could barely believe it. My former work colleague—June Smith—had once been my saviour at Glenrothes College at a time when I wasn't coping well, and here she was about to rescue me again. Would I like to visit her and George in Botswana for two weeks after Christmas?

Ever since John died I had dreaded New Year. This would be a brilliant opportunity and I would still be back in time for the start of the school term and the childcare. To tell you the truth, I had no idea where Botswana was—but that was a mere detail. I had worked with both George and June for most of my college life, George as a fellow section leader for many years and June in the Communication Faculty. Although they were a couple, they were both unique individuals to me.

Aware of June's spirit of enterprise and adventure, and her organisation skills, I knew she would plan an amazing itinerary.

And so she did.

Chapter 49: Botswana

The kindly travel agent in Inverkeithing had arranged the journey to make it as easy as possible. From Glasgow to Dubai to Johannesburg to Windhoek ... where June and George would meet me. Easy-peasy?

I didn't think so. Heather and Stewart would see me off and George and June were going to meet me but—what about the bit in-between? I wasn't exactly a seasoned traveller. So yes, actually I was terrified.

When I arrived in Dubai, my eyes kept popping out of my head. I was used to the mainly white, middle-class families of Wormit and Dalgety Bay. But here the men were dressed in white 'thobes' (long, loose, white robe-style garments) and the women in burkhas. Even I, ignorant as I was, could spot the difference between well-off and not so well-off ladies by the quality of their burkhas. Some were made of beautiful silky material with discrete, exquisite embroidery, while others were simple and plain.

From Dubai I flew to Johannesburg and from there to Windhoek. After my experience with Janette failing to meet me in Toronto, I was apprehensive, and heartily relieved to see June and George waiting for me at the airport. They had three weeks holiday from work around the Christmas period, the first of which they had spent together. Now they were spending the next two weeks with me!

So I had arrived safely and found my hosts. That was the main worry over, I would be fine now. Our first meal in a restaurant was a first in every sense (like so much of my holiday)—crocodile meat with monkey gland sauce and a glass or two of Pinot Grigio to wash it down. I remember it as delicious, but I was starving and—perhaps it *was*?

I hadn't enjoyed New Year celebrations since John died. However hard I tried, I found it an emotional time. Memories of loved ones kept resurfacing. If there was dancing, that made it even worse (I had loved to dance with John so very much).

But New Year in Africa did the trick. On December 30, June, George and I drove across the Kalahari to Swakamund on the Namibian coast. It was a beautiful resort, with its pink sands and salt pans. The following evening (Hogmanay) we sat in a restaurant built on stilts, with a view of the picturesque Walvis Bay, tucking into the most mouth-watering seafood platter I have ever tasted, while we watched literally thousands of flamingos and pelicans flying overhead.

After the meal, the guests, the waiters and waitresses danced to the music blaring out from upstairs. No partners required—just dance badly, with abandon, and enjoy the music! There were Afrikaners, Germans and Namibians and, of course, June and I 'giein it laldie'—not to mention George.

To sing Auld Lang Syne (albeit two hours before the new year arrived in Scotland) in such mixed and friendly company filled me with powerful and happy feelings. I slept soundly that night, not wakening until late the next day.

What else had June got planned for the three of us? On the second day of January, we set off for Etosha, a National Wild Life Safari Park. George had to drive for six hours on a long, straight, dry and constantly rising road. At one point we were 5000 feet high and the temperature was 35 degrees. Our luxury hotel in Etosha was located beside a waterhole in the 2000 square miles of parkland.

Having been brought up in Glasgow, studying nature from a radio programme, my knowledge of wildlife was non-existent. I don't think as a child I'd ever even been to the zoo. Sitting at the waterhole in Etosha in the darkness of the evening was my first taste of spotting wild animals. To start with I found it really difficult to see anything at all, but I soon learned to look for the slightest movement. I absolutely loved the giraffes, the most cautious, timid, fragile-looking creatures ever. They would approach tentatively. Slowly, and step by step, they would look in every direction, stopping at every turn to listen intensely. Then, more often than not, they'd turn around and retreat. Sometimes a lion, the king of the jungle, would appear shortly afterwards. But giraffes, like the rest of us, must drink sooner or later, and when potential predators had finally gone, they would return as slowly and hesitantly as before. Watching their legs fold and cross, as their long necks somehow reached the water—for me, this was an absolute wonder!

On our safari the next day, we were lucky enough to come across female lions in a culvert. George parked his car nearby and we just sat and waited. Guess what? In a forty-minute time span, the lionesses paid at least *eight* visits (for mating purposes) to the male lion not far away. I swear I heard George mutter under his breath, 'lucky bugger'—but he's always denied it—and who am I to disagree with my host, chauffeur and one-time fellow section leader?

As we drove through Etosha Park, we were stopped at one point by zebras blocking the road. Not a zebra crossing, then, but zebras crossing?

With the help of George and June, I managed to spot a kudu, a black-faced impala, a red hartebeest, and a steenbok which looked just like Bambi. (I couldn't wait to tell my grandchildren that I'd seen Bambi.) I loved the baby elephants too. I watched them travel around in packs, all of them female and led by an older experienced matriarch. The young elephants only stay with the herd until they're mature.

And as for the older males, when it comes to mating time, they don't hang around after the deed is done. They're off and away, leaving the females to take on the nurturing role.

I certainly had no problems spotting elephants. They were huge—approximately three metres tall, and at least two and a half tons in weight. The elephant procession had a majestic look. Each beast walked slowly and regally, taking its place in a long line, with the young ones holding on to their mums' tails.

Next day we set off for Rindu and the Caprivi Strip. On the way we passed small settlements, with women carrying water jugs on their heads and selling pots and small woodcarvings from roadside stalls. When we finally found a reasonably priced bed for the night at the Ngepi Camp, I learned we were to sleep in a bush hut. I was no stranger to ordinary camping, but this would certainly be another first.

As we stood at the Camping Reception, we heard one of the other campers graphically describe an experience at night. She had woken up in the middle of the night to find a hippo at her door—or, to be more specific, at her entrance (there was no door).

My bush hut had two single beds and June and George were in the next hut. There were no doors or windows—just a stone floor with an open shower and a loo outside. Visiting the loo during the night, I found it hard to avoid thinking about lizards, snakes and mosquitoes but I resolutely never looked down and survived to tell the tale. June had clearly seen how scared I was. At about midnight, she slipped into the other single bed to reassure me, just in case a hippo did show up. That was a never-to-be-forgotten act of kindness! Mind you, I'm not sure exactly what she would have done if one *had* arrived. Same as me—run?

It was twenty-five years since I'd been on a canoe in Loch Morlich with college students—but that was a piece of cake compared to our canoe trip down the Okavango with our guide, Cosmos. His mission must have been both to entertain and scare the living daylights out of us.

And he did. He stopped rowing to allow us to watch a croc slither off the sandbank on which we were about to land. At one point, we were thirty metres away from not one—not two—not three—but *four* hippos. I couldn't help but notice some children playing in the water at the edge of the river. The attraction to water was of course understandable because it was so hot—but it was so *very* dangerous.

Thankfully our guide delivered us safely back to the camp, promising to take us to see his village nearby in the afternoon. It was run by the Grandma, the matriarch, and Cosmos told us to give our 'donation' to her. Otherwise, he said, he would end up spending it in the Shebeen, a kind of bar that was the centre and focal point of the village. Here the men, many of them AIDS victims, drank copiously.

In each village, there was huts and one special one, with a barrel for beer-making, as well as tin containers of various sizes for scooping, measuring and tasting the brew. There was nothing else. Just litter, a pot, some bowls and one small child dipping his fingers hungrily into a dish of white gruel covered with what looked like little black ants. Outside, the other children kicked a football about. I was horrified. I'd never seen such poverty. But the children were full of smiles; they looked happy and friendly.

The following day we set off on the next part of our trip, the 300-kilometre journey to June and George's home in Francistown, where George was working in the brand-newly-built college. Eat your heart out Glenrothes College—it was a state-of-the-art building, both inside and out. They had no worn-out computers for their 'Computer Support' course and had to buy new ones just to take them apart and build them up again. Staff had ample time, too, to develop teaching materials.

School teaching jobs were reserved for Botswanians only, but June had realised there were things she could do to help. On a recent visit home, she'd collected much needed batteries for the solar panel that provided the electricity for the school's only television. She'd also brought calculators, pencils and footballs for the pupils. I knew this, so I'd also brought a supply from Dalgety Bay, and we went together to give them to the pupils at Matsitama School.

The teacher at Matsitama told me how the first time June visited the schoolchildren, they burst out laughing and couldn't stop. What were they laughing at? Well, they had never seen a white person with red hair before. Perhaps they had never seen a white person, come to that. I'm sure they would have something to tell their mums when they went home that night.

June wasn't entirely convinced that the batteries wouldn't be appropriated for the Head Teacher's personal television. She planned to go back at a later date to make sure they were actually being used for the solar panel.

On my last evening in Francistown, I met some of June and George's friends. It was fascinating to hear about their lifestyles—completely different from my safe life in Dalgety Bay. The main topics of the evening were the challenge of security, and the fear of burglary. The next day June drove me to Gabarone to catch the plane home.

My hosts couldn't possibly have packed any more into my two-week visit. It was utterly brilliant!

Chapter 50: Dalgety Bay—The Years Go By

I thoroughly relished telling the kids and my Dalgety Bay visitors all about my African adventures. I brandished my holiday photos until they were bored to tears.

The years went by. I fitted visits from old friends and family around my childcare commitments. For example, Angela and I spent a nostalgic weekend in Glasgow exploring old haunts. But she and I also had a totally unexpected piece of good fortune when Catriona invited us to go to Carlton Bingo Hall in Fife Leisure Park in Dunfermline.

With obvious reluctance Angela agreed, possibly thinking it was 'beneath her'. I noticed she didn't tell her partner, or her sister—or indeed anyone at all—where she was going. When we arrived we got our 'Dobbers' and settled in to mark our cards. But first, according to the custom, we agreed to share our winnings. The numbers were called fast and furious and if you lost concentration for a second, you missed them.

Lucky Number Seven!
Knock at the Door—Number Four!
Cup of Tea—Number Three!
Man Alive—Number Five!
Garden Gate—Number Eight!

Angela and I were just getting the hang of it, when we heard Catriona shout 'BINGO!' We didn't realise at the time (but she did) that it was a regional competition with a big regional prize. She was to collect it at the end of the session.

You simply won't believe this—but what a windfall! It totalled £2800. That was £933 each, and it had only cost us a tenner. We had trouble taking it in. Angela, by now, was a lot more enthusiastic about bingo. We had struck lucky. *That* was exciting.

When we told Keith, my son-in-law, that we'd won something, he started by asking if it was a fiver. From there, he increased his guess by tens. We finally got bored with the guessing game and just told him. I'd never won any money before, and I've never won any since. But easy come, easy go. I phoned my family and invited those who were around to join me for a free (to them) meal at Aberdour Hotel. My lasting memory is my brother Sandy asking, 'Can I really have a steak?'

I noticed Angela was now keen to tell her friends at home all about her Bingo Adventure.

I still kept in close touch with my Wormit friends as well. Pat and I visited each other, and Jan and David asked us both for dinner. On one memorable occasion, Pat, Jan and I spent a Saturday in Edinburgh helping Pat to buy an outfit for her son's wedding. Pat didn't 'do' fashionable clothes (one of the many things we had in common) and had no idea how prices had risen since she'd last bought anything. It proved an almost impossible task to find something she liked at a price she was prepared to pay. Before long, Jan and I would have paid for it ourselves if it had meant we could stop trailing from shop to shop and go for a coffee.

Needless to say, we didn't. Buying clothes with Pat, nevertheless, pushed our friendship to the limit. She may have been a loyal friend, wonderful mother and a highly competent A&E doctor, but she was the most infuriating shopper I have ever known.

John's daughter Jane used to visit me too, and we sometimes met for lunch. Once she brought Cath, John's sister. Every year after Christmas, both families would get together, either in Dalgety Bay at my place or in St Andrews at Jane's. I think we preferred Jane's because she was—and is—such a brilliant cook. How delighted John would have been to see the different generations from both families bonding so well and enjoying each other's company.

Throughout my life, my Glasgow friends have always been around, one way or the other. Fridays were frequently prioritised for Glasgow or Edinburgh lunches with Heather and Christine. One of my worst decisions, however, was being persuaded by Heather to participate in a Glasgow Girls' High School Golf competition. It was a woeful occasion for me because my golf was still awful and I suffered the ignominy of being awarded the Booby Prize. As a result, what little confidence I had gained simply disappeared overnight. I certainly never ever *ever* played again in that competition.

About this time, another former school friend—Diane—had returned from Newcastle to live in Pittenweem. Since she now lived so much nearer, we worked together on preparing a DVD for our 'Glasgow School Jolly' in London in 2009—nine of us meeting to celebrate knowing each other since schooldays in 1954.

Diane and I even made a trip to the school itself (girls-only in our day but now mixed and private and named 'The Glasgow High School'). Here we were given access to the Alumni section and took a photo of ourselves in our old school hats and scarves. We poured over school magazines and memorabilia and giggled like the school kids we once were as we prepared a spiel about each of our nine classmates: Heather, Diane, Doreen, Angela, Janet, Jean, Liz and Pat and *me*.

I sat for hours in the evening struggling with the technology for the DVD, and Keith, my son-in-law, helped us quite a bit, especially with the sound. Our best (and worst) struggle was recording the school song. I can't remember how many attempts there were but definitely too many. The piano that my mother once played in the drawing room of Colebrooke Terrace took a real battering.

Diane was the pianist (because of her MS, her dexterity wasn't the best but she was the only one who knew which notes to play) and we both sang the words of the school song. Our DVD told the story of the nine of us who were going to be in London for our reunion dinner, with photos of us all from the age of seven onwards drawn from our yearly school magazines.

Our sound technician (son-in-law Keith) recorded our favourite hits of the time, and now and again there was a bit of commentary from Diane. The DVD finale was to be the recording of the school song, the idea being that after our London dinner and lubricated by wine, everyone would join in. Which, in due course, they certainly did.

The date for the reunion arrived, and we all met up in London as arranged. After dinner and a few glasses of wine, Diane and I proudly played our DVD. Talk about reminiscing! We made merry for hours and had to be reminded by the staff that there were other guests in the hotel trying to sleep. Shocking I know, but fun. Thank goodness the hotel had given us a dining room to ourselves.

In fact, I was well into making DVDs in these years. I learned by trial and error—mostly errors really—and with frequent mistakes having to be sorted by an ever-patient Keith. I made one for Kirsty on her fortieth in 2010 which included photos, videos, music and commentaries about her life hitherto; and one for Fiona in Southampton in 2011. I didn't really like sitting all alone in my huge sitting room when the children had gone home. It was so much better to have a project to absorb me in the evening.

Elizabeth and Craig, and Sandy and Sheila visited me too during these years and we enjoyed catching up with family news. Once, when James, Annabel and David were playing together in my study, I heard them suddenly start screaming. I rushed to find out what was happening.

A strange looking creature, dressed like a spaceman, his features partly hidden in a balaclava, was pressing his face against the window. No wonder the kids were terrified! A lifelong lover of sailing, with his keel-boat moored in Blackhall, my brother Sandy had decided to sail across the River Forth. After anchoring in the little bay opposite, he plodded across the road and peered in. The children were only calmed down once it was revealed that the monster really was Uncle Sandy grinning from underneath his layers of sailing clothes.

It wasn't long after this, that Kirsty and Richard decided to move north. I thought it was a good move for them and by the summer of 2010 they were settled outside Kinross. Since Annabel wasn't at school yet, and Ali and Jenny were still at primary school, I now travelled between Kinross and Dalgety Bay for my childcare duties. I was also visiting Fiona as often as I could in Southampton, and she and the boys loved coming to Dalgety Bay—although it wasn't quite the same as when all the cousins lived within walking distance.

But nothing ever stays the same. I knew that better than anyone. Before long, Catriona too had changed her job and they were planning to move to the Kinross/Milnathort area. For about a year I lived a nomadic life, staying over with whichever family needed me, while carrying on my own life in Dalgety Bay. I was lucky: I only had myself to consider. But once again I was faced with tricky choices and decisions. Should I remain in Dalgety Bay or would it be better to move to Kinross?

I thought about it long and hard. The most important people in my life were my children and I had already bonded firmly with my grandchildren too. I enjoyed being part of their life. I could still be useful because all four parents were working very hard. If I spent less time travelling, and bought a house and garden with minimum maintenance, I would be readily accessible for after-school care and also have more time (and money) to travel and enjoy myself. I was 68, young enough to cope with a move. I put my house up for sale.

To my great surprise (and despite the adverse publicity at the time about radioactive particles found on Dalgety Bay beach nearby), I found a buyer quickly. All the same, I was grieved to leave my lovely neighbours, the Vroliks: good neighbours are like gold. But I'd already moved house at least nine times in my life. How hard could it be to do it once more?

What I knew for sure was that location was everything. This time I knew exactly what I was looking for. First, I had to get rid of masses of possessions that I didn't need and no longer wanted.

My children, who now lived in bigger houses, were more than delighted to give a home to some of Granny Wilson's rather grand old Victorian furniture from Colebrooke Terrace. The piano my mother used to play was sent to Fiona and Paul in Southampton to bring some music into their house.

Then there was my mother's bedroom suite, given to her as a wedding present in 1938. When it didn't fit into Mum's sheltered house in Newport, Catriona had offered to have it in her Wormit bedroom—that way, when Granny came to visit she could sleep in her own familiar bed. Guess where that furniture ended up? Yes—

in Catriona and Keith's new house in Milnathort. The grandfather clock went to Richard and Kirsty because I knew they would nurture it. I organised for the piano to be tuned, the grandfather clock to be checked and the bedroom furniture to be french-polished and, where necessary, refurbished.

What about my wall of books? I carefully went through them. I kept reference books, and books belonging to my father, and to my brother Jimmy who died so young. I couldn't bear to part with some of my favourite authors and children's classics like *Anne of Green Gables*. I also kept old and possibly valuable and irreplaceable books. The rest I gave away.

My glamorous and fashionable friend Angela helped me clear out my clothes. She didn't mince her words. 'How long have you had that? *Bin*! That? You can't possibly wear it! Don't even bother to send *that* to a charity shop?'

And so we filled black bin-bag after black bin-bag. It wasn't long until I ended up with a modest wardrobe of garments I might actually wear.

Meanwhile, in my attic, there were boxes untouched since moving from Wormit in 2004. In principle, I didn't need any of them but naturally I still had to check through them. I had five criteria when it came to deciding whether to stow or throw.

1. Would it increase significantly in value?

2. Was it of sentimental value?

3. Was it of historical interest?

4. Was it of practical use to me or someone I could give it to?

5. In my new house, was there ANYWHERE TO PUT IT?

Meanwhile, I was journeying between Dalgety Bay and Kinross to help with the children when their parents were at work. Each time I passed the charity CHAS, I dropped off a load of stuff, and so slowly—very slowly—I cleared my house. After a while, there was no emotion attached to parting with possessions, simply relief that I'd finally got rid of yet another unwanted box. Anyone who has downsized will recognise this feeling.

John and Lucy's sitting-room suite—which had been re-upholstered at least twice over its forty-year life span and had been jumped on, and occasionally even sat on, by John's children (Amanda and Jane), his grandchildren (Jamie, Katie and Stuart), my children (Kirsty, Fiona and Catriona) and indeed my seven grandchildren (Ali, Jenny, Thomas, Cameron, James, Annabel and David)—*finally* went to the tip.

It was all very well selling my house and getting rid of possessions but I still needed somewhere to live in Kinross; it had to be the right house for me. Fortunately, Catriona and Keith's new house in Milnathort had a spare bedroom with an ensuite and a study. I was happy to stay there until I found something suitable. My presence made it easier for Catriona to get to her new job in the morning. It was win-win.

By May 2012, I had bought a three-bedroomed bungalow in Lathro Park, Kinross. It was near the High School, the bus stop, the swimming pool, the golf courses, the shops and the Health Centre. I had a family bathroom and my own tiny ensuite bathroom—ideal if I had visitors. All the same, the house wasn't quite big enough to host the whole family. So—with Diane's help again—I decided to install a conservatory. My new addition stretched the full length of the rear of the property. Once that was done, I had an elastic home: it could expand when I needed it and shrink back to a cosy size when I was on my own. Perfect!

But what was life in Kinross going to be like? I knew I'd like being close to my daughters and grandchildren. That was a given. Another plus was the fact that my brother Sandy and his wife Sheila lived in nearby Milnathort.

On the downside, I'd miss being close to my sister Elizabeth who lived near me in Dalgety Bay. For me at least, life is almost always swings and roundabouts. A good experience is often balanced by one of the opposite kind.

What did the future have lined up for me this time?

Chapter 51: Losses & Gains

My new house was rather bare, I had only two bean bags to sit on. After school, the girls used my new large, and still unfurnished, conservatory as a dance studio. Slowly it began to take shape but there were one or two hiccups. My tea sets had all gone to CHAS, apart from my mother's wedding tea set which was in Kirsty's attic. I hadn't used cups and saucers for thirty years but—horror of horrors—I was invited to take part in putting on an afternoon tea with all the paraphernalia that goes with it. Kirsty had to retrieve the china tea set.

I would have *so* loved sharing this experience with my Wormit buddy Pat Morton. How she would have laughed at my predicament! But she wasn't there any longer. Pat had died of cancer in St Andrews Community Hospital. She was a daughter of the manse with a deep personal faith, so her funeral was a church ceremony where the minister read from her personal writing, and her youngest son Douglas confirmed, through a range of funny stories, what a devoted mother she had been.

She wasn't the only Wormit friend to go. Sandy Harvey's lungs had finally petered out. We watched his three sons set sail from Wormit Boating Club to scatter his ashes in the River Tay—a fitting farewell for a sailor. Both Sandy and Pat had been in their sixties—far too young to die. They left gaps that couldn't be filled. Our former dream-plan for seven of us to share a retirement home one day was shattered once and for all. Only three of the TGIF Wormit gang remained—me, Jan, and David Winch.

Thank goodness for all the cheery children in my daily life. In many ways, I felt glad I had moved away from Wormit—so much had changed there. And yet here I was living in yet another house in yet another place, after only eight years in Dalgety Bay (which was a mere half hour from Kinross). Most folk thought I was off my head. But that was nothing new, and easily ignored.

Why did I do it? My reasons were sound and mainly to do with quality of life. I wanted to be a useful childminder for the next generation and that was easier and more practical when I lived locally. All seven of my grandchildren were now at school, even the youngest (David), who had just started Primary 1. Some of them would come to my house for breakfast, as well as after school on certain days. Then there were in-service days, and school holidays, and days when they were unwell.

Contrary to expectation, I loved the 'sickie' days and so did they*. With only myself to look after, I found it not a chore but a treat—a pleasurable experience to pander to the needs of a not really *very* poorly grandchild. On one occasion, James (aged twelve) was off school and I had an appointment at the opticians in Glenrothes. It was important to me not to miss this, for very good reasons. I have glaucoma and in order to keep my driving licence, I have to pass a Field Vision Eye Test every three years.

So the two of us set off together, James coughing occasionally. Just as we were approaching Loch Leven Larder, I put my foot on the clutch to change gear and—there was a horrible grinding noise. My wee red Fiat Panda ground to a halt, leaving us stuck in the middle of the road.

With difficulty, James and I pushed the car to the verge and I phoned for help. I also rescheduled my eye appointment. Thanks to a mobile phone and Green Flag rescue assistance, our breakdown was less stressful than back in the sixties. When assistance arrived, the car couldn't be repaired at the roadside, but it was duly loaded onto a recovery vehicle while we sat in the front.

For James, the day was turning out to be considerably more interesting than anticipated—*so* much better than going to school or sitting around Specsavers while I had my eyes tested. We were dropped off at my door in Lathro, in good time for David's arrival from school at 3.00 p.m. Meanwhile, my car was towed away to the garage to be fixed.

And the good news? James was well enough to go to school next day, his cough having miraculously disappeared. Neither of us could understand where it went.

Childcare during school holidays is always a challenge for working parents. By 2012, Catriona (my youngest daughter and mother of James and David), was Procurator Fiscal, Sheriff and Jury North. In this post she was responsible for court cases in the entire North Federation and she wanted to visit her staff as far north as Wick and Orkney—but it was school holidays.

Since her husband Keith had to work too, she and I came up with a plan. My former college boss, John Carder, was fond of the maxim: 'Mix business with pleasure whenever possible'. We followed his advice and rented a holiday house in John o' Groats. I would entertain the boys during the day when Catriona was working, and she would be there in the evening.

It was a brilliant break for me, and the boys were still young enough to share my interests enthusiastically. We spent hours, for example, at Skara Brae, one of my favourite places.

It had changed and improved enormously since I'd visited it in 1969, not long after David died. For a start there was a café now—definitely an attraction. The boys enjoyed getting a sense of life five thousand years ago in a stone village, when boar and wild deer roamed the hills, and the folk ate wild berries, and sea birds and their eggs. As I sat clutching my paper coffee cup, they tried, with not a great deal of success, to build their own house with stones from the beach.

We visited a nineteenth-century farming croft too. That gave us an idea of life without supermarkets, transport, telly—even a phone. Living without electricity, growing your own food, collecting your water, making your own bread and clothes—this was a novel idea to a twenty-first century child. None of us fancied it much. We agreed we liked our modern comforts.

We were based in John o' Groats and I was determined to swim at Dunnet Head, the most northern point of Scotland. To this end I had brought my own wetsuit and Catriona had borrowed two for David and James. These didn't fit; they were too small, and I think the boys were pretty uncomfortable—but we did swim. Like little Trojans, the kids bore the whole experience with fortitude. Even with wetsuits it was cold, and there were no amenities like changing rooms or hot drinks. Never again!

We looked unsuccessfully for sightings of puffins, guillemots and fulmars, perhaps some of them flying south from St Kilda. But no luck. However, just down the road from where we were staying was Puffin Farm, recently featured in Ben Fogle's TV programme *New Lives in the Wild*. The boys loved the animals. Also they had never before come across a shop with an 'honesty box' instead of a shopkeeper.

It reminded me of Aunt Isabel in the fifties when we were on a Glasgow tram together and the clippie hadn't collected my fare. Isabel, not the clippie, held up the whole 'get aff the caur' queue while she ensured I put the correct fare in the red honesty box. She was without doubt an excellent role model.

This was the same worthy Aunt Isabel who had long ago taken Elizabeth, Mum and me on a girly holiday to St Andrews and, as they say, history often repeats itself. So when an opportunity arose during the school vacation for *me* to take my oldest daughter Kirsty and her two daughters, Jenny and Annabel, away on holiday, I seized it.

It was the summer of 2014 and Kirsty had a week's break but her husband Richard and their son Alistair were going to a sailing event. Kirsty, Jenny, Annabel and I—all desperate for a little sun— booked a bargain week in Tunisia.

The girls, Jenny (aged twelve) and Annabel (aged nine) were delighted not to be hanging around sailing venues. They were a joy to be with as they literally danced all around the room in the Premier Inn. They couldn't wait to go on an aeroplane, and stay in a hotel where they could choose what they wanted to eat.

I loved every minute of that trip. It wasn't very warm (there was a chilly wind) but the swimming pool was certainly warmer than the now defunct open-air pools of my youth. I swam outside every day and Jenny followed my lead. Kirsty and Annabel were not so intrepid and much preferred the indoor pool.

We all went to the market, which was a bit scary because the stall holders could be aggressive if you dared to walk away from their stall without buying anything. Wisely, we followed our travel company's advice and stuck closely to the guide. Jenny was over the moon when she managed to buy a fake designer bag at a bargain price. It never left her side for the rest of the holiday! And you can't go to Tunisia without going on a camel so we did just that, with little Annabel hoisted up to sit in front while Kirsty hung onto her tightly from behind.

At home, I also had a lot of pleasure on my childminding excursions. This was simply because I took the kids to places that I wanted to go to myself. Wouldn't you?

Accordingly, just before Annabel and James started High School, I bribed them with coke and cakes to pay a visit to the newly renovated Carnegie Museum in Dunfermline. David, being the youngest, was probably more open to the idea. This was fortunate because he was never a bribable child.

Among other interesting bits of history in the museum, we saw pictures of twelve-year-olds—and even younger children—working like adults in textiles and in the mines. Tongue-in-cheek, I suggested that going to school—even a new one—wasn't as scary as working in a mine.

My life in Kinross was improving steadily.

Chapter 52: We Become A Formidable Family Gang

Our family get-togethers were generally much enjoyed, I think. There were now so *many* of us—seven grandchildren, six adults and, of course, me. And quite often we made a trip as a family party, some of them more ambitious than others.

And not everything always went to plan. Once (and only once) we managed to get everyone together to see the sights of London, although on the first night we were unnerved by what seemed to be an earthquake. The building was vibrating and juddering, the coffee mugs rattling on the table. How could we have known that the four-level property sat above Edgware Road Underground? Those on the ground floor didn't sleep too well. And to this day they can tell you the times of the early morning underground trains. Was that possibly why it was such a bargain price?

On the occasion of our trip to the open-air museum in Beamish in County Durham, I'm not sure any of the family—even my own children—realised that although this was history for them, it was remembered reality for me. All too well, I recognised the trams (from my fifties childhood), the dentist's foot treadle drill (an excruciatingly painful experience), an old-fashioned sweetie shop, a draper's shop, and bicycles without gears.

Then in July 2013, the excursion was farther afield. I was invited to my niece's wedding in Poland but the invitation was for me and a 'plus one'. The whole family was going: my three girls, their husbands and the seven grandchildren. What should I do? Travel on my own, or with one of the families, or seek out a partner? Then I had a brainwave—I would ask Heather. She knew all my family and ever since 1958 she'd always been up for an adventure.

And so at 6.00 a.m. on 26 July, we boarded our flight to Krakow. It turned out to be a whirlwind weekend. Fiona, Paul and their boys Cameron and Thomas had arrived ahead of us. We had a bit of time for some local tourism. Where did we decide to go? To the World War II concentration camp at Auschwitz. I was concerned about traumatising the boys but the sun was shining and—I don't know why—that made a real difference.

In photographs and in the film *Schindler's List*, the camp always looked dark, dismal, wet, and gloomy. But standing in a queue in sunshine, chatting to the boys about their football and the wedding to come—somehow this made the experience OK. Nonetheless, seeing the gas chambers, the watch towers and the death block, it was—and still is—impossible for us to comprehend the scale and the horror of the holocaust. It was the little things that brought tears to my eyes—the child's doll, a little girl's dress, the evil obligatory Star of David patch, and the baby shoes.

Thomas (aged eleven) didn't believe that he was looking at the actual hair of the holocaust victims—he still remembers feeling sick at the thought. But seeing the rest of our family waiting for us when we returned to the hotel, we managed to put all that behind us. Our relatives were all so healthy, so exhaustingly full of beans and energy and vitality—it made me yet again count my blessings. It took about five minutes for all seven grandchildren to escape to the hotel garden, while we grown-ups made haste to the bar.

Heather and I knew we were unlikely to return to Poland so next morning we decided to make the most of our time. After a delicious breakfast, we asked Reception whether we had time to visit the 700-year-old Wieliczka Salt Mines before the afternoon wedding. We did, they said, but only if we moved fast. Within fifteen minutes there was a pick-up driver waiting for us. He drove at what felt like a hundred miles per hour.

When we arrived, thankful still to be alive and too terrified to speak, there was a long queue. Our driver took one look, said a few words in Polish and escorted us to the front of the line, where he talked animatedly to the doorman. I don't know what he said, but we were fast forwarded. Within minutes we were struggling down the 380 steps required to reach the first of nine levels.

What we saw was worth the effort. Since then, I have looked at table salt with a new respect. The mine was enormous, with multiple chambers, shafts, labyrinth passageways—even salt lakes and numerous statues carved out of salt. We photographed a statue of Pope John Paul II for Heather to take home to her husband Stewart, who had brought up, like us, in sectarian Glasgow. What we didn't know then was that John Paul was a strong influence for good in the world. The first non-Italian Pope for 455 years, he had travelled abroad extensively to promote greater understanding between countries and religions, campaigning against political aggression, violence and materialism.

The guide kept us moving and when we emerged from the mines two hours later, our driver was waiting for us. We made it back in time to have lunch and get scrubbed up for the 4.00 p.m. wedding of my niece, Jennifer Helen Campbell, to Bantoz Jacek Bojdo in the beautiful and historic St Mary's Basilika. It goes without saying that the bride and groom both looked magnificent. For most of my grandchildren, ranging in ages from five to thirteen, a church service was a new experience, and the wedding ceremony (which seemed long—*very* long) was yet another first. What would we do without sweets to keep children quiet?

I thought drink flowed abundantly at a Scottish wedding but this Polish traditional wedding surpassed even Scottish excess, and the food just went on and on—at least five courses with appetizers, cakes, pastries and fruit, accompanied by wine, more wine and a river of vodka. At one point in the evening, the children were excited to spot a dead man under the table. They were pretty disappointed when they were told it was just a Polish relative who'd drunk too much vodka.

Heather and I managed a sight-seeing tour of Krakow the following day, enormously impressed by Poland and its people. As I write this, Russia has just invaded Ukraine and the Poles have already admitted over one million Ukrainian refugees. If ever a nation understood the unspeakable horror of occupation, it is Poland. The Krakow museum (which we didn't have time to visit) documents life under Nazi occupation from 1939 to 1945. That period was bad enough—but after 1945, the Poles were steadily crushed by a repressive Russian Communist government. Since that time, they have fought long and hard for their current freedom, democracy and economic growth. No wonder they've shown such empathy and support for the Ukrainian refugees!

As Heather and I toured the Polish city, we simply couldn't believe how hot it was (over 30 degrees). Next day we set off home, relieved to escape some of the heat by getting onto the plane. Emerging from Glasgow airport five hours later, we were actually *pleased* to feel once again the familiar, chilly Glaswegian rain.

Chapter 53: Old Friends & New Experiences

My first few years in Kinross were like having a flexible part-time job, with weekends off if I wanted (and mostly I did). Generally on weekdays I was able to go out for coffee and lunch and—a glutton for punishment—I joined Kinross Golf course and played during school hours.

I even managed to learn how to crochet at the Hookers' Club at Loch Leven Community Centre (AKA Kinross High School). My granddaughter Jenny thought it hugely funny that her granny was meeting some Hookers in a classroom at lunchtime; she got a row for trying to peer through the glass window-pane in the door. Sorry Jenny!

During this time, I continued to enjoy playing bridge with my Dalgety Bay pals and some golf with Linda from Aberdour. But it was the social outings of the GHSG Old Pals Group (eight Glasgow High School friends) that flourished most after I moved to Kinross.

We no longer just met occasionally. Getting together was a break from routine and families and years of responsibility and so we made the most of it: racing weekends at Kelso with single rooms at the Buccleuch Arms; weekends in London at the theatre; lunches and dinners in Glasgow; and at Christmas, a lot of bubbly and a Secret Santa at Jean's house, followed by lunch in a west-end restaurant.

We were all Glasgow girls, so the banter was good, we shared problems and laughs; sometimes we even had serious and philosophical conversations. I think in modern jargon it might be called a 'friendship group'.

The Old Pals Group rarely managed to visit Scotland's capital city, Edinburgh. But on one occasion we met before lunch for cocktails in Harvey Nic's, which is conveniently placed for senior citizens right next to the bus station.

I'm not convinced we did much for the image of the store's supposedly élite customer base. We were eight ladies of a certain age, well-dressed of course, and perching with difficulty on high stools (the occasional walking stick happily discarded on the floor), who knocked back some interesting cocktails, laughed a lot and made too much noise. It felt good.

My schoolfriend Angela visited me in Kinross, just as she had everywhere else I had lived, and we enjoyed a wee holiday together. For the first time ever, we didn't hit the big time in the city, but instead revisited the west coast of Scotland. We called in at the renowned Green Kettle Café in Whistlefield and walked down to Portincaple which had changed since I was last there in 1949 and transformed itself into a select and beautiful village. It was definitely no longer a cheap place for a holiday.

We carried on to Dunoon, and then to Portavadie on the shores of Loch Fyne in Argyll and Bute, where in 1960 we had camped as girl guides. It was now unbelievably different. It boasted a sailing marina, a restaurant, a spa complex and upmarket holiday accommodation.

My brother Sandy (and his friend Tony) met us in the marina, then took us out in Sandy's most precious possession—his Moody 31 Keelboat, 'La Cerise'. Not only did we enjoy our wee sail, we were also treated to a delicious lunch in the posh restaurant. A sharp contrast with our first visit over fifty years before when all our food was cooked on an open camp fire.

It was during my early years in Kinross that I grew close again with another friend from my past—Beryl Gale from Sunderland. We'd shared a room in University Hall in 1964, as well as a flat in Union Street, St Andrews during my final year. Since then, we'd done what university friends usually do: we exchanged Christmas cards and phoned occasionally. But now we were both retired, we chatted more frequently on the phone.

Beryl and I had been in the same Latin class at Uni. Of course, I told her about my holiday to Tunisia and my Carthage Hannibal flashback. We remembered ploughing our way through parts of Virgil's *Aeneid*, and decided there and then to do some travelling together and get a bit more 'educashun'.

Beryl's husband Roy preferred to stay at home anyway, so the pair of us made plans, just as Heather and I had done in our teenage years—but they took us further afield than youth hostelling round Loch Lomond.

We began by exploring each other's home territory. When I visited Beryl, our day trip to Roman Vindolanda in Hexham inspired us further. Despite studying Latin over forty years before, and being fans of Mary Beard, we realised how little we really knew. So we decided to remedy this. Working round my childcare commitments, we planned the first of several trips to Italy organised by the Riviera Travel Company.

We were interested in the Romans and so we began with Pompeii, Herculaneum and Rome itself. Our fellow travellers were often classical scholars (retired Latin teachers mainly). With vivid memories of my scary sarcastic Latin teacher, initially I avoided them like the plague, but as the week progressed and we got to know them, things changed. Another maxim of my one-time boss

John Carder was 'Never Assume'. He was right. They turned out to be good company *and* fun.

Besides, this wasn't just history. It was the history of epic catastrophe! On August 24th in 79 AD (or 79 CE if you prefer), shortly after noon, Mount Vesuvius erupted. It literally buried the city of Pompeii, as well as neighbouring Herculaneum, Oplontis, Stabiae and other smaller settlements. Two thousand people died in Pompeii alone. They suffocated in their homes, in the streets, and in cellars where they had hoped to escape the destructive fury of the fire and the poisonous fumes. Archaeological excavation work through the years has unearthed an astounding amount of information about their way of life.

Somehow as I struggled through Virgil in a dreary lecture theatre in St Andrews, I never considered the Romans as real people. I just thought of them as warriors and very irritating speakers because they always put the verb at the end of the sentence. 'Out I'm going.' How silly was that?

We are accustomed now to watching harrowing scenes of terror, destruction and human misery on television, but nothing prepared me for the sight of the numerous skeletons that were excavated in Herculaneum in the belt of land separating the city from the sea. Men, women and children of all social classes were caught in the deadly flow of ash and hot gases as they attempted to flee, some clutching jewellery and other precious objects. It was a dreadful end to what had been—for the wealthy at least—a lavish existence.

In those Roman towns, just like today, the size, furnishings and location of a house were an indication of wealth and success and often power. In excavated Pompeii, we saw the affluent patrician villas enriched with artistic furnishings, paintings, mosaics and small sculptures in bronze and marble. There were other smaller houses too, e.g. shops, taverns etc. Where did the slaves live, I wondered?

We saw an interesting building in the suburban baths outside the walls of the city of Pompeii. These baths weren't divided into distinct sections for men and women. They might well have been a 'health' centre with additional services,going by the sexual subject matter of the frescoes that decorated the various rooms.

One of the rooms—the dressing room (*apodyterium*)—was originally frescoed with sixteen erotic scenes, although only eight now remained, and, below each one, there was the picture of a drawer where clothes were placed.

More intriguingly, various sexual positions and services were shown, interpreted by scholars as a sort of 'catalogue' of what was on offer in terms of sexual gratification. Only one picture of sexual interaction between two women has emerged so far.

Graphic images may well have been essential for purposes of clear information. In ancient Pompeii, communication could have been a problem, the brothels probably being staffed by female slaves from countries conquered by Rome. The difference between then and now is that the enterprise was legal.

I think it's true to say that Beryl and I didn't exactly enjoy our visit to the Sistine Chapel in the Vatican City. We wanted to see it, and we knew how important it was, and is, for the Catholic Church, not least because the Pope prays there and it's where the next Pope is chosen. And the Sistine Chapel has the most amazing Michaelangelo murals. Nevertheless, the display of wealth and magnificent grandeur *in the name of religion* made us uncomfortable. I was brought up as a Scottish Presbyterian and Beryl as a Methodist. Both these denominations, arising from the Protestant reformation, promoted simplicity and lack of adornment of any kind. Perhaps this was the reason we felt it distasteful and simply wrong.

Or perhaps we just didn't know enough about art or religion to appreciate it properly? But we loved the Colosseum. Perhaps you have to actually stand in the Colosseum to appreciate the magnificence of its amphitheatre and the techniques, knowledge, and materials from across the Roman Empire that were used in its construction—not to mention the captured slaves who built it.

Apart from all that, picture the spectacle of an audience of fifty to seventy thousand cheering people watching gladiators being slaughtered. Mind you, Wembley can hold ninety thousand but at least they're not quite killing each other. The roar of the crowds today when a goal is scored is similar, I'm sure, to that of the Romans in the Colosseum when a gladiator finally bit the dust.

We now had a thirst to see new countries. From that time on, we visited loads of places, savouring local dishes, drinking delicious (and not so delicious) wine, meeting some fun (and some not so fun) company, but best of all visiting interesting places.

Neither of us liked sitting in the sun for long, and I always swam wherever and whenever I could.

Chapter 54: Travels With Beryl

Finding out more about the Romans kindled our interest in the whole country of Italy. We visited Sicily, Naples, Lake Garda. And then there was Capri—a small but beautiful island. As we were ferried out to visit the famous Blue Grotto, our attention was drawn to the villa of Gracie Fields, star of cinema and music hall, darling of the troops during World War II. It's hard to believe that at one point during the war the Allies classed her as an 'enemy subject' because of her Italian film-director husband (and Hitler also designated her 'enemy of the Reich' because of her brilliance at raising the morale of allied troops). Dame Gracie Fields died in 1971 in Capri aged 87.

Compared to Capri, the island of Sicily was huge. I remember well our visit to the Villa Casa Cuseni in Taormina, a favourite haunt of Oscar Wilde, Greta Garbo, Coco Chanel, Pablo Picasso, Bertrand Russell and Roald Dahl. I was tremendously surprised by what we were shown. The secret dining room had been opened to the public for the first time in 2012 and on its walls were paintings which showed the story of a gay couple and their son, the first depicted adoption by two men in the local history of art. To us in the twenty-first century, it was hard to believe that family life with the child was limited to the one secret room.

At some point in our holiday planning, we decided to learn a bit more about a different culture. Our next jaunt was to Turkey and Islamic Istanbul (originally Constantinople). There, too, we saw magnificent and dazzling displays in the name of religion, but not on the same scale as the Vatican City. We visited the Hagia Sophia, knowing nothing really about its history. We soon learned it was the largest Christian church of the Byzantine Empire and for a while even a Catholic Cathedral. After Constantinople fell to the Ottoman Empire, the building was converted to a mosque until the secular republic of Turkey turned it into a museum. This all changed after 2014 when President Erdogan converted it back to a mosque, despite the opposition of many Turks. In a way the Hagia Sophia symbolises the divisions within Turkey itself.

Our Turkish guide was clearly opposed to the many pro-Islam changes taking place in his country. Istanbul is a sea port on the Black Sea and stands on a triangular peninsula between Europe and Asia. From our river boat we were able to look on both continents. Is the Bosphorous a crossing? A bridge? Or a barrier dividing or integrating two very different cultures? It remains to be seen.

Turkey was officially recognised as a candidate for full membership of the European Union in 1999, and in 2005, negotiations began. Progress has been slow—Turkey has so far only completed sixteen out of the thirty-five conditions of membership. Under the current Presidency, negotiations have effectively come to a standstill. Our long-suffering guide had a hard time trying to explain all this to us, but we clearly understood his concern that Turkey would be subject in future to stricter Islamic law.

In Istanbul we walked through the famous Grand Bazaar, a huge covered market with sixty-one streets and almost four thousand shops—noisy, vibrant, colourful, full of exotic sights and smells. Standing at the entrance, you didn't really know where to begin or what to look at. I was scared of getting lost, but so was everyone else and we met up at the end of each street. Most of us had about two kilos of spare capacity in our homeward-bound suitcase and in the end we bought very little. We sat drinking Turkish coffee and enjoyed people-watching. We didn't spot a single burkha or a thobe, unlike in Hyde Park in London.

When I got home after my various trips, I shared titbits of information with the grandchildren, and brought home inexpensive souvenir 'tat' that I thought might stimulate a bit of interest and possibly the odd question. After visiting Florence, for example, I proudly placed my tiny replica statue of Michaelangelo's David on the conservatory ledge. However, the human David, my youngest grandson, wasn't impressed with his nudity, and I had to turn him round so we could only see his back.

I bought rulers marked on one side with a time-line of Roman conquests, pencils topped with a centurion helmet or a Roman coin, drink coasters with Latin quotations: *In vino veritas, Carpe diem, Nunc est bibendum*. Perhaps they might realise that the Scots although very accomplished at drinking, didn't actually invent it? Shakespeare's no longer mandatory in Scottish schools—and I certainly didn't appreciate it when I was at school myself—but after my visit to Stratford, I enjoyed displaying the poster with all the popular words and phrases derived from Shakespeare's plays, terms like 'puking', 'wild goose chase', vanish into 'thin air', 'break the ice', 'the green-eyed monster', a 'heart of gold' and, needless to say, 'too much of a good thing'.

Time flew past. I was pretty busy with the grandchildren, my travel adventures, my ongoing uphill and largely unsuccessful struggle with learning golf and, of course, my GHSH outings.

But something else happened during these first years at Kinross which opened many more doors for me. It was called SNISO.

This stood for: *She's Nae In She's Oot.*

Chapter 55: SNISO

It was when I was visiting the Farmer's Market at Kinross with my daughter Kirsty, that I was invited to join SNISO ('She's No In She's Oot'). What on earth was it? All I needed in order to join was an email address. Was it a club? No, definitely not!

What *was* it then? It had no joining fee, no committee, no rules, no constitution. Although memories are hazy about events at that time, it seems that when a few ladies met together for a blether, Morag McKenzie was responsible for the inspiration. That same woman, Morag McKenzie, somehow became an informal facilitator. She dubbed the network SNISO.

Thereafter, if a SNISO member wanted to go to, say, a particular film, they would email Morag and she would send the request out to the email list. If someone on the list was interested, they would email the initiator. In due course, those who were interested were able to organise a group outing. Simple, yet so very effective. If you weren't interested, you simply ignored the email.

SNISO grew and grew and grew. Just before lockdown, there were eighty-two people on the mailing list and a regular coffee morning. Various SNISO groups would join together in holidays, weekend trips, day trips, visits to museums and places of interest, as well as lunches and Christmas dinners. It was through this network that I met first Liz, and then Mary, who volunteered her husband Jim as a bridge partner for me. Remembering my bad experience in Dalgety Bay, I was nervous about this at first, but Jim was a sociable, cheery and non-critical partner, and a good player too. Gradually I began to enjoy club bridge. Not only this, I got to know Jim and Mary quite well and this led to another interesting trip abroad.

Having been formerly stationed in Cyprus, Jim and Mary were planning to revisit the island, staying in Jim's brother's villa. They kindly offered to find an apartment for Liz, Morag McKenzie and me and show us around. Warm-hearted and friendly folk, Mary and Jim Cowan really looked after us. From the very start it was a responsibility-free, fun and historically interesting trip.

Arriving at the airport, we spotted Jim almost immediately. There he was, with one hand brandishing a placard reading *The Three Amigos,* with the other grasping three large paper sunhats. His car was sitting outside, and we were whisked off to our apartment which had been checked and stocked with necessities by Mary. He left us to unpack, then came back to take us to their villa for a barbecue. What a welcome!

Most mornings, Jim would turn up, armed with snorkels for us all and drive us to different beaches. The water was so deliciously cool for swimming in the very hot weather. If it was a particularly warm day, Jim would produce chilled beer from the cool bag and we drank it while we sat in the shallow water, blethering and putting the world to rights. In the evenings we were mostly invited to a barbecue prepared by Mary. We ate, drank wine and jumped in and out of their swimming pool. What could be better?

As you know, I like a bit of history in my holiday and we got that too. Mary and Jim had been stationed in Cyprus in 1974 and they took us to Famagusta. On the way there, we were entertained by their first-hand account of the Turkish invasion in 1974. We had a brilliant day, fascinated by the brand-new casino right next to the abandoned hotels and houses. We had to get out our passports to travel into the Turkish occupied north of the island, where we visited a Greek Orthodox Church, now stripped of its distinctive décor and transformed into a bare and very plain mosque. The abandoned homes and bombed buildings were still there as a reminder of the horror of that time when so many Greek Cypriots lost their homes*. Mind you, the Turkish Delight we bought was delicious.

Another trip that came about through SNISO was my visit to Belfast. I was really keen to go. After all I was from sectarian Glasgow and had been married to a middle-class Scottish Presbyterian for ten years and an English Catholic for twenty. Not surprising that I found the city absolutely fascinating. I understood the ignorance, the hate, the violence, the prejudice, the bigotry, the discrimination. I had been brought up with it.

My brother Sandy remembers that 'Caffliks' were fair game when it came to ringing their door bell and running for your life. You wouldn't get into trouble from your mum, not for that. However, when I went out with a boy from St Aloysius, a Glasgow Catholic school with a green uniform, we had to make sure we weren't seen by either family. Angela was spotted once by her very strict mum just *talking* to a Catholic boy. 'You'll just nip that in the bud straight away', she was told.

Decades later at a Kinross SNISO coffee morning, I found myself next to Jo Middlemiss, Glasgow-educated at Notre Dame High School for Girls. With much hilarity, we remembered incidents connected with the unconscious sectarian conditioning of our childhood. She also mentioned how a job application by her father had been adversely affected by institutional discrimination. We agreed sectarianism was complex, and more concerned with identity than religious faith.

So it was both fascinating and terrifying to visit Belfast and see for myself the consequences of extreme sectarian and political tensions between pro-secession Catholic loyalists and pro-UK Protestant loyalists. The murals that we saw told their own stories. Most striking of all was the depiction of the ten political prisoners who died in the H blocks of Long Kesh prison, protesting against the refusal of the authorities to accept their political status. Their heads encircle a plaque which says, 'I want my memorial to be peace with justice'.

I was surprised and shocked to find there was still a curfew, as well as locked gates (or 'peace walls') between some Protestant and Catholic areas in the city—I had thought the troubles were over. I was so wrong. As we looked at the site of the much-bombed Europa Hotel, our Irish Guide joked that after the troubles when the new Belfast was legitimately demolishing old buildings, they had to send to England for a bomb expert. He laughed so much at his own joke that we all joined in.

Other murals portrayed Catholic and Protestant heroes, or innocent victims of the troubles. There was evidence too, right across Belfast, of community efforts since the Good Friday Agreement to rebuild the city and weaken the sectarian divide. Only time will tell how successful this is.

Belfast is well-known, too, for building the famously doomed passenger liner, The Titanic. A visit to the docks allowed us, the tourists, to feel and hear and see the story of the construction of a magnificent ship. But as we all know, it sank. Dare I joke about such an appalling tragedy? Only the Irish can make history and drama and money from a failed enterprise.

It was also through SNISO that I met Jean Miller. We had been on a day out to Edinburgh and we sat beside each other on the way home on the bus. In the course of our chat we discovered we'd both worked full time for most of our working lives and depended strongly on our mothers to help us. We agreed with hindsight that we weren't particularly grateful at the time. We both laughed at Jean's story of how on one occasion she was hard-pressed to get to work (she was the local pharmacist). As she prepared to leave, her mother observed that she might have some difficulty changing nappies with her arm in a sling. 'You'll be fine,' said the pharmacist as she strode out of the door. This rang a chord with me!

But we both were, and are, strongly aware of how difficult it still is for working parents to survive without family support. And on the same one-hour bus journey from Edinburgh to Kinross, Jean and I discovered that we shared an ambition to write. So we made a plan to visit creative writing workshops during the Edinburgh Book Festival.

After that, we would meet occasionally on a Sunday and read each other's stories. I found it difficult to put feelings into writing but I was OK with spelling and reporting facts in a formal, grammatically correct style. Jean was better than me at description, which I found well-nigh impossible.

I often used to say to my grandchildren, 'You can't be good at *every*thing but if you try hard enough you can do *most* things. You may never be the best—but you can always improve'.

Perhaps it was time to pay attention to my own advice.

Chapter 56: Living With A Teenage Boy

After I'd tried to write a few short stories, I discovered I had vivid memories of numerous past events. In fact, I was surprised how much detail I could remember. On the downside, I wasn't motivated to write fiction—not in the least. I reckoned my own life was interesting enough as source material. So I began to use it.

My first effort was a photo-book publication for my daughters Kirsty, Fiona and Catriona. I wanted to give them a book about their father. David had died so young that his girls never properly knew him. David's friend John Hunter helped me enormously with this task and we produced the book in time for Kirsty's fiftieth birthday. It's still a thrill to handle and read and show it around. And for me the writing was undoubtedly therapeutic. Odd as it may sound, I had never really talked about David's tragic death.

Would I ever write anything else, I wondered. Life in Kinross was keeping me pretty busy, what with the grandchildren and my golf and bridge. Then there were the GHSG Old Pals group outings which continued to blossom and—as we had done for many years—Heather, Christine and I met frequently for lunch and a glass or two (or more) of wine. Why break the habits of a lifetime?

And as most folk do, I kept up with former college colleagues. After all, I'd spent thirty years of my life in the workplace. June, with whom I had shared so many experiences (not least the Botswana holiday), organised a General Education Department reunion. What a joy to meet up again with many of my favourite people! It was fun to reminisce and delight in the fact that we were all free agents now, able to control our own lives. Evelyn Snowdon and Helen Kuzyszyn were running their own little businesses, while Helen Beaton had set up a small press, specialising in publishing poetry.

Adapting to the constant changes of Further Education had primed every one of us for retirement and mostly we had been glad to leave college work. It was about this time that I began to think seriously about writing my memoirs and found to my delight that Helen would edit and help me publish my story—if I ever got round to writing it. However, as often happens in life—and certainly often in *my* life—the unexpected happened.

And what happened this time, you may well ask.

My teenage grandson, Thomas (Tom), had been given an opportunity to train as a professional footballer in Scotland but—being under 16—he still had to attend school. How was this to be managed when he lived in the south of England? Naturally, he would move in with me (I invited him). This was a culture shock for both of us. Kinross was very different from Hampshire, where Tom had spent his entire life. He had to adapt to a wholly different existence. As for me, I was really ignorant about boys. I had only ever brought up girls!

My own girls, and my other grandchildren, had enjoyed school and studied hard enough—but Thomas was different. At the age of fifteen, when he arrived, he had already passed his GCSEs in Southampton, and he did (somehow) manage to leave the Scottish system with a couple of Highers. However, his main resolve was to do as little school work as possible while spending as much time as he could playing football. When he was living with me, he did, nonetheless, acquire the sort of life experience and resilience that I hope will stand him in good stead for the rest of his life.

As for myself, the learning curve was steep, fraught with problems and hard work. I didn't know that teenage boys could eat a whole chocolate cake at one go. I didn't know that they discarded *all* their clothes on the floor every day. I didn't know that they never washed a dish, shifted an *Irn Bru* can, an empty crisp packet, a mug, a glass or a cup from its last resting place.

Did he even realise that dirty clothes go in the washing machine? That towels hang on a towel rail? That grannies aren't chauffeurs?

And what about the business of him arriving home in the middle of the night? And watching endless episodes of *Love Island?*

Tom's kind heart and sense of humour probably saved him from an untimely death. He could make me laugh (his saving grace) and life finally improved for both of us when he learned to drive. Taking him to his driving test was one of the worst days of my life— and believe me, I've had a few. I knew life would be so much easier both for him and me if he could only drive—but the day he was offered a cancellation slot, I was forced to accompany him in a car to the venue.

Against my better judgement, and after seriously considering taking a sedative (me, not him), we set off. Tom was a perfectly good driver really but I'm a nervous passenger. Until we got to Perth, I sat on my hands and closed my eyes. I opened them at a set of traffic lights in the town centre and—as they turned to *red*— Tom put his foot on the accelerator and moved forward. It was a bad moment for both of us, but perhaps worse for the lady in the Ford Fiesta, who swerved wildly to avoid hitting us. Ignoring the car horns blaring all around us, we bravely tootled on to the testing centre. Tom disappeared for his test. I sat chewing my nails and wishing I still smoked.

And guess what?

He passed!

After that, there was no looking back. He was mobile, and shortly afterwards he achieved his ambition to be a professional footballer. Mission accomplished! Now that he had an income, he moved out. This independent young man no longer lived with his granny. Soon he returned home to Southampton. Of course, I missed him—but not his mess!

I celebrated my freedom by going off on a SNISO holiday to Iceland, a place I'd always wanted to visit, its biggest attraction being the thermal swimming pools. I couldn't wait to swim outside on a cold day in a warm pool. I had known the stuffy Arlington Baths in Glasgow, the freezing cold Step Rock Pool in St Andrews, the open-air pool in Dunbar and the icy fresh-water pools in Glen Fruin. In Cyprus, I'd experienced the joy of swimming to get cool—but this was totally different. There were outside geo-thermal pools with saunas, steam baths, and numerous hot tubs, the water temperature ranging from 36 to 44°C.

Although the initial attractions were the thermal pools and the good company, Iceland turned out to be markedly different from anything I'd ever seen before. It was a land of ice and fire, with dramatic geological formations. It's only a six-hour flight from New York, three hours from London, and so the capital—Reykjavik—was teeming with tourists, the houses colourful and low and fresh-looking—nothing like Glasgow in the fifties.

We ladies of SNISO (Jean, Laura, Mary, Morag McKenzie and myself) enjoyed our Iceland holiday so much that we made a forward-thinking plan.

We would go to Budapest in the spring of 2020.

Chapter 57: Lockdown

On the last day of December in 2019, the World Health Organisation was informed that a cluster of pneumonia cases had been detected in Wuhan, Hubei Province, China. The cause was unknown.

We had no idea then how our lives were going to change. No idea that soon we'd be wearing compulsory masks. That shops and restaurants would be closed. That nobody would be going to work or school. That we'd be stuck in our own houses, only allowed one walk (without meeting anybody) once a day.

If anyone had told us that this was going to happen, we'd have thought it was a wind-up. But as we all know, the corona virus called Covid 19 did happen. It affected each of us in a variety of ways. Some lost loved ones or suffered life-threatening illness, or death. For others, there were job losses, poverty and loneliness.

We should never forget those who protected us throughout the pandemic, endangering not only their own lives but those of their families—not to mention the scientists who worked round the clock to produce a vaccine, and the government that commissioned the vaccine and then ensured its speedy and fair distribution.

I was one of the fortunate ones who suffered nothing worse than a restriction of freedom. My recent move to Kinross certainly paid off during lockdown because my whole family—apart from Fiona—lived close by. The grandchildren were much older now, so I no longer had them arriving for breakfast or after school (or any time at all) and I could play bridge online.

At certain stages I was even allowed to take up my golf clubs with a friend, Alison Morrison. What I had learned at the Hookers'

Club—my crochet class—came into its own and I made loads of 'granny squares' into a bedspread for my granddaughter Jenny to take with her when she was allowed to return to university. But I finally understood Laurie Lee's words: 'Never in my life had I felt so fat with time, so free of the need to be moving or doing.'

So one day during lockdown—for no other reason than I felt like it—I started to research my father's wartime experiences. I'd been only fourteen when he died but my older brother Sandy had showed me Dad's paintings of trenches, tanks, and scenes from Italy and Africa. That's when I decided to find out more. The paintings were all I had to go on, because Mum had got rid of his war trunk when she sold Colebrooke Terrace. Still, Sandy told me what he remembered of Dad and that was my starting point.

It was a long slow journey of discovery over many days, hours and months. When I was writing and researching, I was totally engrossed and the time flew. Some days it was dark before I remembered that I'd intended to go out for a walk in the fresh air. I ate when I was hungry and I ate what I felt like eating. For me, that lockdown was a timeless existence, something I'd never experienced before.

Mostly I liked it. It was okay having nothing and nobody but myself to think about. I even discovered new tastes and foods and ordered food I'd never tried before. For me, shopping had always been a nuisance. It was something to get out of the way and finish as soon as possible—there were so many better things to do. Now I sat for ages studying my shopping list choices.

But I needed more than that. I needed people. We all do. And although technology can't replace physical human presence, we can use it to communicate. The young have galloped away with this.

As a result, we have FaceTime, Skype, Zoom, Messenger, Twitter, FaceBook, WhatsApp, SnapChat and TikTok—as well as the tried and tested methods: mobiles, landlines, letters and cards.

Lockdown had nipped in the bud the plans of a particular SNISO group (me, Jean, Laura, Mary and the other Morag). We had meant to go to Budapest but the pandemic stopped all that. So we used WhatsApp to keep in touch via our own 'Budapest Group'. We sent posts every morning and evening, and often during the day too. Once a week, too, there was a group video call, but mostly it was just text messages.

Sometimes the posts were particularly apt and funny. Mostly we would write in various versions of Scots. Here's a message that offered a perfect description of the lockdown syndrome (posted by Mary Cowan on 10 June, 2020):

> Injoay yer gowf, Morag, it micht stay dry
> Am haen a dinnna wanty dae
> A dinna wanty stiy in
> A dinna wanty gan oot
> A dinnae wanty dae hooswurk
> A dinnae want tea. A dinnae want coffi
> A dinna want tae be here
> A dinna want to be ony where else
> So am sittin here no kennin what a wanty dae the dae

Jokes and posts like this helped us through lockdown. We exchanged information and recommendations for films and series on Amazon, on Netflix, on i-Player. Like so many others, for the first time in my life I binged on box sets. Did it matter when you went to bed or when you got up? Not really. The next day held no commitments, no work to get through, no grandchildren to look after.

It was a strange time, but it didn't last forever. I celebrated the beginning of the end of lockdown by travelling to Madeira with Beryl in January 2022. It was a magnificent deal because the tourist industry was desperately trying to persuade us to go on holiday abroad again. We had a week in a five-star, all-inclusive hotel in Funchai, boasting a spacious twin-bedded room with a sea-facing balcony. Flights from Edinburgh, transfers, excursions and spa sessions—everything was included for the total price of £1254.27 for two.

When I was in Madeira, I fulfilled another wish on my bucket list and swam in the hotel's 'infinity pool'. It was cold and really scary because you feel like you're going to swim over the edge and topple into nowhere. But it was also an unbelievably exhilarating experience, and I topped it with wine, a tasty lunch and a good chat with Beryl.

Before our flight home, we were apprehensive about having the correct paperwork, the vaccine passports and the 'passenger location information form'. We did manage—but Beryl's blood pressure was undoubtedly higher than it should have been.

Back home again, meeting up with Heather and Christine was another joyous thing. We even managed a sentimental journey back to Tighnabruaich on the Waverley paddle steamer.

Above all, what the lockdown year did for me was create the time and opportunity to begin writing this memoir. At times, I found it distressing having to relive painful experiences. But I also found it therapeutic.

Hang on though: I've almost finished.

All I have to do is write the last chapter.

That's difficult because—well—endings are hard.

Chapter 58: Has Life Taught Me Anything?

NAH!

When you meet new folk, particularly older people, they're curious about you. Are you married? A widow? Divorced? Have you got any children? As a woman, you're not normally asked about your job or your hobbies.

The younger generation don't seem to me to stereotype quite as much. On the other hand, I may be wrong about that too. Old age, they say, brings wisdom. But the more knowledge and experience I acquire and the older I get, the less I feel I know. I was once sure about much that time's proved wrong. Perhaps that *is* a kind of wisdom—knowing you don't know. Knowing you aren't always right.

I've lived a full and eventful life, full of ups and downs and twist and turns. How my life ends is of little interest to me, although I hope it won't be painful. Will my death be sudden like it was for Jimmy or David? Or will I die from cancer like John, or my Dad, my Granny Graham and my two Wormit buddies, Lis and Pat? Or will it be a slow crumble like my mother? How can I know? For me, aged 78 as I write this, it's definitely a case of *carpe diem*. Seize the day!

Right now, I plan to continue to enjoy my children and grandchildren. I am so very proud of every single one of them. Each in his or her own way enhances the quality of my life. One of my great delights is having lunch with my grandson Alistair, currently a fourth-year medical student. I take a wicked delight in telling him of the shockingly non-PC terminology used in 1976 by his dead consultant anaesthetist grandfather in handwritten case notes. I'm not sure he believes me—which is not so very surprising when you consider that David's terms included:

ATL [Aff The Legs]
—The patient has problems with mobility
ATH [Aff the Heid]
—The patient has problems with cognitive functioning
A CRUMBLE
—Most of the patient's body systems beginning to fail

Then there was his term 'cauliflower heids'—a non-medical description but one of my well-remembered favourites. It describes a waiting room full of old ladies with permed white hair (this *was* in the seventies—many of us are now 'blonde').

Another of my favourite occupations is playing golf with my grandson Cam. He's a seriously good player and I am seriously bad, but we hire a golf buggy when he comes north and play eighteen holes of the Kinross Montgomery Golf Course. It's mostly banter. 'Did you know you were supposed to aim for the flag? The idea is to avoid the trees or the bunkers, or the water'.

I love golf because each shot is so interesting and varies according to the conditions. And I can *talk* about golf—the shots, the right club, the strength of the wind, angles, slices, hooks, distance, and the state of the green—I just can't play it very well.

If I win a hole or play a great shot, which occasionally I do, it's the best feeling in the world, worth all the misery of the hooks and slices. I'm confident Cam enjoys our shared games too—at least for now. I enjoy playing the game, I really do, but like my life story, my golf journey has been full of highs and lows.

If you've read the previous chapters, you'll know I'm interested in history and in this regard I now have a kindred spirit, my granddaughter Annabel. She loves history and was awarded the school History Prize last year. Sometimes, when she tells me about what she's learning, I'm able to contribute a first-hand account—because I'm so old I was alive and I can remember it—for example, the decline of the mining industry in Fife.

My grandson James has just passed his driving test, so for the first time in many years I have a chauffeur again. I never did like driving so I'm thrilled. Recently I had dinner with my grand-daughter Jenny and a friend. What a delight and what a joy to get all their lively young chat. I begin each morning by using the Strava App to check David, my youngest grandchild's long-distance running speeds.

So far as I'm concerned, talking and listening to your friends, your children and grandchildren is one of life's great delights, and the best way I know to stay mentally alert and well. Of course, one of the consequences of lockdown was an increase in mental health problems, something nobody ever talked about when I was a youngster, even although I'm certain that many—young and old—suffered from undiagnosed problems.

When my Dad returned from the war in 1945, it's obvious to me now that he was suffering from PTSD (post-traumatic stress disorder) and—like so many others—he self-medicated with whisky to help him forget. The husband of our family cleaner, Willie Kirk, tried to obliterate the horror and deprivation of his prisoner-of-war experiences in Japan by drinking himself into oblivion. Was that the Scottish solution to mental health problems in the fifties, the sixties, the seventies, and maybe even now—alcohol?

In the past I was dismissive and ignorant about mental health, like most of my generation. Aware of my lack of understanding, I read up on the topic, and what did I discover? That I myself seem to have suffered from an anxiety disorder called 'Selective Mutism'. Symptoms? It's when a child 'freezes' in certain settings—totally unable to speak—but can speak fine in other places. It's not caused by wilful refusal to talk, or by autism. It's a relatively rare childhood condition, often confused with shyness. If it persists into adulthood, it can cause anxiety in social situations.

Since I didn't know the term (or the concept of) 'selective mutism', and nor did anybody else, I was never labelled. Would it have made any difference? I have no idea. I do know that I never opened my mouth to speak unless I was comfortable with the people I was with. Ask my Sunday School teacher, Miss Rolland, or my Greek teacher, Miss McLellan. It even applied, surprisingly, to my own family. I barely talked to them. I was more comfortable with friends from school and fellow Girl Guides.

In unfamiliar situations I never spoke in a group, although there were one or two people I could talk to. And yet I survived holiday jobs, and university—even teaching. Am I imagining a mental health condition? I don't think so. I haven't changed much really and to this day, I'm more comfortable and communicative with one or two people I know well. I tend to shut up when the group's more than three or four in number, particularly if I feel they're not interested in me.

I realise now that when I married David, he talked for me in unfamiliar social situations. No wonder I missed him so much. In his family, the dinner tables were almost rowdy, with everyone trying to speak to me at the same time. Ella (his mum), his Auntie Dot and his sister Belle would all try to get me to listen to *their* version of the same story. I would nod at each one in turn. I think perhaps this is how I overcame my condition—by becoming a good listener. I *must* have been good at listening because in order to be able to write this memoir, I drew on over seventy years of it.

I have listened to many people. Have I learned anything worth passing on, I wonder? I'm not really sure.

But maybe there are a few things.

Like that you should never take yourself too seriously, though occasionally you should push out of your comfort zone.

That you should be kind.

That you should look forward and not backward.

That you should prioritise what's important to you.

That you should accept differences.

That you should enjoy your life while you can.

And that you should listen.

Talking only repeats what you already know—but to listen, to *listen,* is to learn.

Epilogue

When Amber, the new care worker, trolleyed the Christmas tree into the old folks' lounge, she spotted an elderly lady with wispy white hair sitting peacefully in the corner, her hands resting on her lap as she gazed into space.

As the girl started to hang the various decorations on the branches, she noticed the old person was watching her. Not only that—she was getting agitated. In fact, tears were coursing freely down her wrinkled face.

Straightaway Amber went across and took her hand. 'Would you like a cup of tea?' she said. 'Is something wrong?'

'I can't do it. I just can't do it. It won't sit straight.' The old lady's voice was panicky. 'The lights won't work. I can't sort it. It keeps falling down. I need *David*.'

Amber turned the old lady's chair so she could no longer see the Christmas tree.

That did the trick. Slowly she grew less distressed. Within five minutes, she'd forgotten what had upset her.

Later Amber reported the incident to her boss. 'I'm afraid I don't even know the resident's name,' she said.

'It sounds like old Mrs Ridings,' said the Care Home Manager. 'Can you believe she had a really eventful life? It was full of drama, twists and turns, tragedy and fun. Do you know she even wrote a book about it? It made me laugh and cry. There must be a copy lying around somewhere....'

The Dalrymple Family

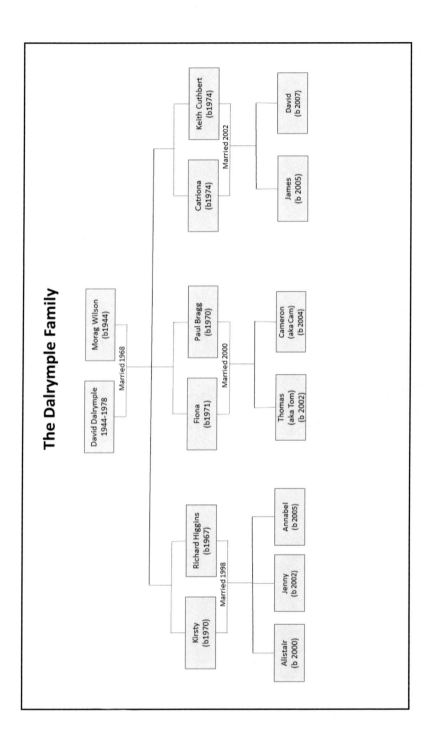

The Wilson and the Graham Families

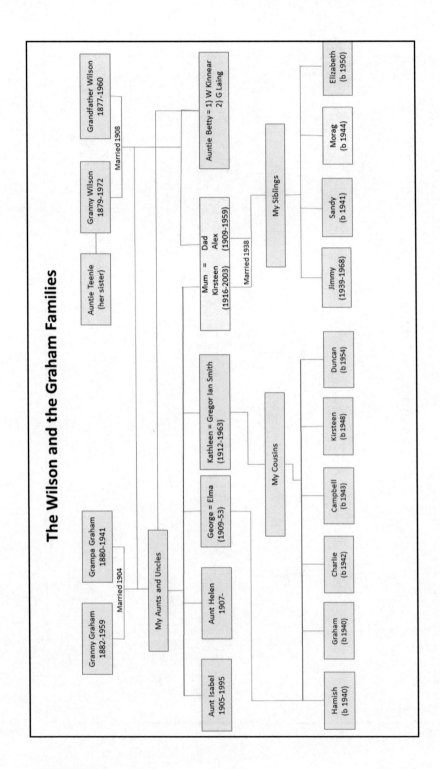

John's Family Tree

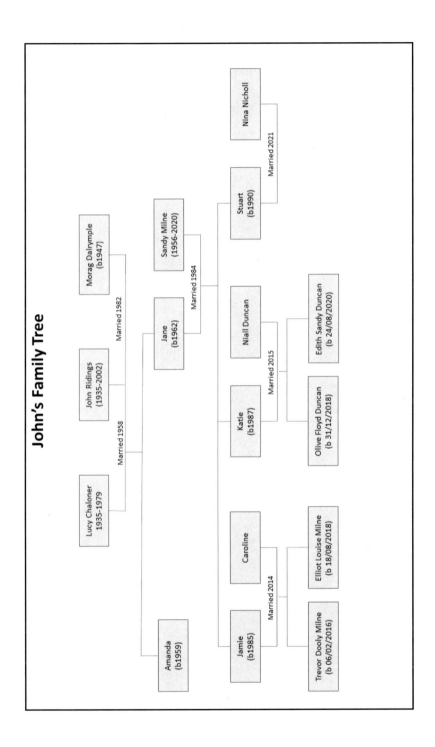

NOTES

Chapter 16

p. 119 My friend Pat Whitton remembers lessons with Miss Loudon:

I used to be so scared that I started to feel sick the night before. If I could persuade my mother I was ill enough to stay off school that was a bonus. When we got to the class, I was in the 'tall' group, along with Elizabeth and Jean, and we were routinely and sneeringly informed by our kind teacher that it was a pity we had such long legs and yet could do nothing with them. So much for encouragement! She was a vindictive, compassionless bully with an eye for an easy target. Humiliation was the name of the game. Of course, back in the day, we just sat there and took it. I sincerely regret not having the balls to take her on, call out her behaviour but such a course of action was unthinkable—even perceived as a death wish.

I remember Elizabeth Dickie trembling and wringing her hands when waiting in line to jump over the buck (often called the horse because it had four legs and the top part the saddle was leather) The legs were extendable but the minimum height was about four feet. Elizabeth would run up to the horse then stop dead, frozen with fear. From the back of the gym, we would hear the fatal words, 'Into the hamper, Miss Dickie. NOW!'

I don't think anyone who had the misfortune not to be good at climbing ropes or balancing on an upturned bench with a bean bag on her head (the futility of it all astounds me now) will ever forget Miss Loudon.

[The 'hamper' was the big basket in which our gym equipment was stored.]

Chapter 19

p. 138 The Rev Johnston McKay (Senior), that same church minister who was there for Angela in her time of need, was also the Education Correspondent for the Glasgow *Herald*. Aware of the availability of grants and scholarships, he made sure that Angela and I, with widowed mothers, had our school fees (£4.00 per term) paid by Glasgow Corporation.

Chapter 21

p. 159 Duncan Smith, my youngest cousin and youngest child of my mother's sister Kathleen, was born in 1955. I can't resist saying a little about Duncan because he has had such a successful and interesting life.

What were the highlights of Duncan's career, I wonder? Was it singing at the memorial service of Sir Michael Redgrave? Or working with Barry Manilow? Or having Julie Andrews make him a cup of coffee? Was it working with his equally talented brother Campbell? Was it the national tours of *Kiss me Kate, Chitty Chitty Bang Bang, The Sound of Music,* and *Phantom of the Opera*? Or was it singing the part of Jesus in the St John Passion conducted by Sir David Wilcox? Or perhaps it was successfully auditioning for the baritone in *Evita*? This last year has been quiet for him because of Covid but his most recent work was an international tour in the cast of *Fame*, starring Mica Paris. At 65, he was the oldest member of the cast.

It was Andrew Kinloch, Head of Music at Hermitage Academy, Helensburgh, who first introduced him to music. From then on, Duncan was blessed with—undoubtedly loads of talent—but also encouragement and support from dedicated teachers and much needed finance from scholarships. (I love hearing about teachers who inspire their pupils with a love of their subject.)

Chapter 26

p. 194 The Indian caste system, used to categorise people by their place in society, although officially outlawed in 1948, continues to permeate Indian tradition.

Chapter 39

p. 277 The TGIF Wormit pals were Pat Morton, Lis and Sandy Harvey, Jan and David Winch, John and myself.

p. 281 At Christmas 1999 at Sandy and Sheila's in Milnathort, each of us had to make up a rhyme for one other family member. Sandy wrote the following lines for my sister Elizabeth in the voice of her devoted dog Bonzo:

Elizabeth's Tale

I'm small and brown and hairy
And I've a tale to make you cry
Cos I'll tell you 'bout my mistress
From my kennel in the sky

I was cruelly called BONZO
Which was a frightful start
(Though it's true I often widdle, piddle
Retch and belch and fart)

At Colebrooke Terrace door I'd sit
I was a loyal fool
And wait for wee Liz Wilson
To come on home from school

She'd throw her school clothes on the floor
And change to strange apparel
Then take me out along the road
To see her wee friend Carol

Carol's dog it was a Shetland
Though I didn't like it much
For it used to sniff at my rear end
And then around my crutch

Liz and Carol gossiped endlessly
About things beyond their years
Their mothers never heard the talk
Or they'd been near to tears

She had two awful brothers
Who seemed to mean her harm
So I barked and growled and ran about
If they grabbed her by the arm

Though really I was frightened
Cos they were bad and didn't care
But my barking brought the Mother out
Who sorted out the pair

Now Liz had an elder sister
And I heard the Mother warn her
'Don't you smoke and kiss the boys
Along at that street corner!'

But Liz was growing older now
And neglected me my dinner
Spending hours at the looking glass
'Oh no I think I'm thinner'

But nature works in wondrous ways
And she grew up tall and fair
Attracting glances all around
With her long and golden hair

Now as a spaniel I love water
And through it I can swim
But my mistress felt embarrassed
As she hadn't learned to swim

So Heather taught her how it's done
Which made Elizabeth cheerier
But I swam better than them both
And I felt much superior

Liz qualified at teaching
And taught herself to dance
She traded walking dogs about
For dancing and romance

I guess the rest you all know well
And need not a dog's preamble
She met with Craig, they fell in love
And now she's Mrs Campbell

But a dog's long ears can hear for years
    and hear from far away
Of Jenny's mutterings and Morag's utterings
    from London and the USA
And what I hear from far and near is so much
    like a daughter
'Let's have a wrap and cut the crap. Let's see
    the gift you bought her!'

Chapter 51

p. 372 Grand-daughter Annabel remembers 'sickie' days in an essay written for school:

Granny Morag

Granny Morag is no ordinary granny. Granny Morag always has a full biscuit tin, with a label on the side saying 'maximum two chocolate biscuits'. Granny Morag's house is open to anyone and everybody, so much so that she has a spare key for anyone who needs to use her house. Granny Morag treats everybody equally and cares for everyone she meets.

When I was young, sick days with Granny Morag were always my favourite. I would get dropped off in the morning while Mum rushed off to work. Granny Morag would tuck me into bed in her spare room and make me freshly squeezed orange juice. 'It's good for you,' she would say.

If I was actually ill, I would watch television all day, but the days when I wasn't *really* ill were the best. Endless games of Rummikub and Monopoly (the Edinburgh edition, of course).

If I was really lucky, we would have a trip to the garden centre. We never bought anything, we just looked at all the weird and wonderful things that it would have. In the afternoon, between the occasional cough to keep up the act, I would help Granny Morag on whatever project she was working on. This usually involved sorting through old photographs and Granny Morag explaining to me who everyone was and stories about them (this was my favourite part of the day). Finally, Mum would come and pick me up and suddenly I felt really 'sick' again. The day was a little secret between Granny Morag and me.

I have always remembered Granny Morag being really interested in history; I think this is where I get it from. Granny Morag's house is filled with trinkets from all over the world, some beautiful and some horrendously tacky, but all are welcome, and all will be put pride of place on her windowsill.

These objects are from all over the world, each with a different story to tell. It's almost impossible to keep up! There are giraffes and tribal figurines from her time in Botswana and a light-up glass Big Ben from our family trip to London, each one of equal importance.

In her cutlery drawer there's silver family cutlery with little Ds carved into the handle, they must be antiques. While some people may hide away their antiques so they don't get damaged (and to keep them safe from children), Granny Morag uses everything—no matter what it is worth or how old it is, because 'what's the point in having something if it's never used?' I have always admired this.

Even as little children we were always trusted to be around fragile things. We were, and still are, treated as equals by Granny Morag. The only thing that she used to hide away was a preserved crab in glass, but only because one of the grandchildren had a phobia of crabs.

Granny Morag is one of the cleverest people I know. Not just in the conventional way of academia (but that too). Granny Morag always knows exactly what to say to everyone and somehow knows what everyone is feeling just by looking at them. Nothing ever gets past her. She can always tell immediately if something's wrong, but she isn't nosey and won't push for an answer. She simply makes you feel comfortable and produces a cup of sweet tea. This strategy hasn't changed since I was about five years old: she is to blame for my caffeine addiction.

Granny Morag never pushes anyone to talk. Yet somehow she always manages to get me to speak freely, just by making me feel comfortable and being unjudgmental. She truly listens—not just nodding but really taking it in. She's genuinely interested in all aspects of my life and listens to anything I have to say, no matter how big or small

She always keeps cans of full calorie Coca Cola in her fridge because I once said that it was my favourite drink. She remembers all of the little details and, of course, the big things. She's the first person I want to share any good news with because I know she'll genuinely be happy and excited for me.

Even in bad times, I know Granny Morag will drop everything like a shot—no matter how inconvenient—to help anyone that needs it, but especially her grandchildren. She's always there for us, no matter what.

Granny Morag is no ordinary Granny. Granny Morag has Snapchat and Instagram so she can keep up with her grandchildren's lives. Granny Morag's house feels like home as soon as you step through the door

Granny Morag is kind. Granny Morag is selfless. Granny Morag is intelligent. Granny Morag is *my* Granny.

Chapter 55

p. 393 Mary Cowan remembers 1974 in Cyprus:

I can still picture Mum and Dad as they stepped off that plane in Nicosia airport. Dad, a miner, and already too hot in his Sunday best suit, shirt and tie, was waving enthusiastically. It was 1974 and they were glad to get away from the misery caused by the National Miners' Strike which had ended only three months before. However, it had been a right struggle to persuade them to come. Fly in an aeroplane? Dad was more used to being under the ground, not flying above it. But in the end it was the need to see us again (and maybe a bit of curiosity) that forced them out of their comfort zone.

As we sat at breakfast two days later, we were suddenly deafened by military music and as far as we knew there was no festival on July 15. It turned out there had been a military coup on the island. We could hear explosions in the distance and soon—outside our house and in the streets—there was hand to hand fighting, between Greek and Turkish Cypriots. The Greek Junta had backed Eoka B to overthrow the elected President Makarios. Mum and Dad had travelled from their strike-torn home Fife village of Wellwood for a holiday but suddenly home felt much more peaceful—and safer.

Mum was determined she was going to visit the NAAFI, even though we were under curfew and not allowed to go far from home. So of course we went and she instantly spotted something she'd never seen before—a cauliflower the size of a large marrow. Despite the chaos all around her, she was going to buy it and she did, tucking it under her arm and defying anyone, friend or foe, with or without a gun, to separate her from her cauliflower. That was my mum all over.

That was just the beginning. A week later on the 24 July, Turkey invaded the island, and the Greek Cypriots were now fighting the Turkish army mainly in the north. Jim and I were living in Limassol and were immediately evacuated to the base at Akrotiri and told to take enough stuff for 24 hours. But what about Mum and Dad? Well, Britain couldn't intervene in the war, as both Greece and Turkey were members of the NATO alliance so they flew all British holiday makers home straight away from their base in Akrotiri. Mum and Dad were home in no time at all and although they were still really worried about us, and it had certainly been a holiday to remember, they were very glad and relieved to be making a cup of tea in the safety and familiar comfort of their own kitchen. They had good reason to worry because we weren't having an easy time.

Denise and I had to share a room with twenty other people, living on compo rations (mainly corned beef), sleeping on a camp bed, with only one blanket, toilets to be flushed as infrequently as possible, and a shower every two days if we were lucky. Not knowing what was happening or what was going to happen was probably the scariest part of it all. But two weeks later we were sent back to Limmasol with a box of compo rations because the base simply couldn't cope with the water, electricity and sewage for so many people. Our first trip to the NAAFI in Limmasol was eerie and scary—there were hundreds of us but as not one person spoke, it felt like that deathly silence you get in an aeroplane when it's coming in to land.

My husband Jim remained in Cyprus until 1975, but it was twenty years before I could go back and even then, every time I thought about it, I got that sinking feeling in my stomach

I no longer feel like this. I think I was cured by the 'Three Amigos' when they visited us in Cyprus in 2015.

NB Turkey occupied 37% of the territory of the Republic of Cyprus and displaced about 200,000 Greek Cypriots from the occupied northern part of the island. Turkish troops still illegally occupy the northern part of Cyprus despite international condemnation of Turkey and the acknowledgement of the rights of Cypriot people drafted by the United Nations and other international organisations. Negotiations are ongoing but nothing is resolved.

Photographs

p. 151: Jimmy's model boat, The Arisaig

My brother Sandy and I knew this model was made by Jimmy but some online correspondence in a website for former service personnel confirmed it. See below.

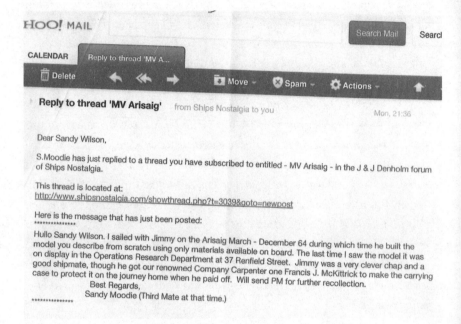